TICTIONARY

A Reference Guide to the World of
Tourette Syndrome, Asperger Syndrome,
Attention Deficit Hyperactivity Disorder
and Obsessive Compulsive Disorder
for Parents and Professionals

By
Becky Ottinger

Foreword by
Fred C. Engh
Founder and President
The National Alliance for Youth Sports

The Building Bridges Project

AAPC

© 2003 by Autism Asperger Publishing Co.
P.O. Box 23173
Shawnee Mission, Kansas 66283-0173
www.asperger.net

Publisher's Cataloging-in-Publication
(provided by Quality Books, Inc.)

Ottinger, Becky
    Tictionary : a reference guide to the world of
Tourette syndrome, Asperger syndrome, attention deficit
hyperactivity disorder and obsessive compulsive disorder
for parents and professionals / Becky Ottinger.
    p. cm.
    Includes bibliographical references.
    Library of Congress Control Number: 2002114207
    ISBN: 1-931282-16-1

    1. Nervous system–Diseases–Popular works.
2. Nervous system–Diseases–Patients–Care.   I. Title.

RC351.O88 2002   616.8
                 QBI02-200764

This book is designed in Caslon, Minion, Century Gothic and Pepper

Managing Editor: Kirsten McBride
Editorial Support: Ginny Biddulph
Cover Design: Taku Hagiwara
Illustrations: Eddy Mora
Interior Design and Production: Tappan Design

Printed in the United States of America

*This book is dedicated to
all the "teachers" who have crossed my path –
the children with neurological disorders.*

Foreword

I first met Becky Ottinger over ten years ago. I can't remember where or why. All I can tell you is that today every time I think of Mother Theresa, Becky Ottinger comes to mind. This woman IS the "one in a million" kind, and thank God her focus happens to be children with neurological disorders. She has been a shoulder I can lean on and I assure you *Tictionary* will be one YOU can lean on.

Having seven children in itself can be a struggle for most families, but for my wife and me raising six was a breeze. Then along came our last child, Patrick. I first started noticing something different about Pat when he was around seven years old. We'd take the kids bowling and he'd do what I thought were silly little things like smelling his hands each time after bowling. My wife, who has her master's degree in social work, was much smarter than me when it came to these things (as is the case in most things), and it wasn't long before she uttered the words "TS" to me. I felt weak-kneed like every other parent who suspects that their child will not be the "norm."

It didn't take me long to figure that dealing with Tourette Syndrome and, as I call them "all the cousins" (OCD, ADHD, LD, ASD, etc.), is not the easiest of life's responsibilities. Not only did Pat have motor and vocal tics, he wasn't doing well in school and his attention span was, shall we say ... lacking. And anyone who knows someone with OCD knows what I mean when I say "nerve-wracking." As Pat grew older, his maturity never seemed to catch up to his chronological age. How frustrating that can be! As a matter of fact, Becky and I have exchanged the word "maturity" when it came to our two sons on several occasions.

However, while neurological disorders pose many challenges, there is help and useful suggestions that can make everybody's life a little easier. And that is why *Tictionary* is such a valuable book. Parents in their frustration need to have a ready place to go to find a quick answer to something that is bothering them THAT DAY. They need to know that, as crushing as the moment might be as they experience another "problem," they are not the first to go through the trials and tribulations of having a child with a neurological disorder. They need to know that their child, like millions of others, will yes, I contend, come out of the whole experience a much better and overall stronger person as age goes on. There are countless examples of successful people who have overcome the challenges they've faced with a neurological disorder. And again, that is why *Tictionary* can and should be a handy guide for every parent who has a child with a neurological disorder.

Just in case you were wondering how Pat is doing ... At twenty-three years old, he is a video photographer, who does his own music writing and edits full-length productions, and his girlfriend is a past Miss Teen Florida. My last bit of advice .... hang in there!

– Fred C. Engh
Founder and President
The National Alliance for Youth Sports

The Joshua Center Story

In 1972 God gave me a beautiful daughter, Sarah. I was so thrilled to finally be a mother. In 1973 God gave me my wonderful Josh. How lucky could I be to have both a little girl and a little boy? I was the happiest mother in the world. Little did I know how challenging our lives would soon become.

In 1983 I became a single parent and returned to the world of teaching once again after staying at home with my family for a number of years. I wanted my children to have a counselor to talk to so I took them to see Jack Southwick, a counselor at a local church. Jack was the first one to suspect that Josh had Tourette Syndrome (TS). Four years later when Josh was diagnosed with TS, the three of us began living in a whole new world we knew nothing about. But with the help and support of Dr. Gary Gaffney, our TS medical expert, Jack Southwick, and many friends we were able not only to survive and deal with our own challenges, but also to grow into better people by sharing our experiences with others.

In 1987, right after Josh was diagnosed with TS – Josh later was diagnosed with obsessive compulsive disorder (OCD) and attention deficit hyperactivity disorder (ADHD) – I became involved with the local chapter of the Tourette Syndrome Association (TSA). There I met Orrilla Clough, mother of three daughters with TS and president of the Kansas City Chapter of TSA. At that time the chapter held bi-monthly support group meetings, and I remember walking away from the first meeting wondering how I was to survive for the next two months without talking to someone who "understood." After a few days I finally got up enough courage to call Orrilla and was totally astounded, and extremely grateful, that every time I told her about a symptom Josh was exhibiting, she seemed to know what I was talking about. I threw myself into the chapter because I wanted to learn as much as possible to help Josh.

Not knowing how to help Josh in the school system with his misunderstood neurological symptoms, I became very frustrated. As the years went by, I learned a lot about neurological disorders and realized that more needed to be done to help the hundreds of children and their families living with these disorders. I didn't want other children to go through what Josh had to go through as a child. Over the years Orrilla answered calls from parents and I helped with educational issues whenever I could. As a parent of a child with the disorders and as a teacher, I felt I was able to help both parents and teachers.

In 1992 I quit teaching so that I could spend more time helping these kids. I knew I could not rely only on Josh's experiences if I was truly going to help other children, but that I would have to observe other children in the classroom. I was scared to death at first, but soon realized that I had more experience with TS than anyone else in the community, so I plunged ahead. I observed hundreds of children in the classroom setting, participating in IEP meetings in every school district in metropolitan Kansas City and many outside the area. Every time I observed a child, I learned something new. Information gained from my observations was shared with teachers, parents and doctors. With over 800 children diagnosed in the Kansas City area we were kept very busy.

Over the years I sent many families to Jack Southwick since he had become the expert in our area on neurological disorders. Jack, Orrilla and several other parents supported me with my dream, a dream of a center where the physician, counselor and educator work together to help children with ND be successful. In November of 1996 the Joshua Child and Family Development Center was opened, proudly named after my son, Josh Oliver.

Since then the Joshua Center has focused on creating programs that provide family-centered care in the areas of diagnosis, counseling, education, publications and a summer camp. Over the years the Joshua Center has helped thousands of families who are dealing with neurological disorders.

There are always those who impact our lives in a positive way, but Jack Southwick not only impacted my life, he saved it. Jack knows our children better than anyone I have ever known. His expertise continues to impact thousands of children and their families. I will be eternally grateful for his support and encouragement. One man can make a difference!

In addition, I wish to thank many others. Without their support this book would never have become a reality. It takes a village to not only raise a child with ND, it takes a village to raise a dream. My village includes my wonderful husband, Jim Ottinger, who taught me how to use a computer, supported my dream and became a friend to my children. Without Orrilla and Richard Clough believing in me and supporting me, the Joshua Center would not be what it is today. Orrilla is the angel every visionary has to have in order to be successful. And to Fred Engh I will be eternally grateful for encouraging me to start the Joshua Center and always being there when I needed help understanding the business world. Elaine and Mark Collins have given me so many good examples of parenting to share with our families. Ginny Tobin continues to be a master at observing our children and working with schools to help our children be successful. Dr. Gary Gaffney and Dr. Bob Batterson have truly made a difference in the lives of children with neurological disorders. And my beautiful children, Sarah and Josh, and my lovely stepdaughters, Jamie, Jackie, Jessie, and Joy – I will always be grateful for their love, support and patience.

I truly believe God gives children with special needs to those who will be able to make a difference in their lives. It is up to us to work together, search for answers, and share our joys and mistakes. Only when we are willing to come together can we truly make a difference. This book is all about making that difference. This resource guide was created for anyone needing information and common sense strategies as they deal with the neurological disorders of Tourette Syndrome, Asperger Syndrome, attention deficit hyperactivity disorder and obsessive compulsive disorder. Written from both a parent and educator's perspective, this guide offers insight into the world of the children and families who deal with these disorders. It is full of funny and sad stories that are intended to educate and give hope to the reader.

All proceeds from the sale of this book go to the Joshua Center. I believe it is the responsibility of all of us involved with a child with ND to make the world a better place for these children. Whether it's money, time or talents – we can all make a difference.

– Becky Ottinger

Table of Contents

C

E

F

I

J

K

L

M

N

O

Q

R

S

T

U

V

W

X

Y

Z

A

ACADEMIC ASSESSMENT

Children with neurological disorders (ND) sometimes have learning disabilities as well. Both parents and teachers may request an evaluation when they suspect a child has a learning disability. Academic screenings are used to identify academic problems that might warrant further, more comprehensive testing. Make sure you also request an auditory and visual processing evaluation when asking for an academic evaluation. In addition to these tests, also request an occupational therapy (OT) evaluation, including handwriting samples. Many children with Tourette Syndrome (TS) and other ND (i.e., Asperger Syndrome [AS], attention deficit hyperactivity disorder [ADHD] and obsessive compulsive disorder [OCD]) produce legible work without time restraints as during assessment, but in a classroom setting it is almost impossible for them to produce a readable writing sample. OT evaluations also address sensory issues. One issue relates to the child's ability or inability to integrate and interpret sensory information, while another may be how the child relates to sensations, like tags on a shirt. Often it takes more time for children to complete a test due to interfering symptoms of sensory concerns, obsessive-compulsive issues, distractibility or tics.

See Auditory Processing Disorder, Handwriting, Occupational Therapist, Visual Processing Disorders

ACADEMIC EXPECTATIONS

Children with ND generally function within the same intelligence range as the population at large. Thus, it is reasonable that parents and educators hold the same academic expectations for these children as for all children. When the symptoms of ND are severe and/or interfere with learning, accommodations can be made to help the child reach her full potential. Good communication between parents and school helps ensure that the child's educational needs are met. While keeping the educational objectives in mind, modifying the quantity of work or allowing extended time for completion of work may be the main accommodations that are needed. As symptoms vary in severity, educational requirements can be adjusted. In brief, students with ND can meet school objectives with a variety of supports, such as allowing them to dictate answers to somebody else (peer, paraprofessional, volunteer) when symptoms interfere with handwriting, allowing them to take tests orally, or keyboarding.

See Accommodations, Communication Between School and Home, Being Flexible, Learning Disabilities, Waxing and Waning

ACCEPTANCE

Once when I was preparing to speak with staff at an elementary school, my son told me, "Mom, it is not about understanding; it is about acceptance. Only persons who have neurological disorders will completely understand." As parents and educators it is our job to learn as much as we can about ND and accept the symptoms. Only with this acceptance can we begin to understand how to help children with ND reach their full potential. In addition, it is our job as parents and educators to help others accept the symptoms too. Rather than getting angry or making others uncomfortable when a negative comment is made, parents can diffuse the situation by how they react to it. When the child is young, he needs the protection of parents to help educate the general population, when appropriate. Teachers also play a role in helping others understand ND. They can help both the child with ND and the general student population develop positive interactions by educating the students and staff.

ACCOMMODATIONS

An *accommodation* is any technique that makes changes to a child's academic setting or environment to help him access the curriculum. An accommodation for a child with ND might include preferential seating, allowing the child to have two desks so he can move back and forth between them, allowing extra breaks to release symptoms, etc.

Alternative school assignments may be necessary for students with ND when symptoms interfere with learning. Many times handwriting is very difficult. Even many adults with ND are unable to write for extended periods. Just accept it; it is part of the disorder. When children write slowly so that their handwriting is legible, they have to expend so much time and effort that they are often unable to complete class assignments. Options that help ensure the student "performs" at his ability level include (a) allowing the use of a computer in the classroom and at home, (b) permitting the child to dictate to someone else including parents, (c) offering the use of a tape recorder or (d) allowing another student to copy his notes. I always suggest to teachers that long assignments be broken into shorter segments because these children often feel overwhelmed with large assignments and have trouble getting started. In some cases it may be necessary to limit the requirements of a project. Teachers need to keep the objective in mind, but modify the quantity of work when symptoms are high.

See Classroom Environment, Getting Started, Handwriting, Individualized Education Program (IEP), Modifications, School Reports and Projects, Written Expression

ACT and SAT ACCOMMODATIONS

If you think that accommodations are necessary to project a true assessment of your child's academic knowledge, you might want to discuss this with your child's counselor, but plan early. The approval process takes time. Both ACT and SAT have policies on accommodations.

See Internet Resources

> Stop and Think

ACTING BEFORE THINKING

Many children with ND have difficulty stopping and thinking before they act. Only after much effort on the part of educators and parents do they learn to think before acting. When a child performs an inappropriate action or says something unacceptable, it is important to review the situation and teach the child new, appropriate ways of saying or doing things. For example, the child may role play the situation or draw the before and after situation. Drawings give the child a mental picture to "draw upon" when placed in similar situations in the future. Some children are able to tell themselves "stop and think" before making choices as they mature. Any of these strategies usually requires lots of practice on the part of the child to be successful.

See Visual Supports

ADULTS AND ADHD

Many adults with ADHD were either not diagnosed or were improperly diagnosed in childhood. As a result, they grew up not knowing they even had a disability or were told their symptoms would disappear in adolescence. Just like their younger counterparts, most adults with ADHD are easily distracted, restless, impulsive and impatient, have difficulty sustaining attention, experience frequent mood swings, have short tempers, are disorganized and have difficulty planning ahead or processing more than one thing at a time. These characteristics are often manifested at work. For example, adults with ADHD may have difficulty finding and keeping jobs, following a routine, and solving problems with self-discipline and organization. Unaware that their problems can be attributed to ADHD, many adults seek professional help, including medical consultations and counseling. Children with ADHD grow into adults with ADHD. This is a lifelong disability. Many parents are realizing through their children that they have had experiences that are similar to their child's.

ADVOCACY

I believe developing good relationships with school staff is one of the most important things parents can do for their child. Most education professionals want to help all their students, including those with ND. But parents are their child's best advocate, so it is up to them to learn "everything" about their child's disability. Parents know their child better than anyone else, although parents should keep an open mind and listen to what others have to say. When parents do not agree with a policy or practice that is negatively impacting their child, they need to advocate for their child's best interest. Become knowledgeable about how the system works and the individuals involved and show respect for the chain of command.

Always put requests in writing and keep copies for your own files. When writing letters, proof them carefully before sending them. You have a better chance of helping your child when you write grammatically correct and respectful letters. Express your concerns, but keep to the point. If you are complaining, don't send the letter until you have reread it the next day to make sure it accurately reflects what you want to say. State in the letter that you expect to receive a response. Keep a file of all correspondence to and from your child's school and periodically check your child's cumulative file at school for accuracy. Finally, document each phone call between home and school in the Parent Journal. Keep each piece of information in chronological order.

See Communication Between School and Home, Parent Journal

ADVOCACY IN COLLEGE

Since parents won't always be available to intervene at the college level, it is important for the student to learn advocacy skills. Most colleges expect students to take the initiative to receive necessary services. Many colleges and universities have offices of disability services. It is a good idea to contact these departments for an appointment so both the parent and child can learn about services that are provided.

See Career Development, College Accommodations, Individualized Education Program (IEP), Transition Planning for Post-High School

AFTER SCHOOL

Ah, how I remember those times. Notice, I didn't say … "fondly." Just "remember those times!" Now that I have hard-earned wisdom to share, perhaps you can avoid my mistakes. First of all, don't wait until your child hits the door after school to run your errands. That is the time to "be there" for your child. He has held it together for the entire day and now must release his pent-up symptoms. Your child may be hyperactive, agitated, exhausted or may be ticcing a lot. Don't take it personally when he blurts out some pretty inappropriate language. One mom shared that when she picked her son up after school, he would enter the van and proceed to kick the dashboard again and again besides being extremely rude to her. When she asked him why he was doing this, he responded, "Mom, I hold this in all day and you're the most understanding person I know, so I give it to you."

Parents are the "safe persons" and home is the "safe place" to unload. Do not overreact to every negative thing that comes out of your child's mouth. If the teachers report he is having good days and you're experiencing problems at home, be thankful that it's not the other way around and talk with your child's teachers about accommodations on school assignments and homework, if needed. Have your child's favorite food ready when he gets home. You might even want to have some milkshakes on hand because sucking sometimes helps calm a child with ND. I know this from personal experience and have been validated by OTs.

You and your child will need to decide when homework will be done. Some children need to be left alone for a while and some need to play before starting their homework. Others do much better if they complete their assignments immediately after school. A consistent routine will make this time of day go more smoothly. Plan, plan, plan. If things aren't working, seek the help of a counselor.

See Counseling - Individual/Family, Homework Strategies, Milkshakes, Sense of Humor, Shopping

AGGRESSION

Children with ND do not choose to be out of control. They are as uncomfortable with aggression (i.e., tantrums, rage, meltdowns) as you are. Building an understanding of aggressive behavior allows you to respond more calmly. These children become easily frustrated, may be dealing with unwanted movements and/or thoughts, and desperately want to fit in so they sometimes become aggressive over the slightest altercation. Recognizing how certain stimuli or situations escalate a behavior allows the adult to plan for intervention when the behavior does occur or even prevents the behavior from occurring in the first place. For example, children with ND can become easily overstimulated by the environment, activities, loud voices or noises. Changes, especially those made abruptly or without planning, can be difficult for both the child and the adult working with her. Planning one step ahead of the child will help ensure that all is being done to prevent aggressive situations.

When a meltdown does take place, keep calm, remove the child from the situation, or remove everyone else, and follow the plan agreed upon beforehand. Attempting to talk to the child during a meltdown is not effective. Wait until the child is calm and you can meet privately to review the situation. (For further information, see Myles & Southwick, *Asperger Syndrome and Difficult Moments: Practical Solutions for Tantrums, Rage, and Meltdowns*). Many times after Josh had a meltdown, he would cry and go to sleep from exhaustion. Sometimes it was not until three days later while on our nightly drive that he was able to tell me what had caused the meltdown. When I learned to keep quiet was when he was able to discuss what happened.

See Consequences, Drives, Rage Stage

ALERTING TECHNIQUES

Sometimes children with ND have a great deal of difficulty waking up in the mornings due to lack of sleep or due to the side effects of medications. In cases like that you may try turning on bright lights, turning on the television, placing a cold washcloth on the child's forehead, gently rubbing the child's skin, or having the child drink ice water.

Sometimes children with ND have trouble staying awake in class. I worked with a boy in high school once who had sleep problems and, as a result, had difficulty waking up and staying awake in school. When he arrived at school he was usually running late and not fully awake. I suggested he be allowed to have some caffeine. It worked, and when he would become sleepy throughout the day he would get a little more. Please note that I am not advocating the use of caffeine in general, but it worked for this young man.

See Medication Side Effects, Occupational Therapist, Sleeping at School

ALLERGIES

Some tics can be mistaken for allergies, but some children with ND also have allergies. Whether there is a correlation between the two is not known, but it is worth exploring whether your child has allergies. When Josh was in the fourth grade, I kept him home one day to give his teacher a break from his sniffing. The sniffing had made me "nuts" by 10:00 A.M. so I called our pediatrician, who sent us to an ear, nose and throat specialist who wanted to remove Josh's adenoids. His advice didn't feel right to me so I ignored the suggestion. Good thing – I learned later it was a tic!

I have known many families who have had similar experiences. I recommend seeing an expert to rule out the possibility of allergies interfering or contributing to neurological symptoms. An allergist specializing in environmental medicine may be able to help identify allergies that go beyond the simple mold, dust and pollen allergies. For instance, if your child has problems with foods, carpets, detergents, car exhaust or perfumes, you may want to consult with an environmental allergist. If your child has been diagnosed with a tic disorder, plan to share information on the disorder with the allergy specialist because chances are he will know very little about TS.

See Alternative Treatments, Internet Resources, Tics

ALTERNATIVE TREATMENTS

Alternative treatments are sometimes called holistic treatment. Including a variety of fields and specialty areas, they address the possibility that allergies, special diets, exercise and health food additives, such as specific vitamins and minerals, may help reduce the impact of specific neurological symptoms. Some families have tried these alternative methods and had great success. Others have found them to be of no practical value. When considering an alternative treatment, the key question to the doctor should be, "Is there anything in the alternative method that will harm my child?" If the doctor says no, you might decide to try the treatment.

AMERICANS WITH DISABILITIES ACT (ADA)

From consumerlawpage.com:

"The Americans with Disabilities Act (ADA) gives civil rights protections to individuals with disabilities similar to those provided to individuals on the basis of race, color, sex, national origin, age, and religion. It guarantees equal opportunity for individuals with disabilities in public accommodations, employment, transportation, state and local government services, and telecommunications. The first part of the definition makes clear that the ADA applies to persons who have impairments and that these must substantially limit major life activities such as seeing, hearing, speaking, walking, breathing, performing manual tasks, learning, caring for oneself, and working. An individual with epilepsy, paralysis, HIV infection, AIDS, a substantial hearing or visual impairment, mental retardation, or a specific learning disability is covered, but an individual with a minor, non-chronic condition of short duration, such as a sprain, broken limb, or the flu, generally would not be covered."

ANGER

Many children with ND have difficulty with anger control. Sometimes they are angry that they have the disorders in the first place, but many times anger is the result of a stressful situation. In addition, certain medications can contribute to agitation and anger. Documenting medication changes and reactions and sharing the information with the child's doctor will help you determine if medication is contributing to the problem. When problems persist, counseling may be necessary.

See Counseling - Individual/Family, Rage Stage, Rumbling Stage

ANXIETY

Many children with ND experience anxiety. Anxiety over upcoming events, birthdays, holidays, beginning of school year, tests, etc., can increase tics, obsessions and problem behaviors. Anxiety can also manifest itself as school phobia, panic attacks, unusual fears and separation anxiety. It is important for parents to communicate the child's symptoms to teachers, medical professionals and counselors. Certain medications can contribute to a child's anger, while others may help tremendously in keeping her calm. For children with high levels of anxiety, it may be helpful to avoid the following: sounds that are too loud or at a certain pitch, visually overstimulating environments, lots of people, rooms that are too large or too small, or situations that may be perceived as embarrassing to the children or others. When children with ND refuse to do something, especially at school, it is often attributed to anxiety. Train yourself to watch for situations that increase the child's anxiety. Once these situations have been identified, share them with teachers and other individuals involved with the child. Always communicate concerns with the doctor.

See Accommodations, Breaks, Fears, Panic Attacks, School Phobia

ARGUING

I like the way Richard Lavoie talks about how to handle arguing in his video "When the Chips Are Down: Learning Disabilities and Discipline" (Bieber, 1994). When a child is misbehaving, Lavoie maintains that you will be able to stop the behavior by saying firmly no more than three times, "In my class, you will …" rather than start arguing. I have used this technique with my grandchildren, changing the line to "in this family we are nice to each other" and it has worked every time. When the adult participates in the argument, the child "will" escalate and you will end up with a whole new set of problems. After many episodes of doing the wrong thing, I finally learned that I was the one who had to change my way of handling the situations.

See Rage Stage, Recovery Stage, Rumbling Stage, Walk and Don't Talk

ART

Some children with ND have artistic ability. It is important to encourage creative expression. For example, when thoughts are racing through their head, many children with ND tell me drawing helps them to relax. When necessary, accommodations can be made if tics interfere with art activities. For example, adults can cut for children who have compulsions about sharp objects, and children who can't touch "gooey" stuff for sensory reasons can wear gloves. If a child has problems keeping her hands off supplies when she should be listening to the teacher, her supplies may be put away and only be brought out when needed. I suggest these children always be seated close to the teacher. Give only one direction at a time, checking for understanding and allowing plenty of time for transition.

See Brainstorming, Sensory Sensitivity, Talking Non-Stop, Transition from One Activity or Lesson to Another

ASPERGER SYNDROME

Asperger Syndrome (AS) is a neurobiological disability that is considered to be on the autism spectrum. Individuals with AS exhibit challenges in social skills and communication deficits and can have symptoms ranging from mild to severe. In addition, they often have obsessive, repetitive routines and preoccupations with one subject, about which they may talk at length. Frequently viewed as odd, children with AS are often the targets of bullying. Treatment may include medication, social skills training, speech-language therapy, educational accommodations, counseling and occupational therapy.

ASSIGNMENT INCENTIVES

It is helpful to develop an incentive program with the child who is having a great deal of difficulty completing assignments due to neurological symptoms. Reinforcers should relate to the child's interest. One child may want to eat with the principal; another may want baseball cards; yet another may want a can of pop. Many children with ND respond better to reinforcers given the same day than having to accumulate tokens to be redeemed at the end of the week.

See Getting Started, Reinforcers, Sensory Integration Issues

ASSIGNMENT NOTEBOOK/PLANNER

Many students with ND fail classes because they did not get assignments properly written down. Ninety percent of all problems I encounter when working with these students, the schools and parents involve incomplete assignments. If "all" children with ND have problems with writing assignments down, getting them home and completing them – let alone handing them in by the due date – we need to accept this as part of the disorder. It is imperative that someone in the school be responsible for making sure the assignment notebook/planner is complete before the student leaves for home. Because students with ND tend to have difficulty staying on task and often have visual-motor integration problems and poor handwriting, I always request that all the child's teachers monitor assignment writing by initialing assignments that have been copied correctly so that parents will know exactly what is expected. At the end of the day a specific teacher or paraprofessional can check to make sure all assignments are entered, initialed and in the backpack. Don't leave it up to the child to get his notebook in his backpack. Any worksheets (with due dates written on them) should be placed in a folder or envelope. Again, it is the teacher's responsibility to see that this takes place. Assignment notebooks/planners usually have a place for teacher comments. Teachers should make only positive notations in these areas, saving serious concerns for phone calls or conferences with parents. When the child arrives home, it is the parent's responsibility to check the assignment notebook/planner and worksheet folder and initial the notebook when an assignment is completed. This lets the teachers know that parents saw the completed assignments. An optional way to handle assignment notation is to email assignments to the child's home.

See Backpacks and Book Bags, Communication Between School and Home, Email, Responsibility, School Supplies

ASSISTIVE TECHNOLOGY

Assistive technology covers a broad range of devices and services that enable individuals with disabilities to function better. Children with ND may need assistive technology for a variety of reasons. For example, depending on the child's needs, he may need (a) computers to compensate for fine-motor problems and, if applicable, written expression deficits; (b) voice recognition software if tics interfere with keyboarding; and (c) spelling and grammar checkers in case of language mechanics or spelling difficulties. Some children benefit from the use of an AlphaSmart (alphasmart.com), a simple, portable and affordable computer companion that enables users to type, edit and electronically store text (for example, reports, essays, email messages or notes), and to practice keyboarding  without having to be at a computer. The text can be transferred to any computer for formatting, or to a printer. Its portability allows students to use it anywhere and anytime in the classroom, at home or on field trips.

See Computers, Handwriting, Internet Resources

ATTENDANCE

Students need to be in school, but there are times when children with ND have difficulty going to and staying in school. For example, medication side effects may contribute to a child's inability to remain for a whole school day or go at all. Sometimes the child experiences anxiety for various reasons. For example, he may have peer problems or be uncomfortable when exhibiting symptoms (i.e., tics, pacing, rituals) in front of others. Teachers and parents need to work together to help the child with attendance concerns. Parents must let teachers and school nurses know of medication changes and the potential side effects. Some medications can cause lethargy, sleepiness, anxiety, etc. In turn, teachers need to let parents know if the student is exhibiting symptoms or behaviors that may be due to new medications or changes in dosage, etc. Parents need to contact their child's doctor and counselor when their child is consistently late for school because she did not sleep well the night before.

Some children with ND experience school phobia-type behaviors that are similar to panic attacks. Others have feelings of claustrophobia, making small, crowded or windowless classrooms a problem. Some students appear to have separation anxiety from a parent and require a great deal of patience from adults to get them to school. Others have to do things over and over before getting to school until it feels "just right." At school this "just right" feeling can cause the child to enter and leave the school building a certain way or have to open the locker a certain number of times. Other students need their mom or dad to walk into the classroom with them at the beginning of the year.

Retreating from using such support in small steps will help the child transition to independence. I have found that a child can usually help with a solution if he is asked to brainstorm options in a supportive setting. In a calm voice describe the situation you are concerned about and ask the child if there is anything the adults can do to help him go to and stay in school every day. Teachers and parents need to be patient and consistent. Allowing the student to miss a lot of school only causes more problems when the child tries to return.

Transition is very difficult for these kids. Providing support and encouragement helps. Create a daily school or home schedule with pictures if necessary and place it in a high-profile area, usually on the refrigerator. If the child is allowed to call home at certain times during the school day, have a picture showing that activity. Reward the child for each step that was successful. Often when the child experiences a successful "baby step," he is more willing and/or able to try the next step. In some situations, symptoms are so severe that a student must receive homebound instruction where the school provides a teacher for several hours a week.

Many children with ND "cycle," that is, they have trouble during a certain time of year or a specific time more than at others. This is especially true at the end of the school year. I would rather see a child receive homebound instruction than escalate and end up in in-school suspension (ISS), out-of-school suspension (OSS) or get into serious situations where law enforcement officials are called. We must help prevent a child with extreme anxiety, behavior changes or depression from remaining in a situation that would jeopardize his relationship with peers or staff, causing self-esteem issues.

See Anxiety, Homebound Instruction, School - End of Year, School - Returning To, School Phobia, Shutting Down, Sleeping at School

ATTENTION DEFICIT HYPERACTIVITY DISORDER

Attention deficit hyperactivity disorder (ADHD, attentive, inattentive or combined types) is a neurological disorder that affects many children. I have observed hundreds of children with TS and OCD in school settings and have only seen three who did not also exhibit attention deficit symptoms. Often children exhibit symptoms of ADHD before exhibiting symptoms of the other disorders. Symptoms include fidgeting with hands or feet; difficulty remaining seated; problems following through on instructions; difficulty shifting from one task to another; difficulty playing quietly; interrupting and intruding on conversations; appearing not to be listening; acting before thinking; doing something that is dangerous or harmful without thinking about the consequences; poor concentration; and failing to finish a task. The symptoms of ADHD interfere with a person's ability to sustain attention or delay impulsive behavior, and peer relationships can be impacted.

Students with ADHD have a greater chance of dropping out of school, being retained and experiencing academic underachievement than their peers without these disorders. However, most children with ADHD can be successful in a general education setting with only a few accommodations including providing visual instructions, copies of class notes, etc. When the symptoms of ADHD interfere with learning, one or more of the following programs may be recommended: a "pull-out" program; self-contained classrooms; additional support personnel; class-within-a-class; or transition interventions. Once believed to affect only children and disappearing in adolescence, certain symptoms of ADHD continue into adulthood.

A comprehensive evaluation by a multidisciplinary team, including a physician, is necessary to properly diagnose a child with ADHD. The evaluation may include assessment in academic, social and emotional development, cognition and peer relationships. Measures of attention span and impulsivity are also collected. Assessment tools may include standardized tests, observation and interviews. Diagnosing adults with ADHD requires a thorough assessment of childhood history, including both academic and behavioral information.

Treatment for ADHD may include any one or a combination of: behavior management, educational interventions, individual and family counseling, medication and social skills training. The most widely used class of medications for the management of ADHD symptoms is psychostimulants, which may decrease impulsivity and hyperactivity and increase attention.

See Accommodations, Adults and ADHD, Individualized Education Program (IEP), Modifications, Section 504 Plan, Social Skills, Stimulant Medications

ATTENTION – NEGATIVE VS. POSITIVE

Parents who are concerned that their child is behaving negatively to gain their attention should try to ignore the child's behavior, if at all possible. Reacting to negative behavior will only reinforce the behavior. Instead, when the child is doing something positive or correct, heap attention on him. The result is likely to be a repetition of the positive behavior to attract the attention that he desires. If only negative behavior is reinforced, the child may feel that he is incapable of obtaining adult attention. Some children decide that if they are going to be considered bad, they might as well be the "baddest baddie" of them all.

ATTITUDE

Receiving a diagnosis of any neurological condition can be difficult for a child to understand. Help the child realize that he is a person with a disorder and that the disorder is not who he is. It is important for the adults to help children realize that there are many children who have other differences and needs. Some children wear glasses, some have freckles, etc. In addition, adults must help children with ND understand that they have to believe in themselves or no one else will. Often I tell adolescents that if they develop a sense of humor about their disorders, they will be more comfortable around other people. When someone acts negatively or aggressively toward a child's disorders, the child with ND should not react negatively, but say, "I have TS, OCD (or whatever the diagnosis is)."

See Acceptance, Advocacy, Bullying, Educating Peers, Educating School Staff, Sense of Humor

AUDITORY PROCESSING DISORDER

Having a central auditory processing disorder (CAPD), sometimes referred to as auditory processing disorder (APD), means that something is adversely affecting the processing or interpretation of spoken language. Hearing and processing are two different things. With CAPD the ear and the brain do not work together as they should. Auditory processing problems are more likely to occur when a child is in a noisy environment or when listening to complex information. In addition to hindering speech and language development, APD can affect other areas of learning, particularly reading and writing. Parents should always request an evaluation by a speech-language pathologist if they suspect their child has an auditory processing disorder.

See Speech-Language Pathologist

AUTISM

Autism is a complex developmental disorder that usually appears during the first three years of a child's life. Autism affects four times more boys than girls and knows no racial, ethnic, educational, income, lifestyle or social boundaries. The diagnostic criteria for autism from the *DSM-IV Diagnostic and Statistical Manual of Mental Disorders – 4th Edition, Text Revision* (DSM-IV-TR, 2002) includes: (a) qualitative impairment in social interaction; (b) qualitative impairments in communication; and (c) restricted repetitive and stereotyped patterns of behavior, interests and activities.

B

BACKPACKS AND BOOK BAGS

Purchase heavy-duty backpacks or book bags. Clearly mark the bag with the child's name, address, home and school phone numbers, and write in big letters "REWARD" in a conspicuous place so the person finding the bag is more likely to return it. Since most children with ND also have ADHD, it is important to designate a resting place for the book bag at home (preferably by the front door). By the time the child is ready for college, the location of the book bag should be automatic! Just in case, keeping an extra book bag hidden around the house is not a bad idea.

It is critical that parents open the bag after school each evening and inspect its contents, including assignment notebooks. By the same token, it is a good idea to have a "last minute before school" inspection to ward off calls from the principal. Remove all sharp and inappropriate objects, which sometimes have a way of getting into the bags. Some children with ND don't think about the items they stash in their bags as being inappropriate or as something that could get them into trouble at school.

It is the parent's responsibility to make sure all completed assignments and supplies are in the backpack each night. It is (or should be) the school's responsibility to retrieve needed assignments from the backpack and to teach students to retrieve their own assignments. It should also be the school's responsibility to designate a person to check the backpack for assignments and needed supplies at the end of each school day and watch the child leave with backpack in hand. This requirement can be written into the student's IEP or 504 Plan.

See Individualized Education Program (IEP), Organizational Skills, Section 504 Plan

BATHROOM CONCERNS

Many children with ND have compulsions dealing with toileting. Sometimes the compulsion involves the child having to see the bowel movement. Sometimes it has to do with the child wiping himself until it feels "just right." Occasionally the child will have a compulsion to touch or smear the fecal material. These compulsions make little sense to us, but like all compulsions it is nearly impossible to use logic to diminish them. Often medication and/or diversionary activities such as finger painting help.

If teachers notice that a child seems to spend an inordinate amount of time in the bathroom, they need to inform the parents. Document the time of day and how long the child stays. Parents, in turn, are to communicate this information to the child's physician. Sometimes a child will ask to go to the bathroom at the same time each day. In addition to a true physical need, this may be an attempt to avoid an activity the child is uncomfortable with or is having difficulty with in the classroom. Also, the bathroom is often the place where the child is most comfortable expressing tics. In addition to talking to the child and encouraging her to stay in the classroom, if appropriate, sometimes it becomes necessary to set a time limit so the child does not miss too much class time.

See Brainstorming, Compulsions

BEDROOMS, MESSY

Josh's room used to be terribly messy, which was extremely hard on me as I was a mom who used to (keywords here "used to") scrub the kitchen floor with a toothbrush. To help Josh and me deal with the mess in his room, our counselor told me to close the door to Josh's room. I did. After many years and many messy rooms, and finally understanding his disorders more, I now know that the mess was so overwhelming that Josh couldn't get started cleaning his room.

I have learned to approach the cleaning task like I do everything else: break it down into manageable steps. For example, tell your child to pick up the action figures, then his socks, then his books, and so on. One thing at a time! Josh really did love a clean room and always felt so much better when his bedroom was neat. Allow your child some privacy, but before the room becomes a "health hazard," help him learn the technique of "picking up."

BEDTIME BEHAVIOR

Many children with ND have sleep disturbances, which may cause difficulty going to bed or staying asleep, sleep walking, or problems arousing in the morning. One of the first things you need to decide is whether bedtime should be set by the clock or by the fatigue of the child.

You might find that even though you think bedtime should be 9:30 P.M., your child would naturally go to bed at 10:30 P.M. Do you enforce the 9:30 P.M. time with the probable hassle it will entail, or do you let nature take its course and go along with the 10:30 P.M. time? You may find that it is much more peaceful for all concerned simply to go with the later hour. The time you go to bed is often dependent on the time you must get up, so if your child is able to get up in the morning and get off to school on time, there is no problem. However, if the later bedtime causes problems in the morning, it is usually better to have the disturbance at night rather than to start the whole day off wrong. I recommend that children with ND who have difficulty getting to sleep at night not take a nap.

Some children have difficulty disengaging and transitioning from one activity to another. Bedtime often causes such transitional difficulties. Try warning your child ahead of bedtime or plan quiet activities to calm your child before bedtime. Activities such as reading, drawing, playing quietly in her bedroom, listening to the radio or watching television may aid in transition. It is important to try to determine why your child is resisting sleep. Possible reasons include bedtime fears and obsessive thoughts, and these may need to be addressed with the child's doctor and counselor.

See Fears, Obsessive Compulsive Disorder, Morning Routine, Structure and Routine, Transition from One Activity or Lesson to Another

BEHAVIOR AND MEDICATIONS

When a child's behavior is completely out of control and her doctor has tried adjusting the medications again and again, the parents and the doctor may decide to take the child off of all medications. Sometimes the medications have run their course and are no longer effective. Sometimes a slight change in a medication will make a dramatic difference. Under no circumstances should parents make such changes without consulting their doctor. I highly recommend that parents document all medication changes and their observations of those changes. Always name the medication, the date, the starting dosage and the observations every few days. See Parent Journal and Medication Changes in the Appendix, developed for just such documentation.

See Behavior, Changing, Medication Side Effects

BEHAVIOR, CHANGING

Children with ND generally learn by seeing and doing rather than by logic and insight. They learn by rote or repetitive performance of the same behavior(s). For example, the child may seem never to be able to remember her backpack in the morning until it has become an established behavior that is repeated every day. Over the years I have noticed that when a behavior has been repeated every day for approximately three months, it has become well established. Luckily, children with ND prefer consistency, which works well with a rote learning style.

BEHAVIOR, ESCALATING AND DE-ESCALATING

See Rage Stage, Recovery Stage, Rumbling Stage, Walk and Don't Talk

BEHAVIOR MODIFICATION

If you have ever tried a point system or rewarded your child with stars on a chart for good behavior, you have tried a behavior modification program. The basis of behavior mod, or B-mod for short, is that you reward for good behavior, causing the child to be more interested in the "good" than the "bad" behavior. It requires that you find a reward that your child will work for, and that you pick out a few behaviors at a time to work on. The idea is that your child will learn to associate doing the "good" thing with a reward, and then eventually like doing the good thing enough so that she won't need the reward. Sometimes B-mod programs are set up to reward NOT doing a "bad" behavior, and rewards are given accordingly. An example of rewarding the stopping of a behavior would be to give your child a star on a chart for every night she doesn't wet her bed.

For children without neurological problems, these programs can work. For kids with ND like TS or AS, unfortunately they don't do so well. These children tend to focus on or obsess too much on the reward and too little on the behavior that the reward is supposed to reinforce. In addition, they sometimes work hard on certain behaviors for a certain reward, only to slide back into negative behaviors after they get the reward. Further, children with obsessions who try to stop themselves from doing a "bad" behavior to get a reward can end up focusing more on the bad thing they are not supposed to do, and do it MORE, instead of less often. In brief, B-mod programs have made many parents I have seen over time feel frustrated and powerless with their children with ND.

See Positive Reinforcement, Structure and Routine

BEHAVIOR PLAN

The 1997 Amendments to the Individuals with Disabilities Education Act (IDEA) state the relationship between behavior and learning must be considered. If the child has behavioral issues, a functional behavior assessment must be conducted and a behavior plan developed to address the behavior and why it is occurring. This plan must be individualized; it cannot be a generic plan used for all children. In addressing the behavioral issues of children with ND, the IEP team must explore strategies to address behaviors that interfere with learning. The IEP team will also discuss how your child's behaviors impact the learning of his child's peers. The team will then develop an intervention plan that includes strategies, accommodations, supplementary aids and supports. Because the disability is neurological, this should not be a plan that relies solely or primarily on consequences for the child's behavior, but should address (a) how the classroom environment and academics should change to meet the child's needs and (b) how the teacher presents and tests material. The objective of the behavior plan is for the child to be successful, so it should include any details that will help to reach that objective.

See Consequences, Functional Behavior Assessment

BEING FLEXIBLE

When you have a child with ND, you must be willing to change your routine and perhaps some family traditions. One mother told me that before her son's diagnosis, the family always ate meals together without the TV on. Her son was very noisy when he ate, and in order to keep peace with the siblings who had trouble with this noise, the family decided to eat in front of the TV to block out the noise. They still give thanks before the TV goes on and talk about the day's events, etc. This did change a family tradition, but the family felt keeping peace in the family was important too.

See Fatherhood, Motherhood, Parenting a Child with ND

BELIEVING IN YOURSELF

Even under the best circumstances, there will be times when parents and teachers wonder whether they are doing the right thing for the child with ND. They must learn about the disorders and then do the best they can for the child, even if it means making some mistakes along the way. If I had listened to some of the "experts" when Josh was growing up, he would have been placed in a residential treatment center for his "behaviors." Luckily, one of Josh's social workers taught me to go with my "gut feeling." It isn't easy, but try to look at the whole picture. Listen to others, reflect on their input, and then make decisions based on what you believe is the best decision for the child. Parents must believe that they can get through the challenges they are faced with. You can learn from other parents who have had similar experiences. They are some of the best teachers.

See Support Groups

BIPOLAR DISORDER

The *Diagnostic and Statistical Manual of Mental Disorders – 4th Edition, Text Revision* (DSM-IV-TR, 2002) describes bipolar disorder as a disorder that causes individuals to experience severe mood swings from very happy (overly high), to severe depression (very low). Periods of normal moods are interspersed with the mood swings. Bipolar disorder is also referred to as manic-depressive illness.

See Depression, Mania

BLURTING OUT

Some children with ND "blurt" out certain phrases or words over and over again, some of them inappropriate. Often they have to say the words repeatedly until it feels "just right." The child may have a compulsion to hear an answer, like when Josh would each night say, "Good night, mom, I love you." I would have to respond many times, "Good night, Josh, I love you," until I said it exactly how he needed to hear it.

When some children blurt out words, whether inappropriate or not, they try to disguise the word or phrase by covering their mouth with their shirt or hand or even try to disguise it with a cough. Some will blurt only to a visual or auditory stimulus: for example, if they see a pig, they might blurt "oink, oink." At school, teachers should allow a child with blurting concerns frequent breaks to relieve his stress level. Teachers should also educate the other children and staff about the child's blurting symptoms. At home family members must learn to accept the blurting, but some strategies that may help include: chewing gum; sucking on hard candy; or redirecting the child to another activity without calling attention to the blurting.

See Coprolalia, Educating Peers, "Just Right" Feeling

BOARD GAMES

Board games and card games are a great way to monitor and encourage social development in all children, but especially children with ND. These children often do not have many opportunities for positive social interactions with their peers, so playing a board or card game with one or two other people can give them an opportunity to learn and practice social skills. The skills they learn while playing can be applied to other activities. These activities require a variety of social skills including: taking turns, voice modulation, learning how to ask for help on understanding the rules, sportsmanship, working cooperatively with others and dealing with competition. These games can be used as positive reinforcers and therefore serve a dual purpose.

See Reinforcers, Social Skills

BOOKS LEFT AT HOME

A complete set of textbooks may need to remain at the child's home during the school year. This way, children with ND won't be penalized for not being able to complete assignments if they forgot to bring home their books. This is not enabling. It is an accommodation for a child with a neurological impairment, and should be added to the IEP or 504 Plan.

BOOKS LEFT IN LOCKER

Is it more important to keep another set of books in the class so the child doesn't miss instructional time by going back to the locker or is it more important for the child to receive a detention for not bringing supplies to class? Which option impacts the child's education the most? We want children with ND to become more responsible and we need to help them in this area. They do have organizational problems due to their disorders. They don't "forget" their materials because they want to be belittled in front of their peers, as often happens in the classroom.

See Acceptance, Locker Concerns, Manipulating Behavior, School Supplies

BOOKS ON TAPE

Textbooks on tape are excellent resources for students with ND by providing audio reinforcement of the printed text.

See Internet Resources

BRAINSTORMING

When a problem arises, ask yourself "Who, what, why, when, where and how." Look at the entire picture. There is usually more than one right answer. Talk to another parent who is experiencing similar problems or talk to a teacher who has worked with another child with ND. And, don't forget to include the children. They are often able to come up with good suggestions.

See Support Groups

BREAKS

At school, recognizing when a student is shutting down, becoming fidgety, etc., and intervening as soon as possible can often prevent the behavior from escalating into a meltdown. Children with TS and OCD can spend a great deal of energy suppressing tics and compulsions while children with other symptoms of ND, like ADHD and AS, can become restless, over-excited, and frustrated with their inability to perform as well as their peers.

A break can make a big difference. Tics, compulsions and pent-up frustrations and energy have to be released. Often, allowing the student to go on an errand, get a drink, etc., will give her enough of a break to continue a class assignment or activity successfully afterward. Also, the student should be allowed to leave for the designated home base to release symptoms when necessary. Planning ahead for these breaks may be necessary. Depending on the severity of the symptoms (tics, compulsions, anxiety), more breaks may be necessary at certain times than at others. Occasionally, a child will manipulate the breaks. In such instances, scheduled breaks may be necessary. Assessing the specific concern (asking the questions who, what, where, why, how, when) is very important in developing the proper break strategies.

See Home Base, Manipulating Behavior, Rumbling Stage

BULLYING

Children with ND are frequently targets of bullying. When your child returns from school relating this type of behavior, contact the school. Don't put up with bullying behavior. Sometimes children with ND are the instigators, but most of the time the child's peers are making fun of his neurological symptoms. School professionals have an obligation to protect all children from bullying behavior. Counselors can meet with the child with ND on a regular basis to monitor the effects of the school intervention plan, and speech-language pathologists can address concerns through instruction in pragmatics. Bullying and teasing is a big concern. Parents must push for these services.

See Counseling - Individual/Family, Immaturity, Manipulating Behavior, Pragmatics, Speech-Language Pathologist

BUS BEHAVIOR

At the beginning of each year I receive calls from frantic parents that their child has been suspended from the bus. I find it appalling that bus drivers are not made aware of the unique behaviors and needs of children with ND. It is difficult enough to be a bus driver. They deserve to know as much as possible about the child with ND so they can make the bus ride a safe and positive experience for everyone involved. Many modifications are possible. Some children with ND have held their symptoms together for an entire school day and by the time they get on the school bus in the afternoon may not be able to suppress tics, impulsivity or anxiety any longer. Giving these children something to do with their hands sometimes helps, such as a hand-held computer game, a book to read, or a Rubics cube. Some children may need to be placed in a seat by themselves if they have intruding tics. Positive role models can also help. It is best to place the child with special needs close to the bus driver so he or she can watch for problems. All the bus riders need to be educated about the effects of ND. If another child is harassing the child with the disorder, that child needs appropriate discipline. Sometimes children with ND do better on the special education bus, but this decision needs to be made on a case-by-case basis. Bus behavior should be addressed in the IEP and 504 Plan.

See Educating the Bus Driver

C

CALCULATORS

There are basically two schools of thought about the use of calculators by students. Rather than spending so much time struggling to retrieve the correct answer and often failing, I think children who have severe math problems need calculators to get the correct answer the first time if at all possible. Others believe that constant drilling is the only way to learn the basic facts. I see so many children in eighth grade performing at second- and third-grade math levels. Letting children with ND use calculators allows them to continue learning higher-level skills while still working on the more basic ones.

CALLING HOME

Children with ND sometimes fear that something will happen to a parent if the child is not at home to prevent it, and therefore may not want to go to school. The parent should make it clear that staying home from school is not an option and try to distract the child by talking about an after-school activity long enough to get him out the door. Sometimes the fear does not show up until the child is in school. In such cases, the child often asks to call home or requests to go to the nurse's office. If phone calls are allowed, establish a time limit for each call and for the number of calls allowed. Sitting the child down with the parents, teachers and other school support and scheduling phone calls home helps the child know that everyone is there to support him. Sometimes hearing the parent's reassuring voice is all the child needs to calm down. When the calls home have a time limit, there is less chance that the child will get involved in a power struggle with the parent about needing to go home. The number of calls allowed can slowly be reduced, as appropriate.

It is important that the parent is supportive of the child and praises her for staying in school. Medication can sometimes play a role in the symptoms. When the anxiety is severe and calling home is not enough to calm the child, the IEP team may consider a limited school day and place the child on partial or short-term homebound instruction. It is important that the child's fears or separation anxiety be assessed by a doctor and counselor so interventions can be tried. A word of caution: Sometimes the child's fears are so strong that he will need to go home, such as when the symptoms interfere with others' learning.

See Anxiety, Fears, Homebound Instruction, Medication Side Effects, School Phobia

CALMING TECHNIQUES

There will be many times when you will need to help your child calm down, for instance, when getting ready to go to sleep, after an intense activity, after birthday parties, etc. Many children with ND are sensitive to light, so using soft lights in the home, especially in the child's bedroom, might help her fall asleep. Visual distractions can be covered with sheets or a room divider. Rolling up in a mat or blanket helps some children relax. I have known several children who prefer to curl up in a box when they need to calm down. One girl I worked with created a hole in her wall just big enough to crawl into when she was stressed. This served as her "home base" – a quiet place to think. Playing soft music or talking softly can also be beneficial. And I swear by milkshakes. Everyone needs a quiet place to think or regroup, even children with ND.

See Home Base, Milkshakes, Occupational Therapist

CAMP

When I was teaching second grade at an environmental science magnet, we took the students to a camp for one night. During the stay I talked with the camp superintendent about how I would like to have a camp experience for children who had Tourette Syndrome. I was convinced this was something these children desperately needed. Due to their symptoms, many of them did not have opportunities for a positive camp experience with understanding staff. We held our first camp in 1994. We wanted to offer a structured, fun experience. The camp was therapeutic for many, but that was not the objective. The experience gave many of the children their first real friends. For some this was their first opportunity to get to know others with the same disorders and be fully accepted. Those who were apprehensive the first day were in tears on the last day because they didn't want to go home. It's probably the achievement I am the most proud of. I would like nothing better than to duplicate this camp all over the country. Parents should contact the national organizations of their child's disorders to find out what camps are available in their areas.

CAREER DEVELOPMENT

Career development involves a combination of assessment of an individual's skills and interests and the training needed to acquire employment in the area of interest. As children with ND age, they need to be exposed to different career options to help them determine their areas of interest. The extent to which their hyper-arousal, social functioning, learning difficulties, and sleep disturbances impact their functionality in a job setting needs to be considered as they evaluate their job interests and the responsibilities involved. Training and education will further enhance the individual's employability once a career area has been chosen.

The employability of individuals with ND needs to be considered as they compete with others in an open job market. While the Americans with Disabilities Act (ADA) prohibits employers from discriminating against possible candidates, job candidates are expected to be able to perform job functions without imposing undue hardships on employers. Once employed, educating coworkers and employers about the disorders may be necessary, depending on the individual's ability to mask or accommodate symptoms.

See Americans with Disabilities Act (ADA)

CHANGES IN FAMILY ENVIRONMENT

Children with ND have difficulty with change, including moving from one home to another, visiting relatives, adding new members to the family, etc. During times of change, it is important to remember to keep the child's routine as normal as possible and to provide structure, including planning ahead with the child. Use a calendar to show when a change will take place. Children with ND like to help others, so when things are changing at home find some way they can contribute to making the transition successful. Educate visitors on what can be expected from your child by handing them something in writing. Be specific on how they are expected to interact with the child. Decide how discipline will be dealt with when visitors are in the home. Also, when at Grandma's house, identify to your child the expectations – that is, the things that are not allowed there that are usually allowed at home. Being very specific about what is/is not allowed will help everyone. Family members who refuse to accept your wishes should have little contact with the child with ND, or when contact is necessary the child will need a parent with him.

See Acceptance, Extended Family

CHANGES IN MEDICATIONS

Often when your child's symptoms change, medications will need to be adjusted or changed. Each symptom requires different medications. It is soooo … important for parents to communicate changes in symptoms to the doctor and ask teachers to communicate to you their observations on a weekly basis. Once a decision is made to change medications, you may see a "honeymoon" period where you will say, "Wow, this is great" or "This is not working!" or notice that your child seems very hyperactive. Good or bad, relay your observations to the doctor. Always let the school know when there are medication changes and ask teachers to communicate to you their observations on a weekly basis. Use the Medication Changes form provided in the Appendix to communicate changes to the teacher, school nurse and other individuals who interact with your child.

See Parent Journal, Teacher Journal, Weekly Reports

CHANGES IN SCHEDULE AND ROUTINE

Change is hard for many people, but especially for children with ND. They desperately need their routines. This means home, school, after-school activities, and family gatherings. Plan, plan, plan, and then plan some more! Don't spring a change on your child without planning unless you love meltdowns. Plan how you will tell the child, where you will tell him, when you will tell him. I could never tell Josh about an upcoming event until right before the event because he would obsess about it and not be able to think about anything else. But other children need to know what is going to happen before it actually occurs. You need to determine where your child fits in. Using visuals (i.e., calendars, lists, stickers, pictures) can help with anticipated change. Tell the child about the change in his calmest setting – for Josh this was on our nightly drives.

This applies to school as well. For example, if a teacher knows a substitute will be needed on a certain day, it is important to try to get someone who knows and accepts the child with ND. If this is not possible, it may be necessary to arrange for the student to spend time in another environment that will provide the support he needs. Sometimes I tell the school to call the parents and allow them to decide whether to keep the child home.

See Structure and Routine, Substitute Teachers

CHANGES IN SLEEPING HABITS

Teachers must keep in mind that children with ND are not always rested when at school, so they may want to provide a physical activity at certain times of the day to help the child be more alert. Parents should always report sleep problems and changes to their child's doctor. Some children with ND are infamous for getting their days and nights turned around. If the decision about sleep is left up to the child, he may stay up all night and sleep all day.

See Bedtime Behavior, Sleeping Habits

CHANGES IN TICS

Josh's tics would change about every three months. They started with eye blinking at about age four. Tics usually start at the head and move down the torso as the child grows. I used to think they couldn't get worse … what little I knew! I remember he was just exhibiting a few facial tics when he was diagnosed with Tourette Syndrome, but the very next week he started having tics so severe that he looked as if he was having full body seizures.

Tics can change, and many times old ones will return. Sometimes the "power of suggestion" will start a tic. I saw this happen to Josh a lot. For example, he would be watching a TV show and all of a sudden would start doing something he had seen on the show. Sometimes parents will voice their concerns about their child picking up another child's tic at camp, for example. While I have seen this happen, the tic usually disappears after they return home.

Your child will pick up tics, both motor and vocal, no matter how much you try to prevent it. Just monitor their impact on your child's life and accept them. Whatever you do, don't point them out. I have noticed tics seem to change during good stress and bad stress (good stress could be a birthday party and bad stress could be a family crisis), and when the seasons change. Over time you may notice that a particular time of year is more difficult for your child than others. Documenting this information helps you prepare for the next year, reminding you of what did and did not work in dealing with the tics.

See Acceptance, Effects of Seasonal Changes and Weather, Tics, Tourette Syndrome

CHANGING BEHAVIOR

Children with ND will have behavior concerns as all children do, but may have more due to their ND. Identify the behaviors that need to change and work on only one at a time. Determine who will be involved. Including teachers, coaches, youth leaders, etc., will provide the structure needed. Positive reinforcement goes a long way. Remember: One negative, hateful remark can undo any efforts to improve a behavior.

In *The Explosive Child*, Ross W. Greene speaks about behaviors belonging to one of three categories: (a) non-negotiable behaviors, (b) negotiable behaviors and

(c) behavior concerns that should be allowed in order to focus on (a) and (b). Parents of children with ND often want to correct all of the child's behaviors (for instance, irresponsibility, cleaning room, following through with chores, etc.) right away, forgetting or unaware that the child may not be able to handle so many expectations at a time.

CHANGING CLASSES

Often children with ND lack organizational skills to prepare for changes between classes at school. Just getting out the door of one class, remembering to take supplies, remembering where to go or how to get there and trying to socialize, too, all at the same time can be quite stress-ful. In addition, children with ND also have attention-al problems and many may have fears or rituals that have to be performed before they can go to the next class. School hallways can be particularly troublesome for children with ND. The child may experience sensory overload with the rush of people and noise.

I didn't find out until one young man had graduated from high school that he hated the hallways because he couldn't stand it when someone bumped into him or stepped on his shoes. When this happened, he became so consumed with anxiety that he was unable to function in class. Hundreds of children with ND every year end up in detention because they are either late to class, arrive without the required supplies or because of conflicts with peers in the halls. It is important to address these concerns in the IEP or 504 Plan.

Helpful strategies include: organization instruction; assistance by teacher, para or designated adult; extra set of books for home; supplies left in each classroom, including textbooks; and early dismissal.

See Fears, Organizational Skills, School Supplies, Sensory Sensitivity, Transition from One Activity or Lesson to Another, Unstructured vs. Structured Environments

CHANGING SCHOOLS

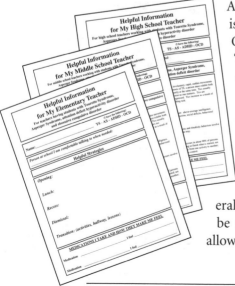

Any time a child changes schools, there are challenges. This is especially true for middle school and high school. Children with ND have difficulty with schedules and "memory demands" when starting middle school. If the child is having peer problems, is immature and struggles academically, the prospect of starting at a new school can be overwhelming.

Before the year ends at the "old" school, the planning for the next school should begin. Many elementary schools take children to visit their prospective middle schools. This should be followed for the student with ND by several visits during the summer, identifying specific staff he will be in contact with. During each visit the child should be allowed to walk the halls, explore and become familiar with all areas that pertain to him. Once the schedule is developed, the child needs to "walk through" his day several times. This should include identifying the locker and practicing unlocking it each visit. Myles and Adreon (2001) provide a helpful transition checklist that can be used with almost all children with ND in their book, *Asperger Syndrome and Adolescence: Practical Solutions for School Success.*

See Educating School Staff, Hidden Curriculum

CHECKING

My daughter, who has OCD, tells me that she would sometimes have to leave high school to go home and "check" to see if the iron was left on. Many people have to make sure the light or stove has been turned off. Some students have told me they have to check a math problem over and over before going on. These are some of the more common compulsions. Unless you know the child well, you may not "see" the severity of this symptom. I once knew a man who, when driving, would have to circle the block to make sure a person he had seen earlier was still alive. He "knew" the individual was OK, but he had to keep checking anyway. It would take him two hours to get home when it should have taken him only 20 minutes.

Adults who have experienced checking compulsions note that sometimes making a list of items to be checked off helps. If your child has a problem with "checking," consult the doctor to see if medications could be helpful. Counseling can also be beneficial.

See Counseling - Individual/Family, Obsessive Compulsive Disorder

CHECKLISTS

When a child appears not to be able to do a task she has been asked to do, it usually means she is overwhelmed and can't get started. At home, work and school it helps to break the task into smaller steps and make a list that can be checked off. Cut pictures out of magazines or use clip art to make charts and place them in "strategic" spots. This can be done for taking medications, doing chores, morning and bedtime routines, etc.

See Getting Started, Visual Supports

CHRONIC TIC DISORDER

Chronic tic disorders are disorders that involve either a vocal or motor tic, but not both. They are differentiated from TS and transient tic disorder in that they can last more than a year and are relatively unchanging.

See Tics, Tourette Syndrome, Transient Tic Disorder

CLASS SCHEDULE

For many children with ND the core subjects of reading, math and language arts should be scheduled in the morning, with quiet activities alternating with more physical ones throughout the day. This kind of schedule will allow them opportunity to release energy as well as tics. Since many children with ND have difficulty with PE, such as the noise and having to change clothes, I recommend PE be scheduled at the end of the day. Students with ND can be slow in getting to the next class, are usually pretty exhausted after the class and often have difficulty transitioning.

The exceptions are children with severe sleep problems who do not start their day until mid-morning. Ask the parents and child what the pattern is in terms of his mood, ability to concentrate, etc. For a student who experiences significant difficulty in the morning, you may want to consider scheduling his first class with high-interest content. In middle and high schools it helps if classes are scheduled in rooms that are in fairly close proximity, if possible. Children with ND can be notoriously late, often having problems with lockers and frequently needing to use the restroom due to medications.

See Physical Education, Resource Room, Transition from One Activity or Lesson to Another

CLASSROOM DISTRACTIONS

I don't know why they call it attention deficit disorder, because the children with ADHD I have worked with are attracted to everything, including windows, bulletin boards, posters, book shelves, noise from lights, children at recess, the children around them, items on the floor, the wall clock and much more. These children do best in environments with few visual and auditory distractions. Sometimes a study carrel can be beneficial if the child is agreeable to using it.

See Classroom Environment, Classroom Seating Arrangements, Study Carrel, Visual Distractions

CLASSROOM ENVIRONMENT

When I was teaching, I loved getting ready at the beginning of the year. I loved creating bulletin boards, hanging up posters and mobiles, and wanted the room to be bright and colorful. While most students welcome such an environment, it can be too much stimulation for some students with ND. The classroom can be attractive and still meet the needs of a child with sensory issues. When arranging the room try to place the child with ND so that he is turning away from as many distractions as possible, facing toward the teacher. It is OK to hang things from the ceiling as long as they are not in direct view of the child with ND. Keeping shelves neat and organized and away from view also helps. Be aware that many children with ND are sensitive to sound and smell. For example, while a flowering plant may be an attractive addition to the room, it may cause problems for a child with ND.

Be observant to see if anything seems to cause the child discomfort. One year I observed a fourth-grade classroom with one very active boy. He had been assigned a seat in the back row, but the interesting thing was that the teacher had placed a swivel chair directly behind his desk so when he was "antsy" he could get in "his" chair and swivel away. It was a wonderful arrangement. I have also seen classrooms that had stationary bicycles where any child who needed to "release" some energy could "take a ride." Similarly, sound machines can help filter out any disturbing noises.

There isn't a classroom in the world these days that has only one child with special needs in it. Planning for those specific needs is crucial. Teachers know from experience that an organized room and a structured schedule can prevent problems for all students, and particularly for those with ND. I tell parents and teachers to plan for everything. Consider how you will have the child enter and leave the room; how you will transition him to and from classes, recess and the lunchroom; how you will transition him from one activity to another; what accommodations are needed for board work and seatwork; how you will handle his assignments; how you will implement the goals and objectives of an IEP; how you will handle seating arrangements; how you will provide breaks; and how you will discipline him. Enlist the parents for help; they really are the experts.

See Accommodations, Individualized Education Program (IEP), Section 504 Plan, Transition from One Activity or Lesson to Another, Transition to and from Recess

CLASSROOM SCHEDULE, END OF DAY

Someone in the school, whether it be the teacher, paraprofessional or a volunteer, needs to assist the child with ND at the end of the day to make sure she gets out the door with important school information and the necessary homework supplies in her backpack. This person also needs to make sure assignments are either written in the student's assignment notebook or emailed to the child's home. One time I was observing a fifth-grade class preparing to go home. The class was divided into teams of four, and each team was responsible for making sure that all team members had the necessary supplies and assignments for home. They were given a grade for this. Many children with ND need this accommodation, and it won't hurt the others. I recommend that parents get a list of phone numbers of responsible students in all subjects for backup.

See Backpacks and Book Bags, Classroom Schedule, Start of Day

CLASSROOM SCHEDULE, START OF DAY

Children with ND have a much better day if someone is assigned to help them organize their day. In middle school it often helps to have them first report to their home base or to have their first class be a study skills class, if possible. In some schools I have seen children report to the resource room when they first arrive. Checking supplies, organizing the desk, returning homework, checking the notebook for neatness, checking to see if the homework is placed in the appropriate folder, etc., are all important activities that children with ND need help with at the start of the day. At home and school it helps to develop a checklist so the child feels a sense of accomplishment when he checks off an item. Parents need to do their part to help organize their child. Parents should always check their child's backpack to make sure he has the needed supplies or books and make sure completed assignments are put in their folder and placed in the backpack.

See Assignment Notebook/Planner, Backpacks and Book Bags, Home Base, Paraprofessionals, Visual Supports

CLASSROOM SEATING ARRANGEMENTS

Some students want to sit close to the front of the room so they are better able to focus and so the teacher can more easily assist them in refocusing or initiating tasks. Other students wish to sit nearer to the door so they can leave without calling attention to themselves. Older students should be allowed to share their thoughts on seating arrangements. If space is not a problem, perhaps the student can vary where he sits, depending on his needs at the time. I have known teachers who have created two seating areas for a student to accommodate his need to get up and walk around. It is important to tell students about seating changes before they occur.

See Classroom Distractions, Classroom Environment

CLAUSTROPHOBIA

Claustrophobia – the fear of small, enclosed spaces – is common among children with ND. It is of little use to try to use logic to talk a child out of being claustrophobic. I suggest using some form of distraction instead. In more severe cases, a good therapist can help desensitize the child using successive approximation techniques. Medication may also help, so parents should communicate claustrophobic concerns to the doctor.

I remember observing a middle school student, one of nine students, in a room so small the desks were touching … and the teacher wondered why the child who had TS was "misbehaving!" This poor young man was ticcing so badly he couldn't sit still, let alone take notes. I usually try to work with the teachers, but I left that room and went straight to the principal demanding the student be removed from that room. No child should be placed in an environment that small. I have been in far too many ill-equipped, cramped special education rooms. Children with special needs generally need more room, not less. They need room to move around in.

See Diversion

CLINGING BEHAVIOR

Over the years I have learned to recognize clinging behavior as an expression of anxiety. Anxiety can be overwhelming. It is very difficult to understand how debilitating it is to have a neurological disorder. My only answer is simply to be there. Children need support, love, compassion and acceptance to get through their anxiety-laden times, no matter what their age is. When no one else in the world seems to understand, the child needs to know that his mom, dad or special caregiver will always be there. This is not the kind of clinginess that's associated with a smothering parent who is afraid to let the child grow. Accept the child where he is at the moment. It's a good idea to consult a doctor and a family counselor when anxiety severely interferes with the child's daily functioning.

See Anxiety, Counseling - Individual/Family

CLOTHING – CHEWING/PULLING ON

It is especially common for children with OCD and/or TS to chew or pull on their clothing. When that happens, you might give them something to chew on such as hard candy, licorice or gum; sometimes they just need to pick at something. Have them wear collarless clothes. Remove all tags. Before purchasing clothes for your child, feel the insides for scratchy seams and rough edges. Also, the child may not be able to wear clothes that others have purchased for him because they have to feel "just right." Josh cut every neck out and every pant leg above the knee. What do you do with dozens of sweat pant legs cut off at the knee? Don't make it an issue, no matter how much it costs to replace the clothes.

See Acceptance, Clothing - Comfort Level, "Just Right" Feeling, Obsessive Compulsive Disorder, Sensory Sensitivity, Tourette Syndrome

CLOTHING – COMFORT LEVEL

Most children with ND have favorite clothes, including socks! Buy stock in the company that makes whatever clothing your child approves of because you'll be buying a lot of the same socks, underwear and jeans. The behaviors of children who are forced to wear "uncomfortable" clothing will deteriorate quickly at school, home or anywhere else. It's not worth it. When getting dressed in the morning it is not uncommon for children with ND to change several times until they find something that feels "just right." You will find yourself washing your child's favorite clothes over and over to help with her comfort level. My grandson won't wear anything with buttons. My daughter finally gave up and accepted that her son would be "buttonless." Not all children with ND experience this level of discomfort, but for those who do, stress can be reduced when clothing accommodations are made.

See Acceptance, Clothing - Chewing/Pulling On, "Just Right" Feeling, Obsessive Compulsive Disorder, Sensory Sensitivity, Tourette Syndrome

CLOTHING – UNIFORMS

Children with ND who attend private schools where uniforms are required present a unique challenge. If a child has sensory issues, the parents should discuss clothing options with the administrator before enrolling the child. Many children refuse to wear anything except sweats. One option would be to allow the child to wear navy sweats instead of slacks.

See Accommodations, Clothing - Comfort Level

COGNITIVE BEHAVIORAL THERAPY

Cognitive behavioral therapy (CBT) is developed out of a set of behavioral theories called cognitive or rational theories that focus on the thinking, beliefs, interpretations and mindsets of an individual. CBT works to incorporate changes by first identifying the thoughts and beliefs that are irrational and negatively affecting the life of a person. Next, through logical discussion, these beliefs and mindsets are explored to see if they are true. During this process some alternative, more rational and effective ideas are discussed concerning ways of interpreting life events and responding to them. A "homework" assignment is developed in which the person agrees to try to implement the new ideas and actions. This form of therapy has been found to work well with anxiety, depression, compulsions and rituals.

See Behavior Modification

COLLEGE ACCOMMODATIONS

Many colleges make accommodations for students with ND, as stipulated by the Rehabilitation Act of 1973. When searching for a community college or university for your child, it is important to visit the campus. The admissions office should be able to direct you to the appropriate advisors to discuss available disability services. Plan to accompany your son or daughter to the college when seeking this information. Since many students with ND have processing problems, they may need an extra set of ears to make sure they communicate their specific needs and, in turn, understand the responses. To determine services, the college will request documentation of your child's disabil-  ity and services provided by your school district. Colleges may offer note takers, books on tape, and extra time and separate rooms for test taking. College personnel will not ask about the disability; it is up to the student to decide how much information to share. Prepare for the visit by identifying problem areas that you feel need to be communicated, but also have your son/daughter prepare a list of what they feel they need from the college and take it to the initial meeting. The child may have concerns different from the parents.

See Advocacy in College

COMMUNICATION, FAMILY

This is a big one. The immediate family members are the ones most impacted by a diagnosis of ND. From my experience of working with hundreds of families, I believe parents go through a process of grieving not unlike that of losing a loved one. While parents may not agree on the way to handle every situation, the really successful children with ND grow up in families where the parents agree to work together consistently for the benefit of the whole family. Parents have to talk to each other, attend support group meetings, get professional help from a counselor who specializes in ND and learn as much as they can about the disorders. A big responsibility has been given to them.

Parents must identify their strengths and weaknesses and use that information to develop a family plan that will work. Single parents need to identify a supportive family member or friend to talk to. You won't learn everything overnight. Parents should not be afraid to share fears and mistakes with other families because that's how we learn. I find that families who communicate and support each other are most successful.

See Acceptance, Counseling - Individual/Family, Educating Parents, Grieving, Support Groups

COMMUNICATION BETWEEN SCHOOL AND HOME

The most important thing to take place between school and home is communication. It takes just a few minutes to share information through email, weekly reports, etc., but those minutes can be life-changing for children with ND. When I see a child experiencing success, I can always identify a wonderful teacher or administrator, someone who believes the parents and is open to learning more about the child's disorders. These teachers are creative when developing strategies to accommodate their student.

I developed a form titled Weekly Report intended to help with home-school communication. Here the teacher notes any incomplete assignments, upcoming projects, field trips, observations, questions, interfering symptoms, social interactions, etc. It is also important to note changes in behavior, good or bad. Don't just communicate about negative behaviors. Often the comments teachers make in these reports contribute more to the overall success of the child than anything else. If appropriate, parents can relay the information to the doctor and counselor. It does take a village to raise children with ND, and we are all a part of this team.

The reports should be sent home on Friday, never on Monday. This is because many children with ND have OCD and may obsess over a comment, incomplete assignments, etc., and not be able to function fully at school for the rest of the week if the information is sent home during the week. By receiving the information on Friday, the parents can address concerns and incomplete assignments over the weekend and the child can return to school on Monday ready for a fresh start. With email so widely available, it is easier than ever to share the information. Don't overreact if the teacher forgets once in a while. Just contact the teacher to remind him. I recommend getting a communication system like this in writing in an IEP or 504 Plan.

See Obsessive Compulsive Disorder, Stuck Thinking, Weekly Report

COMPLAINTS OF NOT FEELING WELL

Children know that when they get sick at school, they can go home. When children frequently ask to go to the nurse's office with complaints of not feeling well, we have to ask if something else is going on. Sometimes a pattern develops when the child wants to go to the nurse at a set time each day. Could it be a class or subject that is stressful for the child? Asking these questions may help you determine what is actually going on. Sometimes high levels of anxiety cause physical problems. Often just touching base with the nurse or resting for a limited time is all the child needs to go on for the rest of the day. A good relationship with the school nurse is very important. While teachers may change from year to year, the school nurse provides some stability across the grades. Documentation of visits must be shared with parents on a weekly basis. Keeping a positive attitude is very important.

See School Nurse, School Phobia

COMPLEX TICS

Complex tics are tics that involve a complex movement or series of movements that affect more than one muscle group. One example would be jumping in the air and spinning around.

See Tics, Simple Tics, Tourette Syndrome

COMPULSIONS

Compulsions are behaviors that are used to reduce the anxiety that is created by obsessions. Most children with ND have more than one compulsion. Compulsions can be confused with tics, so an expert in neurological disorders should be consulted for a definite diagnosis. When compulsions interfere with the child's life, medication and cognitive behavioral therapy may be in order. Compulsions that are either socially unacceptable or unhealthy require professional attention. Your doctor should be able to recommend someone who specializes in this area. Another option is to talk to other parents; they usually know. Common compulsions include: the need for symmetry; counting; checking things over and over; and constant worrying.

See Cognitive Behavioral Therapy, "Just Right" Feeling, Obsessive Compulsive Disorder, Support Groups, Tics, Tourette Syndrome

COMPUTERS

To produce written documents that reflect their true ability, children with ND from middle school on up often need a computer and appropriate training in how to use it. While most children succeed in the basic computer classes that teach keyboarding, many children with ND fail. The strict demands, including time restraints, sensory overload, covered keys, and visual-motor integration, impact their performance such that they often shut down and are unable to complete the assignments.

Students with ND need to learn the skill, but at a slower pace. We offer keyboarding classes at the Joshua Center using the Type to Learn program. This fun, game-oriented, self-paced program allows the children to feel success at every level. Once the children master the keyboard and learn word processing, the demands on fine-motor skills, punctuation and capitalization rules, poor spelling, and editing are minimized or eliminated.

See Assistive Technology, Education Software, Graphomotor Concerns, Handwriting, Shutting Down

CONSEQUENCES

Consequence refers to what happens after a behavior has been demonstrated. In thinking about consequences you are trying to determine if the child was successful in getting what he wanted, avoiding what he wanted, and/or was successful in his attempt to communicate a message by the behavior. Children learn associations between behaviors and consequences. I believe that a consequence can be a powerful motivator for children. For example, when the child breaks something, he has to save money to repair or replace it. Eventually, he will connect consequence with the behavior.

See Reinforcers

CONSISTENTLY INCONSISTENT

No matter how hard you try, no matter how many accommodations you have made, your child can guarantee you only one thing – that she will be consistently inconsistent. The neurological symptoms may cycle throughout the day, month or year. When symptoms are intense, the child's ability to perform is impacted. So when teachers say, "But yesterday he was great," I tell them to accept the inconsistency.

See Acceptance, Changes in Tics

COPROLALIA

Coprolalia is the uncontrolled swearing or socially unacceptable utterances characteristic of TS. Although it is the most sensationalized part of TS, it affects only about 20 percent of individuals with TS. If your child develops this symptom, he should not be punished – this goes for any other tic as well. He may or may not be able to control or substitute another tic. While some children have been able to cover their mouths when they feel swearing coming or turn it into a cough, some children do not have that ability. It has been my experience that sucking on hard candy or chewing gum may help.

I remember a teacher inviting me to observe a little first-grade boy with coprolalia because his behavior was becoming disruptive. After spending time with him he agreed to write the "bad" word instead of saying it. While he felt the need to share the "written bad word" with the class, we came up with a solution. We placed a cigar box on the table and after he wrote down the word, he placed it in the box and closed the lid. That still did not feel "final" to him, so he decided to tear the word into small pieces before placing it in the box and closing the lid. Another young man I worked with had both an expressive language learning disability and coprolalia. When he became frustrated in responding to a teacher's question, inevitably the swearing came out. He was always receiving detentions for this before we intervened and convinced the school of what was actually going on. Teachers became more supportive of him and allowed him to take extra time to answer questions.

Sometimes you are able to brainstorm substitutions, sometimes not. When a child has a severe case of coprolalia, a great deal of education must take place. Many people who exhibit coprolalia carry cards explaining this symptom to be used when they are in public places. Stress can exacerbate the swearing so acceptance is important.

See Acceptance, Brainstorming, Tourette Syndrome

COPROPRAXIA

A complex motor tic of TS, copropraxia is an involuntary, obscene gesture that may include inappropriate sexual touching. It is not a common symptom. I have known children who try to combat this symptom by putting their hands in their pockets, folding their hands together or sitting on them.

See Complex Tics

COPYING FROM THE BOARD

Because many children with ND have visual-motor integration problems, it is difficult for them to copy anything from the board in school. Coupled with poor fine-motor problems, they are truly at a disadvantage. Providing a copy of the notes and helping them write down their assignments are just two accommodations that need to be considered for children who have difficulty with far-point copying. Providing a keyboard, an Alpha Smart (alphasmart.com) or a tape recorder are other possibilities.

See Classroom Environment

COUNSELING – INDIVIDUAL/FAMILY

Of all the things I ever did, finding a good family counselor was one of the most important. I first met our family counselor when I divorced in 1983 and was looking for a counselor for my children to talk to. Jack was the one who first recognized Josh's symptoms. Over the years he was the one person who made a difference in our lives. As a result, I started sending other families with children with TS to him. It was often the little things that Jack said that made a big difference. He helped me believe in myself and convinced me that we would survive – one day at a time. As parents we are so overwhelmed with "living" the disorders that it is hard to step back and see the whole picture. Parents need a support system and someone who can put things in perspective.

I advise parents to begin counseling when their child is diagnosed with ND to develop a good counselor-client relationship. Then when it really gets tough, the problems can be addressed immediately – you won't have to waste time developing that relationship. I have observed that the young adults who are succeeding are the ones who received regular counseling throughout their teen years. One of the best ways to find a good counselor who is knowledgeable about ND is to talk to other families. If a counselor is willing to learn, you have it made. If counselors think they know everything about living with ND, they probably don't.

See Parenting a Child with ND

CRIES FREQUENTLY

If a child cries frequently, she may be experiencing a lot of anxiety. Communicate this behavior to your doctor. I remember so well the times that Josh would end up in tears. These are the times that hurt the most, because more often than not Josh was trying to express something and I didn't understand what it was. I learned over the years to let him "get it out" in his own way. I am a great believer in hugs. Hugs can say "I'm sorry" as well as "I love you." I don't believe telling a child with ND "to stop crying and grow up." There is always something else going on.

See Anxiety, School Phobia, Depression

CROWDS

Agoraphobia is the fear of being in crowds. While most children with ND would not receive this diagnosis, quite a few have problems in crowds. It may be caused by sensory overload when the environment contains too many auditory or visual stimuli. I have known many children with ND who have difficulty going to the grocery store, special events and even restaurants.

See Occupational Therapist, Sensory Sensitivity

CUES TO LEAVE CLASS

Frequently it becomes necessary for children with ND to release tics, obsessions, and/or restless energy or to de-stress. Some teachers are comfortable with allowing the child to leave class for this purpose at any time except during direct instruction. Sometimes simple eye contact is all that is used. Others have an agreed-upon cue. For example, the teacher observes that the child's behavior or symptoms are escalating and walks by his desk, or touches something in the room to make him aware of the situation. Some teachers place a card on the student's desk to hold up or place on the corner of his desk when he feels the need to leave. Often teachers use a pass for all children, who then place the card in a pocket when the need arises. Teachers need to have a plan in place and be sure to include it in the folder for the substitute teacher.

See Home Base, Substitute Teachers

CUMULATIVE FOLDER

Schools develop a cumulative folder for each student, which includes all pertinent academic information such as grades, test scores, IEPs, 504 Plans, etc. This folder is only accessible to the parents and the education professionals. I highly recommend that parents include information about their child's disorders, copies of all letters of diagnosis and any other information that is important to the success of their child. The files follow the child through her public school years. Parents can request in writing to see their child's file at any time.

D

DAYDREAMING

Don't we wish that's all it was! Some children with ND appear to be daydreaming for extended periods, but they may not be daydreaming at all! Instead, they may have symptoms of attention deficit hyperactivity disorder. This disorder is often the most difficult for parents, teachers and children because the children look normal so they are expected to act normal. Their behaviors are not chosen, they are neurological. Accepting the symptoms is the first step. Doing something about it is the next step. Redirect! Redirect! Redirect! I suggest that teachers place really responsible students next to children with ND to assist with staying on task.

See Attention Deficit Hyperactivity Disorder

DEDICATION

Parents, teachers and grandparents can make a tremendous difference in the lives of children with ND. A father I know dedicated himself to helping his child with homework. The mother shared with me that his patience and ways of helping their child was incredible. Father and son became a team with their own way of doing things. Her husband did the writing as his son dictated what he wanted to say. Her son listened while his dad read to him out loud. They would work a short time, break for a board game, wrestle or go outside for basketball. Her husband never complained that this took time out of every evening and weekend. Besides, he still found time for his daughter because he knew how important it was to spend time with her also.

One young man shares how wonderful his resource teacher is. "She's kind of like my mother at school. She tells me what I need to do, but she's always happy to help me." That's dedication!

See Acceptance, Homework Strategies, Parenting a Child with ND

DENTISTRY

It is up to parents and children to educate their dentist about the special needs of individuals with ND. Brochures, videos and specific information about your child's disorder can be obtained from national organizations and shared with the dentist. Also share how the disorders specifically impact your child. An information sheet is included in the Appendix for parents to complete for the dentist. Since a visit to the dentist can be stressful for children with ND, I highly recommend that parents interview the dentist before making an appointment. Depending on the child's stress level, you might need to arrange visits to the dentist's office just to increase the comfort level of your child before the actual dental procedures are done.

DEPRESSION

All children feel sad at times. For some the sadness reaches a high level and lasts for so long that it becomes classified as clinical depression. Children with ND are especially vulnerable to depression. The general signs of depression include depressed mood (children frequently show more irritability and agitation than depressed mood), markedly diminished interest or pleasure in activities, significant weight loss or weight gain, changes in sleep patterns, fatigue, a feeling of restlessness or being slowed down, feelings of worthlessness or excessive guilt, diminished ability to concentrate, and sometimes recurrent thoughts of death. When adults become depressed, they might withdraw and be quiet, often not wanting to be around others. With children, both teachers and parents should watch for nonverbal clues such as personality changes, irritability and agitation, changes in sleep patterns, changes in school performance, lack of interest in playing with friends, low self-esteem, and even talk of suicide. Keep your doctor informed of any of these signs. Certain medications can contribute to depression as a side effect, so keep your documentation of medications and their effects current. Take any thoughts of suicide seriously and call a doctor or therapist immediately. I always recommend that a good counselor be identified early in the diagnosis because when things get rough and you need help, a relationship is already established.

See Counseling - Individual/Family, Cries Frequently, Medication Side Effects

DESK AT SCHOOL

I always enjoy observing the kids at their desks. When I see a desk that is organized, I suspect OCD because otherwise I usually see what I refer to as "mini-dumpsters." All those missing assignments, lost pencils, and "must have" items from home live in the "mini-dumpster." I highly recommend that the teacher schedules a daily "dumpster sweep." I usually suggest that only a few items are left in the child's desk. The rest should be placed somewhere else in the room – in a cubby, crate or shelf. Kids will fidget with anything they can find, including pieces of paper on the floor. Sometimes I recommend turning the desk around (but not the child) so the child cannot fidget with anything in the desk. In addition, I usually suggest the child's desk be placed at the front of the classroom so the teacher can more easily monitor her behavior. With older children I recommend asking the child for input.

See Attention Deficit Hyperactivity Disorder, Obsessive Compulsive Disorder, Organizational Skills

DETENTION AND SUSPENSION

Detention is a form of punishment by which a student is made to stay after regular school hours. Out-of-school suspension involves temporary removal from school, whereas in-school suspension involves temporarily removing the student from classes. Far too many children with ND receive detentions or suspensions for "responsibility" issues. I have seen many kids give up trying at school because of their "forgetting" to bring a pencil or book to class, for "forgetting" to bring an assignment or for showing up late to class, etc. Detentions or suspensions do not make a child with ND "remember" better. This method of "disciplining" only increases stress and humiliation. I also don't recommend children with ND serving detention for talking, when, in fact, it's a symptom of the disorder for some students. Using a similar analogy, we don't make children who are confined in a wheelchair serve detentions for not being able to walk. I do believe, however, that when a child with ND violates serious rules, like all children, he should be disciplined.

See Behavior Plan, Consequences, Responsibility, School Supplies

DIAGNOSIS, INITIAL

Many people go through a lot of frustration, often at great expense, to get a diagnosis of a neurological disorder, sometimes wondering for years what is wrong with them or their child as they bounce from one doctor to another. After such experiences, finally being able to put a name to what is wrong can be a blessing. Upon first receiving a diagnosis for their child, parents may go through a grieving process. Then a thirst for information sets in. As parents' knowledge increases, their comfort level usually increases as well, and they realize that having an ND is not the end of the world. Keeping a file of the information and resources used to educate themselves allows parents to reread information at a later date, and possibly share with teachers and family members.

Attending support group meetings is one of the best things parents can do. I always encourage parents to attend all meetings, what they hear at one meeting may not seem applicable at the time, but down the road they will need that information and be glad they attended.

See Educating Parents, Grieving, Parenting a Child with ND, Support Groups

DIFFICULTY KEEPING HANDS OFF OTHER PEOPLE

Some children with ND have touching tics that are intrusive to others. Sometimes children can be taught to stay within their personal space. One strategy is to teach them always to keep an arm's length from others. Try drawing a circle on the floor (string, chalk) around the child to demonstrate the concept of personal space.

See Hallway Behavior, Inappropriate Tics, Touching Tics

DIFFICULTY LISTENING AND WRITING CONCURRENTLY

Writing and listening are two distinct functions. Individuals with auditory- and visual-motor integration difficulties can usually do one or the other, but not both at the same time. Often children with ND have great difficulty sustaining attention and following oral directions, so a great deal of effort is needed to "listen." When they expend this much energy to listen, they are not able to write. Most children with ND also have fine-motor deficits, so coupled with listening, writing becomes an impossible task. These are lifelong processing deficits. As they mature, children with ND will learn strategies to help themselves but until then, it is up to parents and teachers to help them succeed. For example, having complete notes to follow when oral instructions are given helps the child to follow along. Teachers may copy another student's notes to share with their students with ND, and students who have had a great deal of typing experience can sometimes take notes using a word processor. When deciding how to best help students with listening/writing difficulties, teachers must keep in mind their objective for the class – is it to copy notes or is it to learn the material?

See Attention Deficit Hyperactivity Disorder, Auditory Processing Disorder, Handwriting, Obsessive Compulsive Disorder, Racing Thoughts, Visual Processing Disorders

DIFFICULTY LISTENING WHEN HAVING OCD THOUGHTS

OCD can wreak havoc with the brain. "Racing thoughts" can play over and over like fast-forwarding on a VCR. The thought is the obsession; the compulsion is the behavior. Children with OCD appear normal, but it's what you don't "see" that complicates the child's life. In school children with this symptom may do better listening to a lecture, instructions or presentation if they are allowed to draw or squeeze a stress ball at the same time. Some teachers have an agreed-upon cue for the child with ND when giving instructions; for example, they say, "Listen" or "This is important" to let the child know to listen.

Other teachers walk by the child's desk and gently tap it to help the student redirect and still others give written directions for the child to follow while giving instructions. Other strategies include giving one-step instructions and checking for understanding before going on, and reducing the quantity of work assigned. Finally, sometimes medications can help.

See Obsessive Compulsive Disorder, Racing Thoughts

DIFFICULTY STOPPING ACTIVITY

I remember observing a boy who had difficulty changing classes. He could not leave one class before his work was complete. When he was forced to leave the room for another class, he would immediately complete the previous class assignment even though the teacher had requested that he put the work away and start on her assignment. It didn't take me long to figure out his OCD was involved. After I explained to the teachers what was going on, the student was given more time in class to complete his assignment before leaving and the quantity was sometimes reduced. This type of difficulty is pretty common with OCD. We must accept it as neurological and make adjustments. Teachers and parents should remind the child when an activity needs to stop by using a timer or giving five-minute intervals to help him prepare. Rather than telling him to stop, help the student by praising him when he complies appropriately.

See Acceptance, Obsessive Compulsive Disorder, Transitioning from One Activity or Lesson to Another

DIFFICULTY WITH TICS

Most tics are rather mild. I suggest that parents and teachers ignore the tics as much as possible. When the child tells you she wants help, then it's time to get help. Tics are a part of the child's life. Rarely do they just go away, but certain medications may be prescribed when they interfere with daily activities, including learning.

Under no circumstances should the child with ND be allowed to become a victim of harassment by his peers. Educating the peers about TS helps. Sucking on hard candy or chewing gum may help vocal tics that are intrusive or loud. Keeping a bottle of water close by can sometimes help annoying or loud vocal tics. Using a mouse pad for a pencil-tapping tic can make a classroom environment more comfortable. When a child is ticcing a lot, allow her to go to the bathroom or home base to release. Tics that involve the hands or eyes may prevent the child from writing or reading, so accommodations will need to be made, such as allowing the child to use the computer instead of writing and using books on tape. Give the child more space if a touching tic is involved. At school he might need to have empty chairs surrounding his desk. It is important when making these accommodations that peers are supportive to reduce the stress level of the child with ND.

Children will suppress the tics as much as possible, but eventually they have to come out. Some tics can be as physically exhausting as a workout so the child may need to take several rest breaks. You may be able to redirect or break the cycle by sending the child on an errand. This probably won't work at home – if you send her on an errand from home, she may forget to return! Redirection will work only as long as the child doesn't think you are trying to make him stop ticcing.

Remember, both good stress and bad stress increases tics. Good stress includes birthdays, holidays, new situations, family vacations, etc. Bad stress includes family crises or tests at school. Some parents report that when their child takes antibiotics or over-the-counter cold medications the tics often increase.

See Accommodations, Educating Peers, Inappropriate Tics, Individualized Education Program (IEP), Tics, Touching Tics, Tourette Syndrome

DISCIPLINE

Traditional child-rearing practices may not work well for children with ND. Parents tend to use the same practices with all children in the family. However, different practices are required for each child, whether they have a neurological disorder or not. Some parents feel it is not fair to treat one child differently from the other(s). But "being fair" means treating children in a manner that provides them with the greatest possibility of success. Parents need to agree on which child-rearing techniques they will use and which ones they will need to modify. The same is true for school. Teachers will need to decide which things to do for the child with ND that they will not have to do for other children.

First, parents must look at what environmental modifications are needed in the home to prevent and defuse situations that cause problems for the child with ND. For example, how can the child's stress be reduced at home so he can function more effectively? How can tasks be broken down into manageable steps? Many children with ND have tantrums, rage, and meltdowns. I have not found consequences for these neurological meltdowns to be productive. The child does not want to behave in this way and is almost always sorry afterward. The key is to change the environment.

Schools have suspension policies for discipline infractions, but I have concerns for children with ND who remain at home for suspensions without some type of counseling, as they are often "clueless" about what caused the suspension. When a school places a student in out-of-school suspension for a disability-related behavior, the school must follow steps mandated by IDEA.

I believe when a child with ND needs to be disciplined, whether at school or home, the discipline should be immediate and not carry over to the next day. Children with ND need to start each day fresh; their lives are stressful enough. I am against taking away recess or important events as part of disciplining a child, because children with ND need social opportunities. Further, it is important to be consistent when assigning consequences and to hold the child responsible for any damages he has done. If relationships have been hurt, the child should be encouraged to repair them. Above all, do not humiliate the child.

See Consequences, Detention and Suspension, Humiliation, Parenting a Child with ND, Rage Stage

DISENGAGEMENT

Disengagement refers to when you allow a child to have a meltdown, but don't get drawn into what he says during the tantrum. This is very hard. You can say things like, "I love you" or "I know this is hard for you," or simply "Uh-huh," but the less you say the better. Remember the objective of the moment is to get out of the meltdown.

See Arguing, Diversion, Rage Stage, Rumbling Stage

DISINHIBITION

An inhibition is the ability to put a thought between an urge to act and the action itself. A person has an urge to say or do something; thinks about it for a very brief time; and then either does it or refrains from doing it. Children with ND seem to have more difficulty thinking clearly when they are excited, fatigued, or under stress. As a result, if an urge hits them at these times, they are likely to carry it out without thinking. I have known children who say they know that what they are doing is wrong but they are unable to stop. At these times the child is disinhibited (Wood, 1999). Disinhibition is not an excuse for inappropriate behavior. The child should be held accountable for any damage caused by the behavior. With maturity it gets better; for example, Josh thought nothing of the value of money growing up, but now is budgeting, paying bills on time and making good choices when he purchases something.

See Attention Deficit Hyperactivity Disorder, Counseling - Individual/Family, Immaturity, Impulse Control, Rage Stage, Rumbling Stage

DISRESPECT FOR TEACHERS

Children should not be disrespectful towards their teachers. Similarly, teachers should never be rude or hurtful to a child. I have seen instances when teachers were rude or hurtful to a child with ND – usually out of ignorance. Even in cases like that I believe children should not be disrespectful. Showing disrespect will only cause more problems. The issue of rude teachers can be addressed later with the principal or superintendent.

One of the biggest problems I encounter with regard to respecting teachers is when parents talk badly about teachers in front of their children. Parents need to try hard to bite their tongue. When the child comes home complaining about something the teacher said or did, parents should listen and promise to discuss it with the teacher. Then do it. Ask questions of your child in different ways to make sure you are getting the story straight. I have seen far too many children get upset with school staff after hearing their parents' reaction to a situation they have come home with. Parents are modeling behavior for their child. It should be appropriate. If parents think a teacher has gone too far, they should go through the proper channels. Parents should blow off steam with another parent before they go to the school or write a nasty note to a teacher.

See Communication Between School and Home

DISTRACTIBILITY

Children with ND are easily distracted. Everything around them seems to "catch" their attention so that they become diverted from what they are supposed to focus on. They're distracted by the staple on the floor, the decorations hanging from the ceiling, the beautifully decorated bulletin boards, inspirational posters and, of course, the windows. It's not that they can't pay attention; it's that they pay attention to everything! Stimulant medications may help. To help the child attend better, before starting a lesson or activity at home, the teacher or parent should catch the child's attention by stating the child's name and say, "This is important." Don't require the child to look at you; this may only complicate his ability to attend. I have noticed that when some adults demand that the child look them in the eye while they are talking, the child doesn't have a clue about what was said afterwards.

With a diagnosis of ADHD, no report card should ever go home with the words "Doesn't pay attention" without further clarification. Parents know only too well their child has problems. In this case, "not paying attention" is not a chosen behavior. Accepting ADHD as a neurological problem is the first step. Do not get angry when the child does not pay attention. She does not want to be this way.

Always provide written instructions when issuing oral instructions and give them one step at a time. Use lists, ones that the child can check off when completed. Speak slowly and concisely. Provide models of completed tasks, demonstrating each step. When giving directions, it helps to have the child restate the directions. Sometimes children are too embarrassed to ask for help, so check frequently. Short one-step directions have a greater chance for success than one long project. For instance, when telling the child to clean his room, rather than say, "Go clean your room," say, "Put the dirty clothes in the hamper." Then go on to the next step and so forth. All of these suggestions apply at home, in extracurricular activities, church activities and family gatherings. Above all, everyone must respect the individual – this is a child with ADHD, not an ADHD child. The child will need a lot of positive reinforcement for task completion.

See Attention Deficit Hyperactivity Disorder, Classroom Distractions

DIVERSION

When the storm is rumbling (the first stage of a rage), your child will be thinking less and less and reacting more and more. Do not try and reason at this point; it will only make the situation worse. Help your child get to the designated, pre-planned home base. Some techniques you may want to consider (maybe even frame and hang in a prominent place) include the following: ask the child to run an errand; move closer to the child rather than calling attention to the behavior; give a light touch; make a joke; return to routine if applicable; direct the discussion to a pleasurable event coming up in the near future; redirect attention somewhere else; discuss something the child does well; compromise; express genuine interest in your child's hobbies; take a drive; focus on a relaxing scene. Often the most beneficial is "just walk and don't talk." You must learn which technique works for your child because the wrong technique will escalate rather than de-escalate the problem. Things that may escalate the problem include: raising your voice; saying things like "I'm the boss"; insisting on having the last word; using sarcasm; mimicking the behavior; or comparing the child negatively to his siblings.

See Disengagement, Drives, Home Base, Last-Word Obsession, Rage Stage, Rumbling Stage, Walk and Don't Talk

DOCTORS

Tourette Syndrome, ADHD, obsessive compulsive disorder and Asperger Syndrome are complicated neurological disorders. Doctors who evaluate and manage children with these disorders must be experts in these areas. In many cases parents will be educating their doctor, because it requires a great deal of dedication on the doctor's part to keep up with current research and medications. When you find a doctor who is interested in your child's diagnosis and is willing to learn, you are very lucky. Although communication between doctors and teachers is desirable, I recommend that parents not sign a release for the school to contact the doctor directly. Parents and family counselors should be the only ones communicating with the doctor. Schools can call the parents if they have a concern and parents can then call the doctor or family counselor for help. Similarly, I request that doctors not make recommendations to schools without talking to the parents so they can get both the school's, the child's and the parents' interpretations of the situation.

DOCUMENTATION

I hope and pray that you and your child have nothing but positive experiences during your child's school years and in his community relationships. To play it safe, however, document your child's treatment, strategies and conversations with the school in the event a problem should arise regarding your child's IEP or 504 Plan. If you are involved in a due process or if you are pulled into the legal system at some point, your files could become useful evidence. You must be prepared for the possibility that your child may have problems. Every time you communicate with your child's school or doctor, whether in person or by telephone, do so in writing and keep a copy for your files. Document all medication changes and side effects. Organize your file in chronological order and start a new file each year. Always request a copy of every evaluation and IEP within a few days of IEP meetings. Request a letter of diagnosis from your child's doctor and frequently update your files.

See Behavior, Changing, Communication Between School and Home, Parent Journal, Teacher Journal

DOPAMINE

The basic cause of ND is not known, but current medical theories indicate it is probably caused in part by abnormal genes that alter how the brain uses neurotransmitters such as dopamine, serotonin, and norepinephrine. A neurotransmitter is a chemical that transmits or carries a signal from one nerve cell to another.

DREAMS FOR YOUR CHILD'S FUTURE

OK, so your child has some neurological disorders. Please don't get bogged down with labels. Hold yourself together and start planning for your child's future. What are her strengths and interests? Take that information and build on it. What you do now will impact your child for the rest of her life. Your child's future success depends on this planning. Give her every opportunity to fulfill her dreams. If she thinks she wants to be a lawyer or bus driver or whatever, then arrange for her to shadow an individual in that profession. Josh wanted to be a professional baseball player so I encouraged his ability in that area. Don't pity your child; help him be everything he can be. All of the effort you make now will pay off. It will just take a while.

See Parenting a Child with ND

DRIVER'S LICENSE

Don't push kids with ND into driving too early. One family only allowed their son to drive after he had saved enough money to buy a car and pay for insurance. I was glad Josh wasn't interested for a couple years after he was legally old enough to drive. The emotional maturity of adolescents with ND is approximately two-thirds their chronological age, so many of them are not ready to drive even when they meet the legal age. If your child has severe tics, you must assess if they will interfere with the driving process. Attentional problems also impact children with ND, so they do need lots of practice just thinking about all the quick decisions they must make when driving. You want your child to be independent, but when tics interfere with the safety of your child and the safety of other drivers, having your child drive is not worth it.

See Attention Deficit Hyperactivity Disorder, Immaturity, Impulse Control, Visual Processing Disorders

DRIVES

Of all the things I ever did, and cherish the most now, were the two hours I spent with Josh on "nightly" drives starting at age 13 and continuing into his early twenties. At the time I didn't realize how important it was for him to stop to get a banana milkshake. The drives with milkshakes were the only things that really relaxed him. Who would think my little car could relax this big athlete. It was during these drives that I finally learned to "shut up" and "listen." There were times when Josh didn't say a word; and times when he revealed astonishing insights about what he was going through. At times he would talk about something that had happened three days before – something I had struggled to understand then but that he wasn't able to share at the moment.

After realizing my daughter, Sarah, was feeling left out, I started taking her on drives too, just the two of us. It turned out to be just as beneficial for her as it was for Josh. To this day both of my children take themselves on drives to release stress. Those were truly the "good times."

See Milkshakes

DUE PROCESS

Due process is the procedural safeguard that is given to parents, guardians and children with disabilities to protect the child's rights under federal and state laws and special education regulations. For example, parents and guardians can request voluntary mediation or a due process hearing to resolve differences between them and the school. A good source of information on due process can be obtained at Wright's Law on the Internet. See *Internet Resources*.

See Individuals with Disabilities Education Act, Individualized Education Program (IEP)

DYSGRAPHIA

A child with dysgraphia has difficulty writing legibly with age-appropriate speed.

See Occupational Therapist

E

EATING CONCERNS

Some children with OCD have eating compulsions. Some medications prescribed for tics cause weight gain while some stimulant medications decrease appetite. It is important to communicate your child's eating concerns to your doctor as he will want to closely monitor the child's weight. You have to balance the benefits of medications against their side effects. When children gain an excessive amount of weight, it often causes problems with self-esteem, and possibly health. Providing time for extracurricular activities that involve physical activity and stocking fruits, vegetables and healthy snacks will help your child learn sound recreation and eating habits and therefore help keep his weight down. For compulsive eating I highly recommend therapy by an expert in behavioral therapy. If your child is obsessed with how she looks, you need to watch for eating disorders of bulimia and anorexia.

See Counseling - Individual/Family, Hoarding, Medication Side Effects, Obsessive Compulsive Disorder

EATING OUT

Boy, how I would do things differently if I could! Once in a while we would decide to go out and eat as a family. With Josh's inability to sit still for more than a few minutes, we would go somewhere that had a mega buffet/salad bar. Invariably, Josh would get through the buffet line, return to his seat and finish his overflowing plate before we could even join him. As a result, just as we were beginning to eat our meal, Josh would be begging to go home. He was done and thought we should be too.

Many children with ND have difficulty eating out. It's not that they don't want to eat out with the family; it's a comfort thing. They may have trouble being in crowded places or they may have sensory overload concerns with restaurant noises and excessive visual stimuli. Children need to have positive family outings. Eating out is a life skill that they need to learn. Ordering, waiting for a meal, practicing appropriate table manners and controlling voice volume are all important. Plan in detail how you are going to handle family restaurant outings. You especially need to plan if your child has loud or inappropriate symptoms that might offend others. Contact the manager of the restaurant to reserve a quiet corner or room, alerting him to the child's symptoms.

A wonderful young man I know had a pretty unusual tic that involved throwing a glass of water in the air and hitting himself in the chest before catching the glass on its way down. A startling sight if you're a waiter! The time I accompanied the family to a restaurant, we informed the management of the symptoms and were treated with the same respect as the other patrons. When others glanced our way, we politely told them about Tourette Syndrome. Children with ND need these "normal" life experiences, so let your child plan with you. You're making accommodations just like you expect at your child's school.

See Eating and Sensory Issues, Life Skills, Tourette Syndrome

EATING AND SENSORY ISSUES

Some children with ND have a severe sensitivity to odors and sounds, and some have food allergies. Some children with ND only eat food that has certain textures. When food allergies are suspected, I recommend food allergy testing.

I remember when Josh would not allow Sarah and me to eat at the same table with him because we "slurped" too loud. Sarah and I complied with his request, because it wasn't worth the fight, but we cracked up listening to him "slurp" up his meal. He was supersensitive to sounds at mealtime, not his own sounds, but the sounds of everyone and everything else. Don't worry if your child will only eat certain foods. Usually, she will eventually get tired of the same food. Continue to have available a balance of good nutritious foods for your child to choose from.

See Eating Concerns, Sensory Sensitivity

ECHOLALIA

Echolalia is the involuntary repetition of others' words or phrases and can be a complex tic of TS. I remember when Josh would sit in front of the TV and repeat things he heard. It was difficult watching TV with him at these times, but I just ignored it because enjoying the program was not more important to me than spending this time with him.

See Complex Tics, Tourette Syndrome

EDUCATING THE BUS DRIVER

The bus ride to and from school impacts children with ND. Whether it's negative or positive has a lot to do with educating the bus driver. When the school staff is educated, the bus driver needs to be invited to the program as well. In addition, parents must have good communication with the bus driver. I developed a worksheet for the bus driver, which is included in the Appendix. Children with ND deserve to have their needs met in this environment and this should help.

Meeting the bus driver before the year starts will help the child have a positive experience. Give her specific information about your child's disability. See if the driver will agree to pick up and return your child early in the ride to reduce the possibility of negative interactions, since children with ND are pretty exhausted at the end of the school day. Clear rules, and consequences for breaking those rules, should be established on day one. Let the driver know you expect communication and give her your phone number so if she has questions or concerns she can get help quickly. Don't forget to thank her frequently for her support. The more support the student receives from the bus driver, the better the drive will be for all. Having a supportive bus driver is critical to the success of the child's school day.

See Bus Behavior, Educating School Staff

EDUCATING NEIGHBORS

When the symptoms of an ND impact relationships in the neighborhood, it is the parents' responsibility to educate the neighbors. I highly suggest that you show a video and speak specifically about your child's symptoms, provide some brochures and then have some open discussions. If your child has a meltdown, explain to the neighbors how they are to handle him if they ever encounter this behavior. In addition, you can give neighbors the information sheet I created specifically for neighbors in the Appendix.

EDUCATING PARAPROFESSIONALS

Paraprofessionals have a big responsibility helping children with ND. In addition to attending a school staff inservice on neurological disorders, paraprofessionals must be taught strategies specific to the needs of the child they are working with. Paraprofessionals need to know what is and is not important to document and they need to know what their responsibility is to the education staff. To facilitate communication, see the worksheet for paraprofessionals in the Appendix.

See Educating School Staff

EDUCATING PARENTS

When the staff at the Joshua Center receives a call from a parent of a child newly diagnosed with ND, we encourage them to schedule an appointment with one of our counselors. At this point, parents often feel overwhelmed and want to learn as much as possible. An effective parent program includes definitions of each of the child's disorders and its possible impact on the child. In addition to defining the child's disorders, the following information should be discussed: intelligence assessments; mood disorders; emotional/social delays; sensory integration dysfunction; sleep disorders; enuresis/encopresis (the involuntary voiding of urine and bowel movements); and learning problems often associated with ND such as cognitive processing disorders, dysgraphia, executive function deficits, language disorder (receptive and/or expressive), math learning disorder, memory dysfunction, nonverbal learning disabilities, reading disorder, and written expression disorder. The child does not necessarily have problems in all of these areas, but giving parents this information empowers them to watch for concerns and seek the appropriate help when there are concerns.

See Parenting a Child with ND, Support Groups

EDUCATING PEERS

I usually recommend that once the ND symptoms are noticeable to other children, it is time to educate the child's peers about her disorders. Sometimes when a child has been teased about her disorder, parents and teachers approach the school about educating the kids, but it is best to address the concerns earlier. Adults should gain permission from the child with ND before educating the students.

I recommend that an individual other than the parents give the program. Parents are sometimes viewed as overprotecting or enabling of their child with ND. When I educate students, I usually talk to them first about many disabilities, such as hearing and visual impairments. I ask them how many have red hair, how many have blue eyes, etc. Then I ask if they know anyone who uses a wheelchair or a cane. In all this, I try to show them that we are all born with differences and that we usually inherit our traits from our families. Finally, I show a movie made for children that explains the disorders, allowing them to ask questions. They usually ask wonderful questions. If the child with the disorder is comfortable with it, I let her answer the questions with me because, after all, she is the expert. This kind of information sharing usually takes care of any teasing from peers. If it doesn't, the school administration has an obligation to discipline the child responsible for the teasing. I recommend that the peers be educated and updated in subsequent years.

See Acceptance, Bullying, Educating School Staff

EDUCATING SCHOOL STAFF

When I talk about educating the staff, I cannot stress enough that I mean the "whole" staff. This includes the custodians, cooks, lunch and recess monitors as well as the educators, including the principal. Without such training, invariably, your child will have a confrontation with a staff person who was not able to attend the inservice. The National Tourette Syndrome Association, for example, has developed an educators' inservice curriculum and often the school counselor or nurse is able to give the presentation. Other national organizations have similar material available for this kind of training.

At a minimum, the presentation should include: a description of the various neurological disorders; symptoms that are not "seen"; impact of the disorders on learning; strategies to help the child feel successful; resources; home-school communication; IEP information, including the child's behavior plan; specific symptoms to be concerned about and intervention strategies; transition concerns and strategies; examples of other successful programs; demonstration of what it is like to have an ND; evaluation procedures; behaviors associated with neurological disorders and strategies for handling them; medications; handwriting concerns; and peer relations.

See Academic Assessment, Behavior Plan, Brainstorming, Handwriting, Individualized Education Program (IEP), Support Groups, Weekly Reports

EDUCATION SOFTWARE

I have observed hundreds of children who have problems learning, especially due to auditory and visual processing problems. These kids can usually give you information orally, but have difficulty getting their thoughts down on paper. Often the written page is so overwhelming to them that they can't "get started." Further, some students who have symptoms of ADHD are not able to sit still long enough to learn a concept.

Good education software can make all the difference in the world for children with learning problems. Good education software engages children in the learning process and leads them through a carefully sequenced set of activities – whether it is math, language mechanics, reading, etc. I wish more children with ND had the opportunity to use appropriate software in their classrooms to meet curriculum objectives. So often computer time is used as something that has to be earned, and I think that is sad. My dream is to some day be able to offer a virtual classroom for children who need help.

See Auditory Processing Disorder, Computers, Getting Started, Handwriting, Visual Processing Disorders

EFFECTS OF SEASONAL AND WEATHER CHANGES

Frequently tics, obsessions, moods and behavior change when the seasons or the weather changes. Over the years you may notice that your child cycles at certain times of the year. Keeping a journal will help you know when to expect certain changes and prepare for them accordingly. Your child's doctor needs to know if seasonal and weather changes affect your child. Remember to document any medication changes during these times so in the future you will know how previous concerns were dealt with. For some children light deprivation is a factor. Planning for seasonal and weather changes and how they impact your child may include giving the child more time to get ready in the morning, more time to transition, and more patience.

EMAIL

As an accommodation, many teachers are automatically emailing assignments to students with ND. Some teachers have assignments posted on the school's web page or allow students to email assignments to their homes. The use of technology helps ensure that assignments are available when parents are ready to sit down and help their children. Email is also a good way for parents and teachers to communicate concerns, ask questions, and share upcoming school events and, most of all, inform each other about the positive things that are happening with the child.

See Assignment Notebooks, Communication Between School and Home

EMERGENCY ROOM

Josh sometimes obsessed over a certain pain or infection and would not calm down until I took him to the emergency room even if it was not anything particularly serious. I usually called ahead to let them know we were coming and what the situation was. To be able to let go of an obsession, he needed to hear from a medical professional that he was going to be OK. Depending on the seriousness of the situation, parents should be prepared to share with emergency room personnel the dosages of all medications their child is taking, in case the child needs additional medication prescribed.

ENABLING

Parents must work hard to develop a good understanding and acceptance of the capabilities of their child. Some parents seem to adopt the position that their child can do anything regardless of the ND. Others seem to adopt the position that their child can do almost nothing because of the ND. Neither of these positions is helpful and may even be harmful to the child. Children with ND often need special accommodations and a great deal of support to cope with certain life skills, such as taking medications consistently as prescribed and making and keeping appointments. Failure to provide such support will prove extremely stressful to all concerned and will promote consistent failure. On the other hand, there is also a danger of providing too many accommodations and too much support when it is not really needed. To consistently do for the child what she can do for herself may cause her to become an "emotional cripple," constantly dependent on others. Achieving a good understanding and a balanced approach is hard for parents. If the child sees her parents as anxiety laden, she will become that way too. I urge parents to seek professional family counseling when struggling with decisions concerning what their child can and cannot do in relation to the neurological disorders.

See Counseling - Individual/Family

ENCOURAGEMENT

Out of the clear blue I sometimes sent Josh inspirational cards. I would purchase about 20 cards to keep on hand. Sometimes I sent them when he was down, but often I sent one just because I wanted to encourage him when he was trying something new. Josh always told me how much the cards meant to him. One mother I know wrote words

of encouragement, praise, and love on index cards and put them in her son's room or set them in the dining room for him to find when he sat down to do his homework. Some mornings one was waiting for him at the breakfast table.

END OF DAY

Late in the day is often the most difficult time for children and parents. Parents must give their child time to "unload" without reacting. This can be a painful time, but parents may save themselves from further grief by recognizing the importance of letting the child blow off steam. Providing an evening routine will help the child transition to bedtime. Quiet family activities like reading to and with the child or watching a family TV show lets the child know she is an important part of the family unit.

See After School, Bedtime Behavior, Structure and Routine

ENTERING MIDDLE/JUNIOR HIGH/HIGH SCHOOL

See Changing Schools

ERRAND RUNNER

When a child with ND is fidgety, restless, ticcing, obsessing or distracted, it is often a good idea to send him on an errand. I recommend to teachers that they keep a book, envelope, bucket of supplies, etc., nearby for just these times. Have the child take something to the teacher farthest from his classroom. You'll be surprised how much this helps release energy, reduce tics and generally calm the child down.

See Breaks

ESCALATING BEHAVIOR

See Rumbling Stage

EXECUTIVE FUNCTIONS

Executive functions are the central brain processes that give us the ability to plan, initiate, sequence, organize, prioritize, set goals, and utilize information from our environment. These processes impact the child's learning as well as his relationships with peers. Many children with ND have difficulty with executive functions.

EXPLOSIVE BEHAVIOR

See Rage Stage

EXPOSURE AND RESPONSE PREVENTION

Exposure/response prevention therapy is sometimes used to help reduce or eliminate certain compulsions. In this therapy a person is exposed to the feared situation that prompts the need to carry out the compulsion, but carrying out the compulsion is prevented. For example, suppose a person has a fear of contacting germs by touching doorknobs and therefore has a compulsion to wash his hands immediately after touching a doorknob. The person and the therapist will discuss the obsession and the compulsion several times, moving toward the goal that the person will come to the realistic conclusion that touching a door-knob does not automatically lead to illness as a result of contacting germs. However, even with this logical knowledge, the person will continue having extremely high anxiety if he touches a doorknob and continues to rush to wash hands. Consequently, by mutual agreement the person and the therapist decide to test the situation as follows: The person touches a doorknob and simply sits with the therapist for a period of time. They discuss the level of anxiety experienced by the person with ND but washing hands is prevented. After several such exposures and response prevention sessions over several days or weeks, the anxiety level of not washing hands reduces to a tolerable level, thus eliminating or at least reducing the compulsion. Only a trained therapist should attempt this technique.

EXPRESSIVE LANGUAGE

Expressive language refers to how we communicate with one another, how we put words together to formulate our thoughts, feelings, responses, etc. Expressive language difficulties in children with ND can include difficulty with word retrieval, naming objects, and acquiring the rules of grammar in addition to monotone speech or robotic phrasing of words. At the same time, their nonverbal expressions such as posture, eye gaze, gestures, and facial expressions may be exaggerated.

I have worked with children who have expressive language concerns and have watched their frustration when others are not patient with them. They know the answers, but cannot get them out. One young man only expresses his coprolalia when he has retrieval problems. Some children may understand spoken language but are not able to use it effectively. Stress makes the problem worse and retrieval more difficult. Expressive language problems also interfere with written language.

See Coprolalia, Test Modifications, Written Expression

EXTENDED FAMILY

In the Appendix of this book I have included an information sheet that parents and their child with ND can complete and share with extended family members to help them understand the child's ND. In addition, close family members need to see all of Richard Lavoie's videos: "Frustration, Anxiety, Tension, the F.A.T. City Workshop"; "When the Chips are Down ... Learning Disabilities and Discipline; and "Last One Picked, First One Picked On" (Bieber, 1994). These videos do a great job of showing others what it is like to have ND and how they impact the life of the child. It is a good idea to create a folder with brochures and other materials about the disorders for future reference. Parents can purchase literature on the specific disorders from national organizations of neurological disorders. I have also known children who have written their extended family members in anticipation of an upcoming event to share information about their disorders. The children have done a nice job of educating the family members on their specific concerns.

You may find that you are lucky if you have the support of just one extended family member. Often extended family members will offer advice even when they have no knowledge of the disorders and how they impact the children and families. If certain family members do not accept your child's symptoms and behaviors as neurological in origin, you might have to limit your child's contact with them. I have seen many children deteriorate when left alone with family members who do not support the parents. It's not worth it.

EXTENDED SCHOOL YEAR

If your child has an IEP, then extended school year (ESY) services should be considered. Meant to ensure that they will not lose ground, these services are provided for children who have demonstrated or are likely to experience significant regression in a reasonable time period. These services are not used to teach new skills but to ensure that a child retains material already learned. When determining if a child qualifies for ESY services, parents should think over past summers and how the child did. Did she regress or did it take her a long time to catch up at the beginning of the next year? Talk with your school district about qualifying criteria for ESY services. This will be an IEP team decision and as a parent you are a member of that team.

See Individualized Education Program (IEP)

EXTRACURRICULAR ACTIVITIES

Rather than focusing on what a child with ND cannot accomplish, parents and others working with the child should focus on his strengths, abilities and interests. With careful planning, the child can succeed at many extracurricular activities, adding to feelings of self-worth. If a child is having a rough time at school, knowing he has an after-school activity where he has an opportunity to have fun and excel goes a long way toward helping with self-confidence. Parents will need to help identify the right activity for their child, considering not only the child's interests but also the temperament of the instructor or coach. Extracurricular activities also offer opportunities for a child to develop new interests and new friends. I know a wonderful young man who had a great deal of difficulty at school but has earned his Eagle Scout badge.

See Sports and Disabilities

EYE CONTACT

I think we make a big mistake demanding eye contact from children with ND. Since most have processing problems (difficulty processing incoming information), they often have trouble staying focused on what you are saying while looking at you all at the same time. I believe when parents, teachers and others allow the child to keep his head down when talking to him, the child is able to listen better.

One young man in high school was allowed to draw during lectures because his symptoms were so severe he could not write. He rarely looked up and appeared calm. Afterward he could tell you all about the lecture. Clearly, this accommodation was successful. You can easily test the effectiveness of a strategy by questioning the student for understanding.

F

FAILING

No child with an IEP should be failing. I believe that if a child is failing, the IEP team is not doing what it is supposed to do. I often see well-written IEPs but find they leave too much responsibility for student success to the student (for instance, making the student responsible for writing assignments in planner). If a child has an IEP, it is a sign that she needs help. In working with so many children with ND I have learned that many of them fail because their assignments are incomplete or not turned in. The IEP team needs to make sure that the student with ND receives the necessary help to follow through on assignments and projects. If a child is failing, the IEP team needs to revise the IEP to identify how teachers and administrators need to change so the child with ND is successful.

See Educating School Staff, Individualized Education Program (IEP), Section 504 Plan, Weekly Reports

FAMILY EDUCATION RIGHTS AND PRIVACY ACT

The Family Education Rights and Privacy Act (FERPA) is a federal law that protects the privacy of a student's education records. The law applies to all schools that receive funds under an applicable program of the U.S. Department of Education. Parents or eligible students have the right to inspect and review all of the student's education records maintained by the school. Schools are not required to provide copies of information unless it is impossible for parents or eligible students to personally inspect the records. (Schools may charge a fee for copies.) After inspecting the education records parents and eligible students can request that a school correct records if they believe the information is inaccurate or misleading. Further, after a formal hearing, the parent or eligible student has the right to put a statement in the records that they contest certain information if the school decides not to amend the contested information.

FAMILY REUNIONS

Family reunions can be both exciting and stressful for parents and children with ND. A family reunion requires more planning than a family vacation because you will be in close contact with family members you may have had little or no contact with for years. Plan how you will handle your child's inappropriate and negative behavior, including meltdowns, should it happen. Plan for how you will educate family members about your child's disorders. Also plan how to handle inappropriate comments from extended family members. Identify family members with whom you already have a good relationship and enlist their support during the reunion. Be specific about how they can help. Also consider if other children will be attending and, if so, if there are concerns about how they will interact with your child.

To provide some comfort for your child, take along favorite toys and familiar items such as your child's pillow, blanket and favorite storybooks. Plan some downtime for him with just you and your immediate family. If possible, identify a home base for the child ahead of time. Each morning before you meet with the extended family, sit down with your child and plan the day, discussing any scheduled events, if that is helpful. You know when the best time is to tell your child about the upcoming event. I suggest that once you tell him, you share as many details as possible.

See Extended Family, Planes, Trains and Automobiles

FATHERHOOD

Parenting children with ND is difficult, but for these children to succeed, there are two things I believe a father must always do – love his child unconditionally and love the child's mother, or if divorced at least respect the child's mother. I asked two fathers who seem to always "get it right" to help me write this. The first has a son and the second has three daughters – all with ND.

One father said: "As a father I only wanted the best for my children. I also expected them to always do their best at whatever they did. When my son was first diagnosed with Tourette Syndrome, I was floored, confused, devastated and lost. The first three years of the disorders, I went through a very rough period very much like a grieving process. I went from denial to anger, from anger to sadness, and from sadness to more confusion. Yes, we did search for the right doctors, which also was extremely frustrating because no one seemed to have answers. I got to a point where I didn't take my son's behavior seriously. I didn't understand the medicines and their importance in helping him to control his behavior. Finally, an earth-shattering event occurred that shook me to the core and woke me up to the realities of it all. As young as he was, nevertheless my son had done something that involved the outside world (the authorities) and left an indelible mark on the entire family. It was at that point that I woke up and began to take the disorders seriously. I promised myself that with the help of God my son was going to succeed. By 'succeed' I mean that he would ultimately succeed in life. My goal became to do everything in my power to help him learn to deal with the disorders he was given. While I had always helped him with his homework, it had been on a day-to-day basis. That is, I never looked at the long term. After the incident I began to educate myself about his disorders, his medicines and their purpose and effects, and got him proper counseling. Sitting with him through the counseling sessions and talking to the counselor myself gave me a great deal of insight into the disorders and into my son's mind. I slowly learned to see things through his eyes. I also began in earnest to study him myself. In working closely with him on his homework, I watched for patterns of behavior. I looked for triggers that set him off and for things that were easy for him. I discovered his cycles, how long they lasted and when he might need a medicine adjustment. I began to understand him and his disorders, which enabled me to reassure him when he was having a difficult time. Eventually it got to the point where I would recommend to the doctor what the medicine change should be and he would agree with me. This took an incredible amount of time and patience. It also required sacrifices not only for myself, but also for other members of the family, including my two other children.

I didn't know what else to do. I simply told myself that I was doing the best that I could. My wife was extremely supportive through it all. She made up for the areas that I lacked. We worked together as a team, each using our strengths and relying on each other to make up for our weaknesses. It was very difficult but I think my wife would agree it was worth it. Today our son is almost 18. He is a junior in high school and throughout high school he has made excellent grades with minor modifications. He is a self-advocate and is well aware of his needs regarding his medicines and school. He has plans for college and is already looking at scholarships. In short, his is a success in the challenge of life."

Another dad wrote: "Everyone has his own perspective as to how to deal with neurological disorders. That perspective is dependent not only upon who in the family has the disorders, but upon your own role in the family as well. Make no mistake, the mother and the father of any children with ND will react differently to every problem that they encounter. The main difficulty of almost every father is that problems presented by these disorders usually do not have a solution. They cannot fix the problem with a few well-chosen words of fatherly advice like Ward Cleaver or Robert Young. For a man, this means that he sees himself as a failure as a father, because he cannot fulfill the role he believes is his duty. He believes that he has let down his wife, his child, his family, and even his own father. As a result, he often chooses to ignore or deny every situation that has the potential of being a problem, leaving the mother to deal with the situation on her own. The critical point that every father needs to be taught is that only by ignoring or denying problems does he let down those who depend upon him. While this may seem obvious and simple to every woman, it will strike a man like a bolt of lightening. But this knowledge is only the first step. Putting this knowledge into practice is the rest of the race to successfully raise not only a child with ND, but any child. And that is a long race. But it is a race that you can win, if only you will realize that it isn't important how many times you fall down, only that you get back up and start running again."

See Being Flexible, Grieving, Motherhood

FEARS

Some children with ND have intense fears. These fears are very real to the child, and often no amount of assurance will make them go away. Fears may involve closed spaces, the dark, or being hurt. When the child is experiencing these fears, it is best to try and distract him with other interesting activities or discussion of upcoming events. Talking him out of the fears is often difficult and sometimes impossible.

One way to address fears is to use what is called systematic desensitization – a technique that progressively desensitizes the child to the fear. It is done by taking very, very small steps toward overcoming the fear. I remember when Josh was two years old he was terrified of dogs. He was not afraid of stuffed animals, and he seemed interested in small puppies. So I got him a puppy, which he immediately fell in love with. As the puppy grew, Josh's fear of other dogs decreased. As a result, he has developed a love of animals that has helped him get through some of the really tough times.

See Anxiety, Pets, School Phobia

FIRE

Many children with ND have obsessions and compulsions around fire and sometimes play with matches and lighters. Similar to compulsions that develop around knives and sharp objects, if it results in potentially dangerous behavior, parents would do well to lock up matches and lighters and to talk to the child's doctor about medication for obsessive compulsive disorder. Counseling is recommended.

See Compulsions, Knives

FOLLOWING DIRECTIONS

When giving directions to a child with ND, give them orally and in writing too. It helps if the child can check off the directions on a list so she can see her accomplishments. Also, I suggest standing close to the child when giving directions. I knew nothing about ADHD when Josh was young, but now I know he has this ND. I'll never forget his second-grade teacher telling me about a time when she asked Josh to take something to the office. When he got half way down the hall, he realized he couldn't remember what he was supposed to do or where he was supposed to go, so he returned to the classroom asking the teacher to repeat the directions. She looked at him and said, "Now Josh, you stop and think about what I told you or you can put your name on the board." Josh put his name on the board and the class roared.

Instructions on worksheets often cause students with ND a lot of problems. Don't ever assume that just because the child is a good reader, he has comprehended the instructions. The written page can be as overwhelming as too many oral instructions for a child with ND. Following directions is a processing activity and many children with ND have processing problems. Make sure the child understands each sentence before starting, and remember to give extra time for compliance in following directions. I still can only give a one-step direction to Josh, and when I do, I always check to make sure he understands correctly. Don't get angry. Instead, identify strategies to help your child be successful.

See Auditory Processing Disorder, Visual Processing Disorders

FORGETTING ASSIGNMENTS

How can we expect children with ND to remember to turn in assignments if we don't teach them organizational and study skills? Parents and teachers must model how to organize completed assignments to ensure they reach their destination.

See Attention Deficit Hyperactivity Disorder, Organizational Skills, Study Skills

FREE APPROPRIATE PUBLIC EDUCATION

Free appropriate public education (FAPE) means that a child in a public school who has a disability is entitled to an educational program and related services based on his IEP. An appropriate public education in special education refers to the least restrictive environment. Finally, the IEP must meet the child's unique educational needs without cost to the parents.

FRIENDS

Every child needs at least one friend. Parents and teachers must do everything they can to help children develop and keep positive peer relations. Often children with ND play better with younger children, so don't be concerned if the child wants to play with somebody who is younger. Plan short "play dates" at your house to ensure proper supervision. As you become more comfortable with the friend's parents, share information about your child's ND and how it impacts relationships.

See Peer Relations

FUNCTIONAL BEHAVIOR ASSESSMENT

Functional assessment is the process of determining the message conveyed by a behavior and what causes the behavior in the first place. If you understand the reason for a given behavior, you may be able to make changes to prevent the need for the behavior, or at least develop more constructive behaviors that still meet the child's needs. Asking who, what, where, why, when, and how in relation to the behavior often allows you to determine the reason behind it, enabling you to develop strategies to change it. For instance, ask who is involved, or where the situation took place, etc.

When conducting a functional assessment, you are attempting to understand what the behavior is trying to get, avoid, or send a message about. In thinking about consequences you are trying to determine if the child was successful in getting what he wanted, avoiding, and/or communicating via the behavior. When trying to determine which actions are behavior and which are disorder, you will need to trust your instincts and do what you think is best. For example, a child with ND in middle school appears to be refusing to work in class. How are the disorders impacting this behavior? Is there anything in the environment that is preventing the child from doing his work? When is this behavior occurring? These are the kinds of questions that will lead to answers and helpful strategies.

See Consequences

G

GED (GENERAL EQUIVALENCY DIPLOMA)

The General Equivalency Diploma (GED) is an alternative diploma for individuals who did not complete high school. If children do not complete high school, it is imperative that they enroll in GED classes and work on this diploma, because otherwise they will have a difficult time securing a good job. I do not advocate that any child drop out of high school, but I know from experience with students who have ND that dropping out may be the only choice if the school doesn't "get it." If they are not satisfied with the services their child is receiving, parents can request a due process hearing or mediation, but from my experience the amount of energy and money it takes to go through the process can be very disrupting to family life.

When Josh quit school, it was wonderful not having the hassle of teachers and school administrators constantly interpreting his neurological symptoms as chosen behavior, but he missed out on so much by not being able to participate in school activities, including sports. He missed the opportunities to learn valuable life skills with his peers. It's hard to acquire these skills from a book. I encourage parents to do everything possible to keep their child in school. The GED exam is not easy, and if your child is having academic problems in school, he is bound to also have problems with GED classes. Nevertheless, I am thankful there is an alternative so children can go on with their lives.

GENERALIZATION

Children with ND often have difficulty applying (generalizing) what they have learned from one situation to another. They often misinterpret social situations and have difficulty transferring the skills learned in school to other settings, including home. The school staff and parents need to be consistent when helping the child with ND apply newly learned strategies from one area to another; for example, children with ND may learn to wait their turn at school (at the water fountain, in the lunch line, and at recess), but not be able to apply this to playing in the neighborhood, with siblings, at Scout meetings or sports activities. It's a good idea to role play and make a list to use as a visual support to help children with ND to generalize.

See Visual Supports

GENETICS

When children receive a diagnosis of a ND, the staff at the Joshua Center is almost certain to hear of a family member who lived his entire life with similar undiagnosed symptoms. An incredible amount of research is going on in this area, so I fully expect that scientists will pinpoint the genes responsible for these disorders. Ever since I saw a program on TV about a high prevalence of autism in the small town of Leomenster, Massachusetts, where a factory manufacturing sunglasses was once located, I have been convinced that the environment plays a part in altering our genetic make-up. One week after the program aired, it was reported that a large group of individuals throughout the United States had at one time lived in that town and now had grandchildren with autism.

GERMS

Many children and adults with OCD have obsessions involving germs. Some children are so obsessed that they cannot go into a hallway with other children because they are worried they would bump another child and then would have to get rid of germs from contact with this person. Counseling is recommended.

See Counseling - Individual/Family, Obsessive Compulsive Disorder

GETTING STARTED

This is one of my all-time favorite subjects. Children with ND often have trouble getting started – whether it is with assignments, activities or chores. This is true at home as well as at school. I have observed students at every age from kindergarten to twelfth grade, and it's always the same thing.

When I observed a young man in his high school social studies class, I had a real eye opener. The class was a little laid back and noisy, but after the teacher had given instructions and made an assignment, she allowed the class to use the remaining time to start their homework. Everybody was getting down to work except the student I was observing. He tried to look busy, but stood out like a sore thumb to me, but not to the teacher. She didn't see it. He could not get started. The room was too noisy for him (he reacted to every noise and movement), the worksheet was too overwhelming and no one was helping him get started. So, like hundreds of kids with ND, he goes home with tons of homework every night.

Often auditory or visual stimuli are the culprits. When students with ND become overwhelmed at the beginning of an assignment, feeling there are too many things being thrown at them, they often "shut down," unable to work and not knowing what to ask when needing help. When teachers and parents do not understand that there may be a reason for this, they often think the child is choosing to be difficult. Many don't want to appear "dumb" in front of their peers so they use coping mechanisms like sleeping and trying to look busy, thinking they can complete the assignments at home. They don't realize that by taking all assignments home, they will be even more overwhelmed. That's why it is helpful if they can at least do some of the work in class. Strategies that might help a student begin an assignment include breaking assignments into small steps. For example, the teacher might say to the student, "Do this problem, sentence, etc., and then raise your hand to let me know when you are finished." It's the same at home; cleaning the room, chores, transition. Use pictures or give one-step directions and check for compliance often.

When they feel successful at completing small steps, individuals with ND will be able to accomplish more of an assignment. Other options include covering all but one problem on a worksheet at a time, writing only one math problem at a time on the paper, reading the questions at the end of the chapter first and placing the student in the least distractible setting. Frequently, when these strategies are applied to help her get started, the student can stay focused for a longer period of time, thus helping her feel good about gaining some control over the situation. Just telling children with ND to get their work done won't work. To succeed they really need supportive strategies, along with a lot of patience.

See Auditory Processing Disorder, Checklists, Organizational Skills, Sensory Integration Issues, Shutting Down, Visual Processing Disorders, Visual Supports

"GOTTA GO" AND "GOTTA HAVE IT NOW"

When I was teaching, I usually didn't get home until about 5:30 P.M., at which time Josh was always waiting by the door obsessed with something. He'd usually tell me that I "had" to take him to a basketball court to play with whoever happened to be there. I'd struggle, but not for long, about what to do. Should I respond to his urgent demands or make him wait until later? Some parents would think I was "giving in" to my son's obsessive compulsiveness if I stopped everything and agreed to take him to play ball. Would I make things worse by giving in to his OCD behaviors? If I said "no," would I be pushing him past his ability to handle not being able to go? I always tried to look at the whole picture. I really did know my son best. Josh needed this release! He was an athlete. I "knew" he needed this. If I didn't take him, his anxiety would increase dramatically. To this day, I feel strongly that I was meeting his need to release. He needed to exercise, and because he had so few positive peer interactions, here was a time when he could excel.

See Obsessive Compulsive Disorder

GRADES, MODIFIED EXPECTATIONS

Most school districts use grades as a standard for granting general education credit, so their grading practices apply to all students, including those with ND. Grades provide the IEP team with information on a student's mastery in a certain area to help them make appropriate educational decisions. While many children with ND can succeed in regular education classes with the same expectations as other students, there may be times when it is appropriate to modify their grades. There are times when the neurological symptoms are severe enough to impact learning to the point it becomes impossible for the child to achieve the same level of performance expected of other students.

This is where quality vs. quantity comes into play. Some districts allow alternative grading systems such as pass/fail. Others provide grades based on the percent of work completed. That is, if a child with ND completed five problems correctly, he would receive 100 percent as a grade even though neurotypical students were graded on completing 20 problems. The IEP team needs to evaluate whether the child can master the objectives with less work or alternative methods. For instance, I frequently recommend that children with ND not have homework and that teachers grade on what the student completed in class. I do not believe these children should ever fail. The IEP team should review whether the child is receiving everything necessary in special education to be successful.

See Failing, Homework Strategies, Individualized Education Program (IEP)

GRANDPARENTS

Some grandparents are extremely supportive of the child with ND; others make matters worse by refusing to accept the symptoms as neurological. Parents should do everything possible to educate their child's grandfathers and grandmothers about ND, but the most important goal is to protect the child from humiliating experiences. Grandparents should not offer advice unless asked. The best thing grandparents can do is "to be there" when they are needed. I feel it is the responsibility of all grandparents to do everything that they can to ensure that their grandchildren have every opportunity for success, including offering financial support to research programs searching for causes and cures of ND.

See Extended Family, Family Reunions

GRAPHOMOTOR CONCERNS

The term "graphomotor" refers to a disorder involving problems with skills requiring the small muscles. For example, a child with graphomotor difficulties may not be able to use a pencil at the same level as his peers. An occupational therapist can assess for concerns in this area and develop a treatment plan.

See Dysgraphia, Handwriting, Occupational Therapist

GRIEVING

The stages of grief are: denial, anger, bargaining, depression, acceptance, and hope for the future. I have experienced them all! I remember my first appointment with our counselor after Josh had received a diagnosis of TS. The counselor asked, "So how do you feel to have the diagnosis?" My response was, "It's great, at least I have a name for it!" Ha! No sooner had we been given the "name" for all of Josh's movements, when all of a sudden everything got even worse – Josh started having full body tics that looked like he was having seizures 24 hours a day. That's when the grieving started. Just watching him suffer like this was one of the hardest things I had ever experienced. If I hadn't had a counselor, I don't know what I would have done. He let me cry and get angry, but more than anything, he shared information. The local chapter of the Tourette Syndrome Association (TSA) was another great help to me. I knew I could not do it alone and that I had to do everything I could to make Josh's life better.

Many parents know there is something different about their child. For some it takes a while to accept a neurological diagnosis. From personal experience I can only say to parents that the sooner you get involved and start learning, the more successful your child will be. Allow yourself to learn from other parents. Having a child with ND is not embarrassing unless you let it be. Grief is highly associated with loss. No parent hopes for or envisions having a child with ND. Instead, they have hopes and desires of what their child should and will be like. As parents become aware of their child's neurological difficulties, these dreams sometimes have to be modified. The result is very similar to a grieving process of giving up previous thoughts and wishes and reaching acceptance of the current situation. If a parent has not worked through this grieving process to a state of realistic acceptance, he or she may continue in the denial phase, assuming that the child can do anything he sets his mind to. On the other hand, some parents remain in the depression phase, feeling that they must do everything for their child because he has disabilities. Both of these parental mindsets are harmful to the child and are the result of not having worked through the grieving process to obtain a realistic view of the child. Once parents get through the stages of the grieving process, they are better able to address specific issues pertaining to their child. Parents need to take one day at a time, looking for the positive things in life and encouraging their child wherever they can.

See Acceptance, Counseling - Individual/Family, Parenting a Child with ND, Support Groups

GROUP ACTIVITIES

When planning group activities, remember children with ND do better in small groups, whereas large groups can be overwhelming and too stimulating. It is better for the child with ND to succeed with one other child than shutting down or exploding in a large group. Provide extra adult support when the child is involved in a large-group setting, as is sometimes unavoidable, like field trips, birthday parties or school assemblies.

See Anxiety, Panic Attacks, Peer Relations

GUIDED IMAGERY

Guided imagery is the process of using words and often music to take the listener on an inner journey for a particular purpose, such as a rain forest to help them relax when they are having a lot of anxiety. An experienced counselor best teaches the techniques of rhythmic breathing and focusing on a relaxing scene such as a beach, mountains, or a rainforest. The counselors at the Joshua Center teach children with ND how to utilize this technique so they can use it when they are under stress. I have had children tell me they are able to stop themselves in the rumbling stage by taking themselves to their very own "place" to calm down and regroup.

See Counseling - Individual/Family

H

HALLWAY BEHAVIOR

Transition between classes is difficult for most children with ND. Planning ahead will save not only the teacher's sanity, but the child's too. Many problems occur in the halls of schools, but some of them can be avoided. For example, having the child at the front of the line with a responsible student behind him can help; giving the child something with a little weight that requires both hands keeps the child from intruding on others physically; ignoring vocal tics and constant talking will make the transition easier; immediate, positive reinforcement for appropriate behavior (a smile, sticker, five minutes on the computer at the end of the day, etc.) will go further than paying attention to

negative hallway behaviors such as constant talking. Other helpful suggestions include: sending the child ahead of the other students by a few seconds; assigning an older student to walk the child to and from her destination; and enlisting parent volunteers to assist between classes.

But no matter what precautions and interventions you implement, some tics just have to come out. It has been our experience at the Joshua Center that not until the children are about 15 or 16 do we start to see them having much control over their symptoms. In some cases with severe TS and OCD, it may be even later.

See Accommodations, Auditory Processing Disorder, Brainstorming, Changing Classes, Transition from One Activity or Lesson to Another, Visual Distractions

HANDWRITING

Writing problems occur in a majority of individuals with ND. Poor fine-motor skills impact learning greatly by slow writing speed, illegible writing and inappropriate spacing. If students have time restraints placed on them, they often are unable to complete assignments. Writing for children with ND is not automatic; it takes a lot of effort. In addition to motor problems, they have difficulty thinking and writing at the same time. Some children with ND do a lot of erasing – I mean a lot! Often their papers get torn, and they have to start all over. They shouldn't have to redo their work for these symptoms. To avoid this tendency, you can try having the child use only pencils without erasers, but I think it will be stressful. The best thing is to allow the child an alternate means of completing work, such as using a computer or dictating to someone. Since many children with ND have poor fine-motor control, I often suggest that parents purchase Power Putty, a tool occupational therapists use with patients to strengthen hand and finger muscles. It is a non-toxic silicone rubber compound resembling Silly Putty.

See Computers, Handwriting - Cursive vs. Manuscript

HANDWRITING – CURSIVE VS. MANUSCRIPT

For many children with ND printing and cursive writing skills are slow to develop. For most of the children I have worked with, printing is easier and faster than cursive. We teach the Handwriting Without Tears (HWT) program (www.hwtears.com) at the Joshua Center, starting with printing for all ages before going on to cursive. This multisensory program is fun to learn and is developmentally based, so it works for children of all abilities. Once they have mastered the correct manuscript, cursive is easier for the children. Some of the problems the Joshua Center staff have observed in students include forgetting how to form letters, forgetting how to connect letters, too little or too much spacing, not being able to keep letters on the lines or in the lines, and excessive pressure when writing. The HWT program addresses all of these concerns while still allowing children to be successful when writing.

HANDWRITING, GRADING OF

I do not know of any research that specifically addresses the handwriting problems of children with ND, but in working with hundreds of children I have seen very few without some type of handwriting difficulty. While I encourage good handwriting, I believe children should be graded on effort not the actual handwriting. They should be allowed to use computers, an alternate form of technology, or to dictate to somebody on all papers and projects, including writing weekly spelling words.

See Handwriting, Handwriting - Cursive vs. Manuscript, Occupational Therapist

HEADACHES

Many children with ND have headaches. Doctors don't exactly know why, but stress and muscular tension can develop from tics, for example. Headaches can also be a side effect of medications so it is important to communicate any pattern of headaches to the child's doctor.

See Stress

HEADPHONES

It is often difficult for children with ND to get started on assignments in class. This is not chosen behavior but may be due to oversensitivity to their environment, including general noise, rustling papers, buzzing lights, or even the noises of the fish tank or class pets. Many children wear headphones either by themselves or with the benefit of classical, soft music or white noise, such as sounds of the ocean, to screen out these noises.

See Auditory Processing Disorder, Getting Started

HELPER

Many children with ND have low self-esteem due to interfering symptoms, poor peer relations, etc. One way to help boost their self-esteem is to let them be a helper, especially in front of peers. Most children, with and without ND, love to help. I'm not talking about putting out the trash or cleaning bedrooms, but about helping out at school or in the neighborhood. Doing something for another person for, say, 30 minutes a couple of times a week will help the child with ND feel appreciated and build her self-esteem. One young man visits the nursing home where his mother works so he can talk to the residents and perform little errands for the nurses. He always goes home feeling good about himself.

HIDDEN CURRICULUM

Most people take for granted the dos and don'ts of everyday behavior and typical social interaction. Brenda Myles and Richard Simpson (1999), in an article titled "Understanding the Hidden Curriculum: An Essential Social Skill for Children and Youth with Asperger Syndrome," say, "For some, a generous investment of time is required to ensure that the student understands; other 'rules' can be learned in a matter of minutes. The hidden curriculum varies across location, situations, people, age, and culture." Examples of hidden curriculum items include:

you should not have to pay peers to be your friends; do not draw violent scenes in school; when your teacher gives you a warning about behavior and you continue the behavior, you are probably going to get in trouble; different teachers have different rules – some allow talking only if your hand is raised, others allow talking as long as it is not intrusive; friends do not ask friends to do something that could get them in trouble; and don't tell about personal stuff from home.

HIGH SCHOOL DIPLOMA

All children, including those with ND, need a high school diploma to get off to a good start in the adult world. Schools should try hard to prevent students with ND from dropping out by providing as many modifications as needed to succeed. I have watched several children with ND struggle (depression, getting into trouble with the law, etc.) with too much time on their hands when they have dropped out of school. A word of warning: Don't think your child is ready to be on his own just because he's earned his diploma.

See Career Development, GED, Life Skills, Transition Planning for Post-High School

HOARDING

Some children with ND hoard things. Hoarding can be a form of OCD that can involve excessive saving of items to the extent that it interferes with the child's living space. For example, I know children who hoard food in their bedrooms. One college-aged young man spent hundreds of dollars on shoes his first year in school, creating a financial hardship for college expenses. If the hoarding interferes excessively, consult the child's doctor and counselor.

See Obsessive Compulsive Disorder

HOME BASE

A home base is a place in the school or the home where the child can go to reduce stress. It needs to be a place that the child is comfortable with, so I suggest that the child be involved in identifying it. The home base should be equipped only with items that help reduce stress and should not include items the child could destroy if he is experiencing a meltdown. Some children may wish to draw or listen to a radio in home base while others may need a physical activity. The goal is for the child to calm down so she is able to return to her normal activities. The home base should not be used as a disciplinary tool. The child is not being disciplined; she is being allowed to regain her composure in a special place. The child can usually regain composure in 10-15 minutes, although occasionally he may need up to 30 minutes. When the child has regained his composure, he is expected to return to the previous activity. It is a sign of maturity when a student can identify when he needs to go to his home base. Use of the home base should be monitored for how long, rather than how frequently, the child uses it. I would rather have the child go to the home base four times a day for 10 minutes each than having him go for a long period of time, avoiding a return to class. Schools often state they do not have space available for this purpose, but if they look hard enough there is usually some place that the child and school can agree upon.

See Accommodations, Brainstorming, Rage Stage, Recovery Stage, Rumbling Stage

HOMEBOUND INSTRUCTION

Many children with ND receive homebound instruction at some point in their school years. Homebound teachers are usually school district employees who go to the child's home after regular school hours to work with the student. An important element in successful homebound instruction is that someone is responsible for home-school communication.

If the neurological symptoms are severe enough to interfere with typical school participation, they will continue a home, at least for a while, so accommodations are just as important at home as they were at school. For example, accommodations may have to be made in the quantity of work assigned, and the parents or homebound teacher will need to read and write for the child if this was an accommodation at school. Finally, when the child returns to school, he should not have to complete any extra work that was not made available to him during his stay at home.

See Accommodations, Modifications

HOMECOMING DANCE

Often children with ND do not have the opportunity to participate in school functions because their neurological symptoms prevent them from having many close relationships. As a result, when the opportunity for a social activity arises, the child sometimes needs a little help. I know a wonderful mother who, when her 16-year-old son announced he was attending the Homecoming dance, immediately started thinking of ways she could help this become a successful experience. Like many children with ND, her son had experienced a long stretch with no friends, so she was excited that he was going to participate in a major social event. Before her husband left for an out-of-town trip, he told their son that he would buy a suit for him if he wanted and that he expected him to wear it to church and on Christmas Day. Mom was excited at the thought of how handsome her son would look in all the pictures she would be taking, but her son soon told her that these days not everyone wears a suit even at formal occasions. After her son assured her he would not be the only one without a suit, she reluctantly ironed his Dockers and dress shirt. Both were hanging in his closet the day of Homecoming.

That afternoon her son informed her that he and his girlfriend were going out to look for a "cool" jacket. Nothing could have prepared her for what he brought home. Walking in hours later, he called out, "Hey, I found a suit and it only cost $93.00. You and dad will help pay for it, right? The store has no refund policy." His mother rushed into the room where she found her son holding a long white plastic bag covering his "suit," purchased at a vintage shop. He slowly began pulling up the bottom of the bag to reveal white pants. She immediately envisioned the jacket would be navy blue and her son would look like a sailor. But as he pulled the rest of the bag up, she saw a white jacket. Her first thought was "Saturday Night Fever" and John Travolta. As her son pointed out the thin red stripe down the outer edge of the jacket and the ruffles on the tuxedo shirt, she began to explain that he couldn't possibly wear this tuxedo. But his girlfriend pointed out that it matched the white dress she would be wearing. To better convince his mother of the appropriateness of the suit, the young man tried on the shirt and jacket and his girlfriend put on her dress. The Mom agreed he looked handsome in the jacket. Then she asked him to try on the pants to see the whole look. She had noticed that the coat sleeves were rather long, so she was wondering if the pants were big also. This is when she found out that her dear, impulsive son had only tried on the jacket and assumed if the jacket fit, the pants would too (remember, nonrefundable!). When he came out wearing the pants, they were so loose they began to fall off. Reluctantly, she ironed the tuxedo-type shirt, still thinking about "Saturday Night Fever" and wondering if she should allow her son to wear the suit. Her son's friend and his date arrived early with the friend's dad, who also wanted to take pictures. While everyone waited in the living room, and with her son urging her to hurry (and still asking if she would help pay for his suit), she began working with the pants that were four times bigger than her son's waist and had a self-belt that could not be tightened. The safety pin she first tried broke as she attempted to push it through massive folds of material, so she ended up using a large diaper pin she had saved for years. When she warned her son he could not take his jacket off or the folds that showed all the way down the seat of his pants would be extremely noticeable, he insisted he would be way too hot dancing in his jacket. At first resisting his idea of not tucking in his shirt to compensate for the problem, she decided the most important thing was that he have fun. So she finally put aside her mindset of a "regular" suit or Dockers, and together they figured out that even though the shirt was long, the jacket was even longer, so if he didn't tuck the shirt in, it would not be wrinkled when he took his jacket off. Then they joined the others and had fun taking lots of pictures. Afterward her son told her he did get a few looks but he got even more compliments! And yes, his mom and dad did help pay for his Homecoming suit. Sometimes you just have to go with the flow! These kids may need a little help and do things a little differently, but they need these experiences and they need our patience to help them be successful.

Another parent tells how she and her husband helped their 16-year-old son be successful at the prom. In a nutshell, they tried to lessen any of the stresses that their son would encounter. A great deal of time was spent breaking down the evening into little steps (clothing, flowers, transportation, after-prom activities) and walking through the steps that they could check out beforehand. Even though they did encounter some obsessing and "rumbling" during the planning, the evening went well and their son experienced success in what he set out to do. They are hopeful he will remember this successful experience and be able to draw on it when other things don't go as well. It can be done, just plan every step.

HOME SCHOOLING

Many children with ND do quite well in the traditional school setting with accommodations, but I have observed some school situations that don't give parents much of a choice but to home school; for instance, when excessive bullying of their child is not adequately addressed at the school. When the child's neurological symptoms are treated as behavior disorders and all efforts to convince the school otherwise have failed, parents may consider home schooling to protect the child from emotional harm. Some parents like the flexibility home schooling brings to the family. Home schooling can be planned around vacations, jobs and everyday events, and children learn about real-world experiences by being a part of them.

Home schooling is legal in all 50 states. If you are considering this option, you need to check with the Department of Education in your state for any regulations that might apply. Parents should contact their public libraries to identify home schooling organizations. You can attend home schooling conferences and fairs to look for education materials and to get ideas. Many parents either join a home school support group or start one themselves to provide opportunities for children and parents to socialize and participate in cooperative educational and physical activities. If you are going to home school, do it responsibly. For example, if your child needs accommodations in the traditional school setting, he will need accommodations in the home school setting so you will need to decide how you will implement those accommodations.

See Accommodations, After School, Consistently Inconsistent, Getting Started, Individualized Education Program (IEP), Organizational Skills, Racing Thoughts, Section 504 Plan, Waxing and Waning

HOMEWORK STRATEGIES

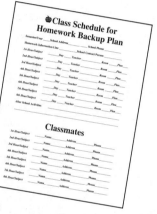

Most parents have had their share of homework woes. Before committing to helping your child with homework, observe him to identify what works and when it is a good time to start homework. Figure out how you can best help. Would it be by reading directions or reading a chapter to the child, or does your child do better by reading by himself? Many children with ND need a great deal of time, attention and patience just to get through one evening of homework. If homework seems overwhelming, they may start to shut down. As a result, you may need to spend a lot of time just talking to your child to build up his confidence. You will also need to break down the homework into smaller tasks and recognize when your child needs a break. Take frequent breaks like watching TV or playing a short game. Set goals like saying, "Let's finish spelling, then we will play a short game." This gives the child something to work towards. If your child does not understand the homework, schedule an appointment with your child's teacher to inform her of the problem and determine how you, the parent, will accommodate your child when it happens again.

Specific strategies to consider when helping your child include the following: establish homework rules that you and your child can agree on; each night review assignments before your child starts her homework; organize homework supplies before starting; develop short-term goals that can gradually be extended; break down large assignments into manageable steps; identify a specific place for your child to work that has good lighting and is free from distractions; praise appropriate work habits; treat your child with respect by avoiding nagging and threats; use highlighting tape or markers to identify important words or directions; and establish a maximum time allotment for homework.

If symptoms are so severe that they prevent the child from completing her homework in one evening, parents must note that in the assignment notebook/planner. Sometimes it may become necessary to reduce, by as much as 50 percent, the amount of homework. If a child can master the concept in five problems, practicing 20 may not be necessary. I tell teachers and parents to work toward 100 percent, but warn them that there will be times when this may not be possible. If a child appears fine at school, he may be expending a lot of energy suppressing tics, managing racing thoughts or even performing rituals in his head. Often the children hold it together at school only to let it all out when entering the front door at home, making homework completion difficult.

See Getting Started, Homework, Stressless, Homework Supplies, Observations at Home, Shutting Down

HOMEWORK, STRESSLESS

Recently I came across an interesting story on how to make the most of compulsions when it comes to homework completion. A boy was terribly anxious one Friday evening because he had so much schoolwork to do that he thought it would be impossible to finish it all by Monday. He began to obsess about not being able to go to school on Monday because he felt he could not go if all his work was not done. Soon he had worked himself up to the verge of a meltdown.

To prevent his behavior from escalating further, his parents suggested that they plan a fun workday for Saturday. They got out pencil and paper and began to plan the next day. They started with getting up one hour later than usual, which made the boy very happy. Next, the mother agreed to a special breakfast that the boy liked. Then they divided the rest of the morning into 30-minute segments with a homework task assigned to each. After each time segment the boy opted to do a fun activity for 15 minutes. These activities were also written down on the schedule. They planned fast food for lunch and then scheduled the afternoon in the same manner as the morning. They even had some time allotted for taking a drive, during which the mother ran some errands and her son got some ice cream. The boy thoroughly enjoyed the planning, and best of all, the threat of a meltdown vanished. The next day the boy followed the schedule as only someone with OCD-type behaviors can do. It was a "fun" day and a "work" day. All the homework got done. The boy went to school on Monday with no problems.

See Homework Strategies, Homework Supplies

HOMEWORK SUPPLIES

Regardless of your child's age, your child's IEP or 504 Plan should always state that the child gets to keep a complete set of textbooks at home for the entire school year. The following are items you may want to purchase and keep stocked up on: a smooth desk or table top, number two pencils, reliable pencil sharpener, colored pencils, recommended size notebook paper, computer paper, large supply of erasers, mechanical pencils, good quality pens, folders, hole punch, paper clips, stapler with plenty of staples, computer ink cartridges, scotch tape, scissors and glue.

See Books Left at Home

HOMEWORK TIME ALLOTMENT

Most schools have a homework policy. It has been my experience that usually 30-40 minutes of homework is expected in the early elementary grades; one hour in upper-elementary grades; and about two hours in middle school and high school. If your child is spending more than the recommended time doing her homework, talk to her teacher about adjusting assignments or changing the method of completion. For example, the child may have to dictate written assignments to parents if symptoms of ND interfere with handwriting, or the parents may need to read the textbook assignments to their child if symptoms interfere with reading. Document the amount of time spent doing homework when discussing possible changes in homework assignments with your child's teachers.

See Homework Strategies

HOSPITALIZATION

In my experience, when children with ND need to be hospitalized, they are usually hospitalized on the child psychiatric ward. Most psychiatric hospitals are set up to provide behavior modification programs. Josh was hospitalized several times due to medication changes and monitoring, but because he was usually in for a short period, it was difficult to educate medical professionals. Right after he was diagnosed with TS, his tics looked like seizures 24 hours a day, so he was hospitalized in a psychiatric treatment center for children to monitor medication side effects. I was not allowed to see him for several days, a typical regimen for psychiatric hospitals, but what Josh needed was nurturing and support from his family – not isolation – at a time when his body was out of control. He has finally forgiven me for that, but it took years. I thought the staff were specialists until just a couple of years ago when I saw the therapist who had worked with Josh and heard her tell a doctor that Josh was her first patient with TS. She had no idea what she had just said. Be careful, hearing the labels is not the same as understanding the disorders. It turned out Josh's biggest concerns were obsessive-compulsive symptoms and they were treating these symptoms as chosen behavior. A little information can be detrimental to your child.

See Behavior Modification, Changes in Medications

HUMILIATION

I'll never forget a boy with ND I was helping in a small-town middle school. The school staff had been educated pretty thoroughly, I thought. One day in art class the student couldn't find the project he had started a couple of days before, until the class was about two-thirds over. When he finally started working on it, he got frustrated and threw it away because it was not perfect. He wanted to start over, but the bell rang. Of course, the whole time he was looking for the project he was talking to himself. At the end of class, the teacher proceeded to give him an in-school suspension (ISS) for talking and not doing his work. He was sent to the assigned in-school suspension room, and after the ISS teacher read the note about the reason why he was assigned ISS, he made the student complete a think sheet by writing 25 times "I will keep my big mouth shut." Besides, he was made to stand in front of his peers in the ISS room and read the sentence aloud. The parents and I called an IEP meeting as soon as we learned about this. To top it all off, the art teacher and ISS teacher did not see anything wrong with what they had done! There should never be punishment for neurological symptoms, and no child should ever be a target of such humiliation.

See Discipline

IDEA DISCIPLINE SECTION

According to the discipline provisions provided for in IDEA, schools can remove a child for up to 10 school days at a time for any violation of school rules as long as there is not a pattern of removal. They do not need to provide services during the first 10 school days in a school year that a child is removed. A child with a disability cannot be suspended long term or expelled from school for behavior that has been determined to be a manifestation of his disability. The 1997 Amendments added provisions that mandate schools assess a child's behavior to determine if the behavior is a manifestation of the disability. Positive behavioral interventions must be developed to address that behavior. In addition, a child with disabilities who has been suspended or expelled must continue to receive services. A child may be removed if he brings a gun or dangerous weapon to school, if he is in knowing possession of illegal drugs or is selling or soliciting controlled substances. When a child's current placement is deemed likely to result in injury to himself or others, schools can request a hearing officer to remove a child for up to 45 days. For behavior that is not a manifestation of a child's disability, schools must provide services for long-term removal to the extent determined necessary to allow the child to progress in the general curriculum and advance toward meeting his IEP goals. The IEP team is required to develop a behavioral assessment plan (or review one in place) when the child is first removed from his current placement for more than 10 school days in a school year or when commencing a removal constitutes a change in placement.

See Behavior Plan, Individuals with Disabilities Education Act

IMMATURITY

Based on our experience at the Joshua Center, we have found that the emotional maturity of children with ND is two-thirds their chronological age. As you watch your child interact with his peers, you may notice that other children seem more mature. It can be difficult when they reach the middle and high school levels when most children are acting appropriate for their age and your child is acting as through she was still in elementary school.

Jack Southwick discusses three factors that affect maturity: the ability to retrieve learned behavior that is filed for future reference; the ability to read, interpret and act on social clues from a situation; and the full development of the nerve path network in the brain. For most children, somewhere between the ages of 9 and 13 the brain undergoes a growth spurt and reaches its full weight and circumference. At this stage the child begins to be able to think more flexibly. From our experience at the Joshua Center, for many children with neurological disorders this development of operational thought is delayed until 14-16 years of age. The good news is that maturity does seem to catch up around 25-28 years of age. This is one of the reasons I stress to parents not to give up on their child in those critical post-high school years.

See Impulse Control, Transition Planning for Post-High School

IMPULSE CONTROL

"Stop and think" is not an automatic message in the brains of a children with ND. If a thought or an action comes to mind, it's immediately out the mouth or it's acted upon. When Josh was about 18, he had gone to the high school to watch a baseball game. (Josh had dropped out at 16 and got his GED.) Josh was a pitcher, good enough for professional ball, so he took advantage of any chance he had to play or watch a game. A professional baseball scout, who was there to watch the game, had told him (I found out 24 hours later) that he wished he could see Josh play. When Josh returned home that afternoon, he said he was leaving again to see a show with his best friend, Roger. When I woke up at 2:00 A.M. and realized Josh wasn't home yet, I figured he was with Roger, so didn't worry. When I got up the next morning at 8:00 o'clock and found that Josh still hadn't come home, I called Roger's house. "No," Roger said, "they hadn't gone to the movies." Now I did worry! About 2:00 P.M. I got a collect call from Warsaw, Missouri, a small town a couple of hundred miles away. Well, Josh had taken himself on a drive (a long one) to think about what could have happened if that scout had been able to see him pitch. At some point on the trip he tried to pass a semi-truck – and almost made it. Unfortunately, he didn't see a car in the opposite lane coming toward him. They didn't meet, but in trying to get back into his lane (farm road lane), the semi went over the hood of Josh's car. The car was totaled, but Josh was OK! The tow-truck driver had been kind enough to drop him off at the nearest Pizza Hut where Josh proceeded to ring up a tab for pizza, his favorite food. Soon he met some girls who were picking up pizza to take to a slumber party while their parents were out of the country. The girls took Josh home for the night! I didn't ask too many questions, but they did drop him off the next morning at, where else, the Pizza Hut. When I went to retrieve my son, my question was, "What do you think I would be thinking if a police officer had come to my door telling me my son was dead in Warsaw, Missouri?" He just shrugged his shoulders! (He later did sign with the Kansas City Royals and played in the Minor Leagues for a while.)

Children with ND are the ones who cannot wait their turn in line or in a game, who cut in line, blurt out answers in class, tend to be too loud, and have poor social skills. They often say the wrong thing at the wrong time and fail to learn subtle social cues that everybody else picks up more or less automatically. They have limited problem-solving strategies. They don't stop and look at the problem and then say, "Well, I do this first, then this second," etc. They often interrupt or intrude on others, start something before having understood the directions, have difficulty self-monitoring their behavior . . . the list goes on. Medications can often help, but some children cannot take the meds due to side effects, for instance, weight gain, stomach distress, or loss of appetite.

In the video "When the Chips Are Down: Learning Disabilities and Discipline" (Bieber, 1994), Richard Lavoie addresses impulsivity better than anyone I know. These children can learn "stop and think," but it takes lots of practice. The best way is to use real-life experiences. Review situations and ask how they could have handled them differently. Our counselor drew several stick figures with the kids so they could "see" a situation. The kids would help draw alternative ways of handling things. Puppets are also a good way to teach social skills. Look at the problem, break it into manageable steps and practice each step until it is mastered. Then, most important, praise the child for each step mastered. Success breeds success! Children with ND need all the support they can get!

See Social Skills, Speaking in Pictures

IN A HURRY TO COMPLETE WORK

Some children with ND seem to hurry through their assignments at school, appearing unwilling or unable to check for correctness and showing little regard for neatness. I have worked with far too many children who do this to view it as a chosen behavior. To improve neatness I recommend using a computer for as much of the work as possible. To teach students to slow down, give them only one paper or task at a time. The teacher or paraprofessional can check for correctness, neatness and completion before assigning another task.

See Accommodations, Computers

INAPPROPRIATE CONVERSATIONS

I have known children with ND who have inappropriate conversations relating to sex, the devil or just weird stuff. If you are concerned, I suggest you talk to the child's counselor and doctor. The child could be having some obsessive-compulsive thoughts.

See Counseling - Individual/Family

INAPPROPRIATE LANGUAGE

After you have read about coprolalia and compulsions and you don't think your child meets the criteria, maybe he is doing it just to be misbehaving. Josh used to say his swearing was voluntary! Sometimes I can understand why the children use inappropriate language with all the stuff that gets dished out to them, but if you are concerned, talk to your child's doctor and counselor.

See Compulsions, Coprolalia, Counseling - Individual/Family

INAPPROPRIATE TICS

I remember observing a second-grade student with ND in a self-contained classroom for students with behavior disorders. The child's teacher was having difficulty with his getting out of his seat and touching another child inappropriately, and the principal wanted to file sexual harassment charges. Inappropriate touching can be a tic. Since I did not actually see the child engage in the offending behavior, I asked the teacher if he directed this behavior at one particular child. It turned out that it was directed at a little girl sitting close to him. I recommended the teacher seat this child as far as possible from the boy doing the touching and that she keep the two children separated throughout the day (as much as possible), including other classes, recess, hall passing and lunchtime. In addition, I recommended that the child with TS be allowed frequent breaks. He was a very active child and needed a lot of room for movement. Reports from the teacher verify it worked.

It is important to educate the other students in the class when tics are a problem for others. Giving the child something to touch at his desk, like a rabbit's foot or a stress ball, may help redirect the tic. Some children with touching tics actually tell others to stay a certain distance from them so they won't be ticced upon. No one has the right to touch another person inappropriately, but with some children the tic is so quick, it is often difficult to avoid it. Some older children and adults who have invasive touching tics are able to ask the person whom the tic is directed towards if it is ok to tic on them.

See *Brainstorming, Complex Tics, Educating Peers, Educating School Staff, Tics, Tourette Syndrome*

INCLUSION

There are strong arguments for both inclusion with resource help and for self-contained special education settings for children with ND. I suggest that as a member of the IEP team, you look at the whole picture when evaluating what is best for a child with ND. An inclusion classroom gives the child the opportunity to be educated in a setting like all other children. Some parents are concerned that inclusion means their child will not have adequate special education support. The social and academic benefits can be very positive if your child's teachers are committed to the program.

Dedicated teachers will ensure that all children understand and respect learning differences and will structure their classrooms to foster mutual respect. A good general education classroom teacher will identify the child's strengths and give him opportunities to demonstrate them with his peers. One of the biggest benefits of inclusion is that it stresses to all children the importance of living in harmony with others in a diverse world. Parents should question administrators about the training and experience of all general education teachers to ensure that their child receives the supports needed to meet his IEP objectives. If you believe the general education classroom setting cannot meet your child's needs, you can request a modification in services or program. General education classrooms should provide the following supports for your child: a clearly defined IEP; professional staff development that addresses the specific disabilities represented in a teacher's classroom, including alternative teaching methods and curriculum; planning time for the teacher to prepare for meeting the child's special needs; reduced class size if at all possible; good home-school communication; sufficient funding to meet the needs of all the children, including those with special needs; support from a special education teacher and any ancillary services needed.

See *Educating School Staff, Individualized Education Program (IEP), Structure and Routine*

INCREASE IN TICS

See Changes in Tics, PANDAS, Waxing and Waning

INDEPENDENCE

The ability of a child with ND to be independent will wax and wane, just like her neurological symptoms. At those times when things are going well, allow her some space not only to develop her skills but to explore her creativity. Don't hold her back from experiences that will allow her to develop into a mature adult. If she does not receive these "foundation" experiences, she will get stuck. I have known mothers who have denied their children wonderful new experiences due to their personal fears that something might happen. When you prepare a child for new experiences, make a list of all the things he needs to know to make the experience a positive one. Encourage him and let him know you will always be there, but lengthen the rope when you can.

INDEPENDENT EVALUATION

Parents may request an independent education evaluation (IEE) as provided for in IDEA whenever they disagree with the evaluation obtained by the district. The school must either provide the evaluation at public expense or initiate a due process hearing to show that its original evaluation is appropriate. During a due process hearing, a hearing officer may at any time order an independent evaluation at public expense. The hearing officer can also encourage mediation at all stages of the hearing process to resolve the dispute.

A qualified professional who is not an employee of the school district must conduct an IEE. Further, IDEA regulations stipulate that the independent evaluator be qualified and that the independent evaluation meet the district's criteria for such evaluations. If an outside evaluation has not been requested from the school district, the parents may seek an IEE at their own expense and, if appropriate, it must be considered by the district.

See Due Process, Individuals with Disabilities Education Act

INDIVIDUALIZED EDUCATION PROGRAM (IEP)

If a child meets the criteria for a disability, an individualized education program (IEP) can be written. The Individuals with Disabilities Education Act (IDEA) was enacted to give all children a free and appropriate public education in the least restrictive environment. A team that includes school district professionals and the parents as equal members writes the IEP. Written to address the unique needs of your child, not a generic plan, the IEP describes a child's current levels of performance and the impact of his disability. The IEP must include a statement of measurable annual goals, including benchmarks (major milestones) or objectives (intermediate steps of the annual goals), and a statement of needed supplementary related aids and services, including assistive technology. IDEA now also requires that every student's IEP include a statement regarding the child's behavior and whether or not it interferes with his learning or that of others. If behavior impedes learning, a behavioral intervention plan must be developed to address the identified concerns. An IEP meeting must be held within 30 calendar days after it has determined that your child has one of the disabilities listed in IDEA and needs special education services. Beginning at age 14 your child's IEP must also include a statement of transition service needs. At least once a year the IEP team will convene to review the IEP.

See Behavior Plan, IDEA Discipline Section, Individuals with Disabilities Education Act, Individualized Education Program Team, Transition for Post-High School

INDIVIDUALIZED EDUCATION PROGRAM TEAM

The members of the multidisciplinary team who write a child's IEP include: one or both of the child's parents; at least one general education teacher if participating in general education; at least one special education teacher of the child; an individual who can interpret the results of the child's evaluation; and a representative of the school system who knows about special education services and has the authority to commit resources, such as the special education coordinator for the district. Parents and the school district may invite additional individuals with knowledge or special expertise about the child. Representatives from transition services agencies, when such services are being discussed, also attend. Finally, the student, when appropriate, may attend, such as when transition planning is discussed or when he wants to explain to the team how his disorders impact his education. I usually recommend that the child be invited to visit with the IEP team at the end of the meeting so that the team can show him support. This usually reduces anxiety for the child.

INDIVIDUALS WITH DISABILITIES EDUCATION ACT

The Individuals with Disabilities Education Act (IDEA) is a federal law that provides for special education and related services to eligible children with disabilities. It mandates that all children with disabilities from preschool through high school receive a free appropriate public education (FAPE).

INSURANCE

If you have a child with ND, most likely you will be communicating often with your insurance company. Sometimes your health care carrier can be difficult to deal with, especially when you decide to challenge a claim denial. Document all conversations, including the date and time; the name and title of the person with whom you talked; all details discussed; and the length of the conversation. It is important to keep copies of all letters you write to your health care carrier. Don't be afraid to write to the company president, if necessary. I know it's not fun, but read your policy carefully and thoroughly. Every insurance carrier has policies to follow in making and questioning claims and asking for an appeal, so learn them. Highlight important points you may frequently want to refer to. Learn the procedures to be followed when making claims, questioning claims, and making appeals. If your carrier doesn't pay a claim you feel you are entitled to, write the insurance commissioner and your legislators (both at the state and national level) to inform them of the problems. If your child needs to see a specialist who is not on "the list," write a letter requesting that your carrier cover the costs of these visits, explaining that their costs will be far less in the long run if your child is seen by an expert in ND rather than someone who has had little or no experience with these disorders.

INTELLIGENCE ASSESSMENT

When the school personnel perform an evaluation of a child, they will most likely administer an intelligence evaluation. This test will yield an Intelligence Quotient (IQ), a score that tells the general cognitive ability of the child. The average range of intelligence is 85 to 115. Eighty-four percent of the population falls into this category.

INTERNAL TICS

Frequently children with TS and related ND complain of stomach spasms that could be internal tics. They can cause considerable discomfort for the child, so parents need to contact their child's doctor when this happens.

See Tics

INTERNET

The Internet is a wonderful educational and communication tool, but monitor your children closely. Many children with ND quickly figure out how to get into the "wrong" websites. I have worked with children who obsess over sexual information they have seen on a website and have a terrible time getting rid of the thoughts. Often children are more knowledgeable about the Internet than their parents and can even figure out some of the child safety blocks.

See Medication Side Effects

"IT'S NOT MY FAULT"

See "Oops, I Forgot!"

J

"JUST RIGHT" FEELING

One of the worst tics Josh ever had involved repeatedly hitting his elbow on the piano until it felt "just right." I remember saying after about 20 minutes, "Josh, I don't care about the piano; I'm worried you will break your elbow." Nevertheless, he had to start over, and I had to leave the room for a tissue to wipe my tears. The "just right" feeling is often associated with how things look or feel, but can also be associated with having to explain a thought over and over in different ways until it feels "just right." Children with ND frequently will wear only clothing that feels "just right."

See Clothing - Comfort Level, Occupational Therapist, Sensory Sensitivity

K

KNIVES

Sometimes children with ND obsess over sharp objects, some even to the point of "having to" cut themselves. I have known children who have used paperclips or staples at school to dig into their skin. When this happens, you need to lock up all knives, scissors, tools or anything else that has a sharp point. Contact the child's doctor because medications may be able to help this symptom. Keep in mind that while some medications may help, others may exacerbate a condition, so it is important to communicate regularly with the doctor. Parents should also consult a therapist for help.

See Obsessive Compulsive Disorder

L

LAST-WORD OBSESSION

I learned about the "last-word obsession" from a counselor at the Joshua Center. So many children seem to "have to" have the last word that one boy dubbed it the "last-word obsession." Some parents have difficulty accepting this because they believe that since they are the parent, they have the right to the last word. Arguments can go on forever when children and their parents both feel they must have the last word. It is far more important to have the *lasting word* than having the last word. When parents realize this, they can state their position calmly and then listen to their child in an emotionally neutral manner.

See Obsessive Compulsive Disorder

LATE ASSIGNMENTS

The IEP should include accommodations for late assignments, if appropriate. The important thing for teachers to remember is the objective of the assignment. If a child with ND forgets to complete a regular assignment, I do not think she should be punished for "forgetting" since "forgetting" is a symptom of ND. The important thing is that the child completes the work satisfactorily. Similarly, when a child with ND returns to school after an illness, I believe he should be given extra time to complete assignments. An assignment that takes most children 20 minutes may take an hour or more for children with ND due to interfering symptoms of the disorders. Children with ND are physically and emotionally exhausted at the end of their school day so any problems with assignment completion need to be communicated to teachers. Parents will need to help the child determine when an assignment can be realistically completed and work with the teachers on an agreed-upon date.

See Communication Between School and Home, Discipline, Email, Individualized Education Program (IEP)

LEARNING DISABILITIES

In the Individuals with Disabilities Education Act (IDEA), a specific learning disability is defined as a disorder in one or more of the basic psychological processes involved in understanding or using spoken or written language. Listening, speaking, reading, writing, and mathematics are the skills that can be affected by a learning disability. Children with average to above-average intelligence can have a learning disability. Learning disabilities affect the way children receive, process, or express information. Learning disabilities last a lifetime.

See Individuals with Disabilities Education Act

LEAST RESTRICTIVE ENVIRONMENT

One of the conditions of IDEA stipulates that states must assure children with disabilities a free appropriate public education (FAPE). FAPE includes special education and related services, provided at no cost to parents, with an IEP designed to meet the unique needs of each child with a disability. Further, states must ensure that, to the maximum extent appropriate, children with disabilities, including children in public or private institutions, are educated with nondisabled children. Special classes, schooling, or the removal of children with disabilities from the regular educational setting should occur only when the nature or severity of the child's disability cannot be met satisfactorily in regular classes with supplementary aids and services.

See IDEA Discipline Section

LEGAL SYSTEM

For the parent of a child with ND, vigilance, dedication, and understanding are key. Do not let your guard down. There are times when your child's behavior may be or appear to be so dangerous or disruptive that the authorities may become involved. Should the child's behavior result in a serious criminal offense, such as major destruction of property, threats or injury to others, or involve a weapon, the police will take the child into custody. You usually will not be successful at trying to talk the police out of taking the child. They will not understand and they are only doing their job.

What do you do? First, depending on the seriousness of the offense, try to persuade the police not to take the child. Explain the child's disorder and how it affects her behavior. For example, the problem may be related to medication; perhaps the medicine has lost its effectiveness. If you suspect this is the problem, explain to the police that you will be able to keep the child under control until you can get her to the doctor, which you will do immediately. If the child is 12 years of age or older, more than likely the police will take her into custody.

Accompany your child, if the police allows it. If not, follow them to the police station. At the police station your child will be isolated, which is a frightening experience for both you as a parent and for your child. From the station, immediately contact your doctor or insurance company to make arrangements for hospitalization for a medical evaluation after the hearing, if possible. The child will be taken to juvenile detention for the night. You will not be allowed to visit him that first night, but he may be allowed one telephone call. During all this, remember to get his medicine to him, if necessary.

Then you need to prepare for the next day because things will happen quickly. You will be notified that there will be a hearing the next day in juvenile court. Unless you have an attorney (contact your state parent advocacy organization for a referral, if necessary), the court will appoint one for the child. Don't expect to find out who the attorney is or have much of an opportunity to talk to him ahead of time, as you probably won't meet him until about 20 minutes before the hearing. You must quickly educate the attorney about your child's disorder and be prepared yourself to address the court as your child's advocate. Prepare notes ahead of time so you will know exactly the point you want to make.

You may also want to have a letter from your child's doctor and counselor. The prosecutor and judge should receive copies as well. It is our job to educate the legal system. The police, prosecutors, defense attorneys and judges have very little information about neurological disorders. The more aware they are and the more education they have about the child's ND, the more likely your child is to receive the appropriate treatment.

You are the best advocate your child has. At the hearing the court will be concerned primarily with whether or not the child is a danger to himself. If he is determined to be a danger, he will be held in juvenile detention, pending trial on the charges. If he is not a danger, he will be released to your custody, pending trial. The only other option, and the one you will need to persuade the court is the best option, is to release the child into your custody in order for him to be hospitalized and get the proper treatment.

If you are successful in so persuading the court, the child will be released into your custody on the condition that you take immediate steps to get a medical evaluation and the child hospitalized, if necessary, and report back to the court within 24 hours what you have done. The court may condition the release on the child being hospitalized and, if he is not hospitalized, you may have to return him to juvenile detention. If the judge does not allow the child to be placed in the parent's custody or admitted to a hospital, he will remain in juvenile detention.

At a later date, usually a month or two depending on the court's workload, there will be another hearing. At this hearing the court will hear evidence on the criminal charges and decide what should be done. The court's primary concern at this hearing is to determine what is in the best interest of the child. It is imperative that you, as parents, impress the court with your knowledge of all associated disorders your child may have; that you know exactly what the child needs; that since the first hearing you have gotten the child the treatment he needs; and that you will do whatever is necessary to ensure the child receives the proper medicine and treatment. Your knowledge, your dedication, and your self-confidence may be the best and only defense your child has to offer the court.

If you stay on top of the medicines, and maintain your child's therapy, hopefully, you will avoid problems like this. If you find yourself caught up in the legal system and don't know what to do, call for help from a lawyer or friend who is knowledgeable about the legal system. Remember, you don't have to suffer alone. Other parents have had similar experiences and are more than willing to help, even if you just need someone to talk to.

LIBRARY

Many children with ND have reading problems. It is a good idea to get your child a library card and consistently take her to check out books. Reading should be fun, so allow her to choose books, with guidance, at her independent reading level. Talk to the librarian or your child's teacher for assistance. Continue to read to your child also.

LICKING TICS

Understandably, schools have big concerns about health issues. If your child has a licking tic, he will have to be taught tic substitution.

See Complex Tics, Tics, Tic Substitution, Tourette Syndrome

LIFE SKILLS

While many children with ND enter college or the working world, they still have a lot to learn when it comes to life skills. Some of the skills that need to be developed include money and time management, how to participate in a job interview, developing a resume, doing laundry, scheduling and keeping appointments, ordering utility services, shopping, preparing and storing foods, following a map, public etiquette, and general household management. You will need to help your child develop the independent skills he did not learn through his high school years. The children whose parents hung in there while their child matured and learned life skills are the proud parents of successful young adults.

See Career Development

LISTENING

Many children with ND can often listen attentively if allowed to doodle or draw. However, they may have trouble taking notes and listening at the same time, so in school it is helpful if teachers make copies of another student's notes or, even better, give the child a set of notes before the lecture so she has something to follow along with. Not until I had worked with children with ND did I realize that I had difficulty taking notes all my life. Now I take a friend with me wherever I go if I need to be particularly attentive!

See Difficulty Listening and Writing Concurrently, Difficulty Listening When Having OCD Thoughts

LOCKER CONCERNS

For students in middle, junior high or high school, I often request that an extra set of textbooks remain in each classroom rather than in the child's locker. I do this for several reasons. Many children with ND have compulsions that require locking and unlocking the locker several times until it feels "just right," or they forget something and are late getting to their classes because they had to retrieve a book or an assignment from their locker. Assigning lockers that are as close as possible to the child's classes is helpful, but this does not guarantee there will not be problems. I have seen far too many children receive detentions because they were late to class or did not bring supplies, so it helps to have supplies remain in the classroom.

See "Just Right" Feeling, Obsessive Compulsive Disorder, Tardiness

LOSES EVERYTHING

Boy, have I had a lot of experience with this! Josh would have lost his head if it weren't securely attached. In an effort to hold on to a child's belongings, print labels that say "When found, please call (phone number) for reward" and place on everything. Label socks, underwear, hats, gloves, basketballs, baseball gloves, shoes, toothbrushes and anything else your child owns. One time I ended up buying an expensive baseball glove for Josh after we had spent a long time trying on every glove in the store until it felt "just right." Nevertheless, shortly afterwards, he and a friend went to play catch, and Josh decided his friend's glove felt "just right" more than his glove felt "just right," so they traded. After a while they sat down on the bleachers to talk. Guess what they both left at the ballpark? And of course neither glove was there when they returned to look for them.

See Attention Deficit Hyperactivity Disorder, Impulse Control

LUNCHROOM CONCERNS

Lunchtime can be a nightmare for both the child with ND and the lunchroom staff if they are uninformed about the child's disorders. There are several concerns to address in this setting. First, often the lunchroom is very noisy and crowded. Second, the children usually have to wait in the lunch line, which can lead to behavior problems. Third, many children with ND have sensitivities to certain foods and their odors.

Allowing the child to be first in the lunch line can eliminate or reduce some inappropriate peer interactions that might otherwise take place. Another concern involves the lunch table. If the child completes lunch quickly, it may become necessary to remove her to prevent deteriorating behavior, while she is sitting around with nothing to do. On the other hand, if a child does not complete his lunch in the allotted time or if certain odors are bothersome, it may become necessary to have an alternative lunch setting. One middle school teacher who has TS, OCD and ADHD herself provides an alternative lunch setting in her room daily for children who require another positive setting.

Sometimes children with touching tics or compulsions have problems going through the lunch line. I once received a call from a school describing a child who kept touching every serving dish despite repeated warnings not to do so. I suggested that the child remain seated while another individual got his lunch for him. It helps for the child with ND to have good role models sitting next to and across from him. Lunch monitors can help by praising appropriate lunchroom behavior.

See Educating School Staff

LYING

Some children with ND have a problem with lying. Some lie just to get attention. Some use lying as a coping mechanism when feeling overwhelmed. Some become pretty compulsive about lying. Professional counseling is important to help the child understand the lying behavior and to determine what needs to be done to reduce the frequency. Many parents make the mistake of asking the child if he is lying when they are in fact reasonably certain that the lie has occurred. Lying can be a terrible stress inducer, and the last thing these children need is to add stress to their lives.

Counseling - Individual/Family

M

MANIA

Mania refers to a significant departure from the child's normal mood. It is an upward shift in mood whereby the child feels more energetic, overly confident and thinks she is more able to focus. The child is not just unusually happy, but almost euphoric. She may not require much sleep during this time and may talk more than usual (is that possible?). A manic episode may impair the child's judgment or cause her to engage in risky behaviors. Some medications can cause an elevated state of mania. If you think your child is exhibiting mania, you need to contact your child's doctor.

See Bipolar Disorder

MANIFESTATION DETERMINATION

A manifestation determination is a process conducted by the IEP team to investigate whether there is a relationship between the student's action of concern and her disability. That is, the team must decide whether the student's action was a reflection of her disability or perhaps the result of it. When your child has engaged in behavior that is the result of his disability, he cannot be expelled from school for that behavior, but his placement may be changed. The IEP team will convene to determine if the IEP is meeting the child's behavioral needs. Modifications may need to be added or an alternative placement assigned. What is important is addressing the behavior so that it does not reoccur.

If the child's disability is found not to be related to his inappropriate behavior, he will be subject to the same disciplinary procedures and consequences as all children in the school. He may have a more restrictive setting for his FAPE, such as a juvenile detention center or residential treatment center.

See Advocacy, Free Appropriate Public Education, IDEA Discipline Section, Individualized Education Program (IEP)

MANIPULATING BEHAVIOR

Over the years I have seen many children develop manipulating behaviors. I worked with a middle school student for several years who had an excellent support staff. During his first year in high school he had a lot of motor and vocal tics and consequently received some services in a resource room while being mainstreamed in others. Six weeks into his second year of high school one of his teachers asked me to observe him in his mainstreamed classes because the parents had said he was doing better and was practically tic free at home, but in school he seemed to be having many tics. After observing him for about 15 minutes walking around the room, I had a hunch about what was going on. I took him into the hall and asked him why he was making up his tics. I just felt like he was forcing himself to tic. It turned out that his tics were a lot better, but during the previous school year he had received so much attention when he had so much trouble with his tics that he wanted to continue to receive the attention and did not know how to accept himself without them.

When I see a child in conflict with manipulating behavior, I remind myself that this is a child with ND. He may not only be struggling academically, but also with social acceptance by peers and adults. Often these children do not know how to be different even when they want to. When teachers and even parents say that a child is manipulative, it is usually said in a negative tone reflecting the belief that the child really could accomplish the task if she wanted to. I usually take the attitude that the manipulation, whether perceived or real, is being done by the child for a legitimate reason. I see the manipulation as a coping mechanism for a child who feels cornered or in a tough predicament without the ability to explain what the real problem is.

How do you stop this behavior? You cannot, at least not completely. But what you can do is try and figure out what the real problem is and help the child to recognize it and deal with it. A functional assessment of the behavior needs to take place and the child has to be taught how to change the behavior.

See Functional Behavior Assessment, Positive Reinforcement, Shutting Down, Social Skills

MASSAGE

Even with medication a mother found her daughter could not relax and shut her mind down. Sometimes after school or when her child prepared to go to bed, the mother would massage her daughter's neck, back, arms or legs. There were three daughters with ND in the family, and each daughter required different massage techniques. One daughter was helped by a firm touch while another required a light touch. Different children with ND require different support and accommodations.

See Parenting a Child with ND

MATH DISABILITIES

While many children with ND do well in school, a number of them have learning disabilities, usually in reading or math, or both. A good evaluation will identify the specific areas of need. For example, many children have trouble memorizing basic number facts in all four areas of operation (addition, subtraction, multiplication and division). Sometimes children need to hear themselves talk through a math problem. Some parents and teachers use stickers to reward mastery of math facts, even partial mastery. Many children with ND hurry through their math worksheets and never check for accuracy. It's important for teachers and parents to monitor these children as they are working math problems to encourage that they check for accuracy.

See Academic Assessment, Math Modifications, Reinforcers

MATH MODIFICATIONS

Math modifications can be added to an IEP or 504 Plan. The most common include: allowing use of calculator without penalty; requiring fewer problems to attain a passing grade; providing a table of math facts for reference; including fewer problems on a worksheet; reading and explaining story problems and breaking them into smaller steps; using graph paper or notebook paper turned sideways to keep problems in columns; using a computer when possible; allowing the student to dictate to a paraprofessional or another student work requiring writing; allowing students to talk through an assignment; and identifying good, interactive software for children to practice their math skills. I suggest they be allowed to use pocket-size facts charts to refer to when needed. As they learn a fact and no longer need the chart, that fact can be blackened or covered with white-out. Older children should be allowed to use calculators. Children should not be held back because they have not mastered basic math facts. Consistently practicing facts in small segments each day is more beneficial than one hour per week. When the child has mastered a small number of facts, add more. Make it fun. See recommended math websites in the Appendix.

See Math Disabilities

MEDICATION COMPLIANCE

Few children with ND can consistently be responsible on their own for taking their medications. I thought I was proactive when I bought those weekly medication containers until I discovered Josh was opening any cap he felt like, without paying any attention to what day it was. So I learned quickly that to be sure he took the medications, I would have to watch him take them. It takes a vigilant parent, but if your objective is for your child to succeed, then monitor medication taking. Sometimes you even have to check to see if the child swallowed the pills because many children try to hide them or spit them out later. Even for young adults it is important for parents to monitor medication compliance.

MEDICATIONS, PARENT-SCHOOL COMMUNICATION

See Teacher Journal, Weekly Reports

MEDICATION MANAGEMENT AT SCHOOL

Parents should ask the child's doctor to write prescriptions for the exact times when medications are to be given by the school nurse. For example, a child taking a stimulant medication at 7:00 A.M. may need to take the second dose before his regular lunchtime, but often school policy is to give all noontime medications to children when they are returning to class after eating lunch. That time span may be too long because the benefit of some stimulant medications lasts for only a few hours. Children who have to wait too long to take the second dose may experience a "rebound effect," whereby the behavior deteriorates to a state of irritability or depression for an hour as the stimulant wears off. Sometimes this is worse than the child's baseline behavior.

See School Nurse

MEDICATIONS MISSED

Some patients can occasionally miss a dose of medication with little impact on the outcome of therapy. Most information sheets given with prescriptions include statements such as: "If you forget to take one or more doses, take your next dose at the normal time and in the normal amount. Do not take any more than your doctor prescribed. If you miss one dose, skip it and continue with your normal schedule." I always recommend that parents contact their child's doctor when a medication has been missed since the medications children with ND take are often very strong. When medications are running low, call the doctor or pharmacist for refills at least one week in advance of needing them. It is not fair for a child to experience an increase in symptoms that can alter his behavior and attention just because he has missed his medications. Ordering prescriptions and monitoring that the child is taking medications as prescribed are the responsibility of the parents.

See Medication Compliance

MEDICATION SIDE EFFECTS

Many children with ND are on several medications at a time, all with potential side effects. To avoid problems, it is important to keep a journal of when medications are started, including amount and time of day given. Then watch for side effects. Some side effects must be accommodated for, like having a water bottle for excessive thirst or having a permanent pass to the restroom for diarrhea. Other medications cause sleepiness so teachers may need to allow children with ND to leave their chairs and walk around for a while. Yet other medications may increase negative behaviors or symptoms. Document everything and report your observations to the child's doctor. Also, when medications change, notify the school nurse immediately. See Medication Changes worksheet in the Appendix.

See Parent Journal, School Nurse, Teacher Journal

MELTDOWNS

A meltdown is the same as tantrum or rage.

See Rage Stage

MENTORING

A mentor is a trusted individual who has an interest in the development and education of another individual and serves as an advisor. Children need someone to go fishing with or provide emotional support during stressful times. As the child with ND faces new challenges or is trying to work through a problem, it is important to have someone to talk to. Boys especially need a father image and girls, a mother image. A mentor can provide the child with ND a little extra encouragement and support. Churches, neighborhood groups and professionals are all good potential sources for mentors. Mentoring can change lives.

MILKSHAKES

For years I took Josh on two-hour drives each night because it was the only thing that helped him relax. On these outings, we always had to stop at his favorite ice cream parlor to buy a banana milkshake. Having heard about this routine, sometimes other parents would call in a panic begging me to take their child for a drive who was either in the rumbling stage or just agitated. Soon I started offering them milkshakes too. It was amazing to watch how all of a sudden the child would become calm. Based on these observations, I began to tell parents and school staff to have milkshakes in their freezer to zap in the microwave when a child's behavior started escalating. I have since learned that occupational therapists sometimes recommend sucking as a means to calm children with ND. It really does work!

See Drives

MODIFICATIONS

A modification is any technique that alters the work required that makes it different from the work required of other students in the same class. Not all children with ND need modifications to succeed in school, but many do. To be effective, the modifications must be individualized, depending on the needs of the child. To make this process a little easier for teachers, I created a Modifications worksheet (see Appendix). Not every student with ND will need all of these modifications, but most will need some of them.

See Academic Expectations, Accommodations, Handwriting, Math Modifications, Organizational Skills, Reading Accommodations, Test Modifications, Transition from One Activity or Lesson to Another

MOOD SWINGS

One mother learned that when her daughter was experiencing quick mood swings, she needed to allow her space and downtime. The girl ended up spending a lot of time on her own, but she needed that to recover from being out in the public (school or social activities) all day. Children with ND, unlike other children, may have quick and unexpected mood swings. Some even receive a diagnosis of a mood disorder such as bipolar disorder or depression. It is important to document the behavior, time of day the behavior appears, how the moods cycle, precipitating factors, etc. When extreme mood swings happen, don't overreact. Try to be supportive and provide structure, and contact your child's physician.

See Bipolar Disorder, Depression, Documentation, Mania, Parent Journal, Teacher Journal

MORNING AROUSAL

Some children with ND require several wake-up calls, responding best to a gradual transition between sleep and awake. Some parents have had success with turning on a radio or TV just loud enough to disturb their child's sleep. One mother rubbed her son's back each morning until he was awake enough to sit up. A couple of times I have even sprinkled water on Josh's face to get him going. The child is not just being lazy; morning arousal can be a real problem for many children with ND. Arousal problems can fluctuate throughout the day (such as falling asleep in classes) and are a big reason for performance inconsistency.

MORNING ROUTINE

Reasons mornings may be difficult for children with ND include: drowsiness from medications, inability to sleep well during the night and difficulty falling asleep. A parent shared how she was able to help her child get off to a good start each morning. Knowing how difficult a school day can be, she wanted the morning to go smoothly and wanted her children to start their day on a positive note. Picking out clothes the night before and getting backpacks ready was a must. She also made sure that lunch money, all completed assignments and signed field trip notices were placed in the child's backpack the night before and put by the door. In the morning she would be up, dressed and ready before she woke up her children. Because her son was easily distracted, she handed him his shirt and said, "Put it on." She did the same for pants, socks and shoes, checking on him frequently. Instead of reprimanding him for getting off track, she simply told him to brush his teeth, or handed him a glass of water and gave him his medications without any discussion. She learned to let go of the idea that her son should be responsible for these things himself. He would have many challenges ahead of him at school during the day when he would have to act independently. She couldn't be at school to help him, but she could help him get off to a good start in the mornings.

Instead of being there physically throughout all the morning routines, parents can make visual supports. Cut out pictures for each direction such as getting dressed, brushing teeth, eating breakfast, etc., and number each direction in the order the tasks need to be completed. You can laminate the list to preserve it and place it on the back of the bedroom door, for example. It is very important to send your child off to school in the best frame of mind possible.

Finally, it is important to make sure children eat something in the morning. Never send them to school without eating – even if it is last night's pizza. As a teacher for many years I know all too well the impact not eating breakfast has on children's learning.

See After School, Parenting a Child with ND, Responsibility, Visual Supports

MOTHERHOOD

One of the wonderful mothers at the Joshua Center wrote the following about motherhood: "When your child receives a diagnosis of ND, you may initially experience intense fear, a fear of the unknown. You will grieve for your child and wonder how the disorders will impact your family. I was determined that my son would know that these disorders were only a part of who he was. Learning all I could was the beginning of focusing on what I could do for my son rather than what I was unable to do. It is important to join a support group to learn more and meet other parents going through the same thing.

The ND will be a big part of your entire family's life, but don't let it completely define who you are. Continue with family traditions and routines as much as possible. Don't constantly talk about the disorders, focus on the positive. Your child, his siblings, your spouse and your marriage are still individual entities.

It's important to accept help and support from family and friends you trust. In the beginning I didn't want to talk to anyone about the diagnosis. But I soon realized I would need a lot of help to get through this. Talking to others made me feel much better. Mothers, remember that fathers often don't open up to others about their feelings like we do. When they do something well to help your child, let them know they are doing a good job and mention how much that means to your child. They will probably do it again!

When your child with ND has no friends to play with, it is very important that you play with him and take him places. This is time consuming but will mean the world to your child. Do continue to spend time with your other children.

Taking the time to do these things will make a significant difference in the way all of your children cope.

Give your child tools to develop strategies for dealing with other kids. You can't always be there to protect him. Role play situations of what other kids have said to your child. Help him come up with responses so he can be prepared, such as 'whatever' or 'that's real mature'. I used to tell my son to put on an imaginary coat of armor and let the insults bounce off. Bullies rely on an audience. Tell your child not to help the bully or the audience. If he doesn't make much of a response, the bully loses his audience and usually backs off. Tell your child this is a work in progress. It doesn't all come together right away. No matter how cruel others might be and how discouraging it was having to deal with the symptoms day after day, my son would know I was always there for him.

You must absolutely be your child's advocate at school, but also let teachers know you want to work with them as a team. Understand that it isn't easy to have our kids in a classroom and that teachers, just like parents, won't always know what to do. Don't say negative things about school staff in front of your child because he may repeat it at school.

When I asked my son what he thought was the most helpful thing I did to help him deal with having these disorders, he said, 'Being patient, not getting mad, and staying calm. When a kid is having a hard time, if the parent stays calm it helps the kid get through it; if a parent panics the kid will too. Also, giving me something to look forward to – doing things with me, taking me places, and encouraging me that things would get better. One of the best things you did was write all those notes and leave them out for me. That helped me so much, encouraged me to keep going. I still have almost all of them in a box.' I used to buy cards, or use index cards and put on stickers, and write encouraging messages and sometimes add a little humor. I put them on his bed or on the table where he did his homework for him to find. I still occasionally do this. Never give up hope!"

See Being Flexible, Encouragement, Grieving, Parenting a Child with ND, Siblings

MOTOR TICS

Motor tics are involuntary, rapid, sudden movements that occur repeatedly in the same way.

See Tics

MUSIC

Some children with ND use background music to complete homework or to calm themselves. Others like to relax listening to a heavy drumbeat. By allowing the music to be the distraction, other things will not distract them. One young man with ND explained it well, "If the radio is on, there is one thing getting my attention. With it off, there are 10 things getting my attention." Keep in mind that one type of music may work for a while, but then it may need to be changed.

See Accommodations

MUSIC CLASS

Music class can be too stimulating for a child with ND. I suggest that teachers seat the child in close proximity to them to monitor for problems. Some children need alternative situations for music, primarily due to sensory overload. I observed a second-grade student one time in a music class who simply could not stay seated. He was all over the room. The room was very small and did not have windows. When nothing else seemed to work, I finally recommended that the student go to the resource room during music class where he was allowed to listen to soft music. He could not handle the auditory stimuli or the small classroom at that time. (See information for the music teacher in the Appendix.)

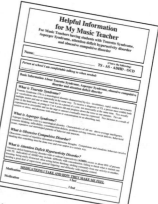

See Claustrophobia

N

NEUROLEPTICS

Neuroleptics are medications used to treat the symptoms of TS and the behavioral symptoms of tantrums, rage, and meltdowns. They target the dopamine neurotransmitter system.

See Dopamine, Neurotransmitter

NEUROTRANSMITTER

A neurotransmitter is a chemical that carries nerve impulses across the synapse (gap) between adjacent neurons (nerve cells).

See Dopamine, Nicotine

NICOTINE

Several studies (e.g., Perry & Gaffney, 1996) have shown the benefits of nicotine in treating TS. Researchers seem to think TS is caused by a malfunction of several neurotransmitters and since it is known that nicotine acts on the dopamine neurotransmitter, some individuals have chosen to smoke cigarettes, chew tobacco or use the nicotine patch as a way to relieve symptoms of TS. Understandably, parents do not like the idea of exposing their child to nicotine. In addition to the well-known effects of nicotine, parents must consider how nicotine reacts with some of the other medications their child may be taking. Anyone who is considering using nicotine as a way to treat the symptoms of ND should discuss this with the child's doctor.

See Dopamine, Neurotransmitter

NONVERBAL LEARNING DISABILITY

Children with a nonverbal learning disability (NLD) have difficulty processing non-verbal information – information that does not rely completely on words or information that cannot be visualized; for instance, when a peer is crying, the child with ND may not pick up that the peer is upset. Assessments of these students usually reveal strengths in verbal tasks and weaknesses in visual, spatial and other nonverbal tasks. As a result, they rely on verbal input and verbal self-direction, usually talk a great deal, but often speak in a rigid way, often interrupt others and stand too close in conversations. Because they tend to focus on details rather than the larger picture, children with NLD may have difficulty taking notes, developing outlines and setting priorities.

NOTEBOOK ORGANIZATION

Children with ND are often disorganized. One way to help them function better in school is to teach them notebook organization skills. Helping a child develop an organized notebook is half the battle. Based on years of experience, I recommend that parents purchase one notebook with velcro fasteners to be used for all classes; for example, Intelli-Gear by Mead. Print the child's name, address, phone number, and a statement that a reward will be given if the notebook is lost and returned, in permanent marker on the inside front cover. Place the following items in a three-ring plastic zipper pouch in the front of the notebook/planner: several pencils (mechanical if breaking pencils is a tic), extra pencil erasers, small calculator (large enough for accurate keystrokes), a portable collapsible hole-punch, and self-adhesive reinforcements for notebook paper. An assignment notebook/planner should be placed in the front of the notebook. Assignments and worksheets can be placed in class dividers or one folder can be designated for all assignments and worksheets as part of the notebook (for both work to do and for work completed).

See Assignment Notebook/Planner, Organizational Skills

NOTE TAKING

See Computers, Handwriting, Paraprofessionals

O

OBSCENITIES

See Coprolalia

OBSERVATIONS AT HOME

One father shares how he learned a great deal about his son and gained a lot of insight into his behavior simply by taking the time to observe him closely. First, he suggests parents look for repeated reactions to similar situations, for patterns in behavior. Take note of the time of day, the season, and even the time of year. The child's symptoms will wax and wane, and by closely observing them parents will get to know how long the cycle typically lasts. This is extremely helpful because it can give you and your child hope to know that, though things seem bad right now, it will be better in the next week or two. In addition, this knowledge can give parents clues about what to anticipate from their child so they can prepare to react in a positive and encouraging manner. Finally, it helps everybody to keep things in proper perspective.

See Educating Parents, Effects of Seasonal Changes and Weather, Fatherhood, Homework Strategies, Motherhood, Observations at School, Parenting a Child with ND, Waxing and Waning

OBSERVATIONS AT SCHOOL

When I quit teaching to help children with ND, I knew that I could not rely on Josh's experiences alone. I had to observe other children. I was hopeful that teachers would trust me because I have a teaching background in addition to being a parent of a son with ND. I remember my reactions the first few times I left a school after an observation. I was absolutely amazed at what I could identify in these children. For example, I would see attention deficit symptoms severely interfering with the child's functioning in school, yet the child had not been diagnosed! I remember walking away in tears after observing an adorable little boy who I did not think was receiving an appropriate education. The teacher knew he was not succeeding, but didn't know what to do. I always shared my observations with the child's doctor and teacher.

After observing hundreds of children I was convinced we needed a clinic where the doctor, counselor and educator were all working together to help the child and his or her family. No one person has all the answers. Out of these observations the Joshua Child and Family Development Center was born. Now our social workers observe the children in their school setting. The observations made all the difference in the world by allowing those of us observing to develop strategies, IEPs and 504 Plans to help children with ND succeed. It is important for parents to work with the school staff and students to educate the school community about the disorders.

See Educating School Staff

OBSESSIVE COMPULSIVE DISORDER (OCD)

Obsessive compulsive disorder (OCD) is a neurological disorder. Obsessions are repetitive, unwanted or bothersome thoughts. Compulsions are the acting out of obsessive thoughts. While the thoughts are often illogical to the child, they are so real to him that they cannot be ignored. They can produce great anxiety. Your child may feel that a certain ritual or action must be performed to keep something from happening; for example, a young boy had to say to his mom every time he went out the door, "I'm going now, mom, OK?" Often rituals and actions take a long time to complete. When young, Josh had to say, "Good night, mom, I love you" over and over until it "felt right" to him. And each time I had to respond with "Good night, Josh, I love you." This would often go on for 15-20 minutes before he was ready to go to bed. The child will feel a sense of relief once the ritual has ended, but soon the tension increases as the ritual or action returns. Treatment for OCD may include both behavior therapy and medication.

See Compulsions, Rituals

OCCUPATIONAL THERAPIST

An occupational therapist (OT) evaluates and remediates problems affecting the motor and perceptual skills required by the activities of daily living and school functioning. These skills include correct posture, body positioning, gross- and fine-motor coordination, graphomotor functioning, visual perception and organization, visual-motor integration, motor planning and problem solving. An OT can also assist students in overcoming sensory defensiveness by helping them to not overreact to the stimuli in their environment. The OT uses special exercises and activities to address deficit areas. In addition, the OT can provide adaptive methods and equipment if needed for successful use of writing implements and computers, adaptive living skills and academic functioning in the school environment.

OFFICE FOR CIVIL RIGHTS

The Office for Civil Rights (OCR) enforces federal statutes that prohibit discrimination in programs and activities receiving federal financial assistance from the Department of Education. Section 504 of the Rehabilitation Act of 1973 prohibits discrimination on the basis of a disability. OCR investigates complaints filed by individuals who believe they have been discriminated against because of their disability.

See Section 504 of the Rehabilitation Act, Section 504 Plan

OFF-TASK BEHAVIOR

Children with ND have difficulty staying on task as part of their disability. In school I usually suggest the teacher surround the child with ND with students who can stay on task as models. Some children with ND do well utilizing a study carrel, while others prefer to use a headset with white noise to block out distractions that keep them from staying on task. As another option, the teacher and child can work together to develop a cue that can be used when the teacher sees the child becoming distracted and off-task.

See Attention Deficit Hyperactivity Disorder, Getting Started, Headphones, Study Carrel

"OOPS, I FORGOT"

I always wanted to have a t-shirt made that said "Oops, I forgot!" on the front and "It's not my fault!" on the back. With Josh I heard these comments often. Children with ND are constantly forgetting because of their attention problems. Accept the symptoms and develop strategies to make things work, like giving one direction at a time and making checklists. This way they can check off a task when it is completed.

See Acceptance, Attention Deficit Hyperactivity Disorder, Checklists, Visual Supports

OPPOSITIONAL BEHAVIOR

Tracy Fisher, a member of Rocky Mountain TSA, wrote a wonderful article about his son, called "Oppositional Behavior: The Evolution of TJ," which we have permission to reprint here.

"I'll bet that most of you TS hardened parents looked at those two words, and immediately your shoulders slump, your eyes roll and you let go an involuntary moan of exhaustion. Following is my experience with my son TJ (and if these things didn't happen to you yet, they will!). After reading a plethora of material looking for information on the subject, I finally realized I was wasting my time. There was no need to try to understand the behavior. 'Oppositional' was the only word needed to know because that is exactly what it is. You say, stand up" they sit down. You say "goodbye" they say "hello" (hummmm, sounds like a Beetles song). It's the unconscious simplicity of the behavior that lets one know that this is indeed an oddity and not simply a childhood phase. Well, now that I recognized the symptom for what it was, the solution seemed simple. I had worked my fingers to the bone and all I had was bony fingers (hummm, another song), nothing complex about this, all I had to do was initiate a parental reverse psychology method and I'll have things exactly the way I want them. Herein lies the seed of oppositional behavior. For three days, I was in complete control. On the eve of the fourth day, things began to get hazy. By mid-afternoon on the seventh day, I was doing TJ's homework while he was eating ice cream and watching 'R' rated movies. Suddenly, as I was running to the store to get TJ more ice cream and another movie, it dawned on me that something had gone terribly wrong. I gathered my wits about me and examined the situation. Obviously, TJ had somehow reversed my reverse psychology without me having a clue. Now that I knew what was going on, the solution seemed simple. NOW was the time to start reading and gathering information to help me thwart the demon, so ..., I did exactly that and mapped out a brilliant plan. I would reverse myself on every third time with a few sporadic reversals thrown in now and then to really baffle him! Obviously this had disastrous results. By the next Friday, I found myself playing Hungry, Hungry Hippo with a bunch of primary school kids while TJ was in the den doing the budget and putting the final touches on our year-end taxes. The next step in the evolution was initiated by TJ. Out of sheer spitefulness, he suddenly became one of the best-behaved children ever. For two weeks I could do nothing but to try to contemplate what he might be up to next. TJ seemed to be in complete control again and I was lost. Then it hit me! On my way to pick up TJ at his school, I suddenly felt a warm and comforting feeling envelop me. TJ wasn't in control, I was! I HAD WON! TJ had succumbed to my greater will and maturity. I decided instantly that the thing to do now was to reward him and thus begin to reinforce my newfound parenthood. Who knows, in a week or two, I might even be able to turn in my Hungry, Hungry Hippo for TJ's tax forms. As TJ got into the car I said, 'TJ, you have been so good, I am going to let you choose which one of the following three things you want to do this weekend and we'll do it together. We can go swimming, play tennis, or go fishing. Which would you like?' TJ said, 'Dad, I hate swimming, tennis sucks, fishing is for girls and I'm too old to do things with you!!!!!'" Sometimes no matter how hard you try it just doesn't work.

OPPOSITIONAL DEFIANT DISORDER (ODD)

Most children display oppositional behavior at some point. The following description of ODD provided by the staff physician at the Joshua Center helps explain this disorder. Child development books teach us that two-year-olds often exhibit oppositional behavior as a normal part of child development. But when a child's behavior is consistently uncooperative and hostile compared to his peers and affects his family and school functioning, it becomes a serious concern for parents and teachers. Some symptoms of ODD include excessive arguing with adults; noncompliance with rules and requests from adults; frequent tantrums; deliberately annoying to and annoyed by others; blaming others for misbehavior; frequently saying hateful things; and seeking revenge. Any child exhibiting these symptoms should be thoroughly evaluated to look for disorders such as ADHD, learning disabilities, mood disorders (depression, bipolar disorder) and anxiety disorders.

See Oppositional Behavior

ORAL DIRECTIONS

Not all children with ND will need accommodations, but many do. Since so many children with ND have attention problems, one area that often needs adjustments is the way materials are presented. The following accommodations have been found helpful: break assignments into segments of shorter tasks; introduce one concept at a time with as few words as possible, checking for understanding and having the student repeat the directions for a task; provide a model of the end-product (completed math problem, finished quiz, etc.); introduce an overview of long-term assignments (written and verbal) so the student knows what will be expected and when they are due; make a visual for the classroom and a checklist for the student; break long-term assignments into small, sequential steps with daily monitoring and frequent grading; alert the student to key points with such phrases as "This is important" or "Listen carefully;" number and sequence the steps in a task; explain the learning expectations before beginning the lesson; allow the student to obtain and retain information by utilizing a tape recorder, computer, calculator and/or dictating to another person; highlight important concepts to be learned in texts; provide outlines, study guides and copies of overhead presentations to reduce frustration with visual-motor integration and encourage concentration on the lesson; shorten assignments based on mastery of key concepts; provide incentives for beginning and completing material; check that all homework assignments are written down correctly, providing assistance when needed; separate assignment sheets from notes to parents about behaviors; provide written and verbal directions with visuals, when possible; give alternative assignments rather than long written assignments; and modify expectations based on student's needs. (See Modifications worksheet in Appendix.)

ORGANIZATIONAL SKILLS

Children with ND have problems with organization; yet rarely do I see an IEP or a 504 Plan address how a child will learn organization skills. IEPs and 504 Plans should include goals and objectives related to organizational skills. The long-term goal is for the child to be an independently functioning adult. Often a student knows organizational strategies, but not how to apply them. Parents and teachers need to encourage children to apply newly learned organizational skills. Children with ND need many years of practice to learn good organizational skills so they will make mistakes along the way. The following are some of the skills children should be taught: notebook organization; how to use a calendar to their benefit; how to plan for tests; how to break a large project into small steps; and how to make lists and prioritize, possibly using the computer. All skills should be taught with both verbal and written directions.

See Assignment Notebook/Planner, Assistive Technology, Individualized Education Program (IEP), Section 504 Plan

OTHER HEALTH IMPAIRED

Other health impaired (OHI) refers to students whose chronic health problems result in limited strength, vitality or alertness that adversely affects their educational performance to the degree that they require special education. Neurological disorders can adversely affect educational performance in all areas depending on the severity of the symptoms, so children with ND should qualify for special education services.

OVERPROTECTING

It is tempting to try and protect children from the effects of a ND. There are ups and downs and lumps and bumps for every person in this world. Parents cannot and should not try to shield their children from every bump in life as they help develop who we are. Encourage children to try new things and don't deny them opportunities that grow out of your own fears. It is also our duty as parents to do everything we can to educate all the individuals involved with our children, while at the same time giving our children the chance to participate in the world the same as all children do. Parents who insist that every time their child has problems it is because of the ND are making a big mistake. Periodically evaluate how things are going and ask yourself if you are overprotecting your child.

See Educating the Bus Driver, Educating Neighbors, Educating Paraprofessionals, Educating Parents, Educating Peers, Educating School Staff

OVERSTIMULATION

Josh had a difficult time going to the movies. I finally realized the stimuli were too much for him – the noise, the crowd, the smells, etc. – so we avoided movie theaters and rented movies for home instead. He would tic terribly when he did try to go and his anxiety would increase. Other areas that can contribute to overstimulation include: too many directions at once; more than one or two people visiting at a time; being too hot or too cold; someone demanding that the child look at those talking to him; or someone touching the child. Parents need to identify what increases anxiety for their child and make modifications accordingly, including sharing the information with others who work with their child.

See Occupational Therapist, Sensory Sensitivity, Shopping

P

PALILALIA

This fairly common Tourette symptom refers to individuals repeating their own words or phrases.

See Tourette Syndrome

PANIC ATTACKS

Many children with ND experience panic attacks, a feature of panic disorder. When a child is having a panic attack, she is experiencing intense discomfort or fear that strikes suddenly. Panic attacks often happen in familiar places where there should otherwise be nothing to be afraid of. One young girl was relaxing on the couch watching TV when she suddenly stood up and began pacing and saying it felt like the walls were coming in on her. There was no apparent reason for her panic. Symptoms of a panic attack include intense fear or discomfort, racing heartbeat, shortness of breath, fear that something terrible is happening, dizziness or lightheadedness, a feeling of being smothered, and a fear of dying. Panic attacks can last minutes to hours and can develop without warning. Panic disorder is fairly common and can often be treated with medication and therapy.

See Anxiety, Obsessive Compulsive Disorder

PARAPROFESSIONALS

Having a paraprofessional assigned to a child can be a godsend to both the child and the teacher, but before the paraprofessional begins working with the child, he or she should be trained. The paraprofessional does not have to know everything about the child's ND before she starts, the main thing is that she accepts the disorder(s) as neurological and not chosen behavior. Paraprofessionals can be very helpful by assisting the child in getting organized, getting started, staying on task, etc. Specifically, they can help with note taking; teaching organization skills; making sure assignments are written down; transitioning the student through activities, classes and hallways; monitoring during less structured activities such as lunch, recess, field trips and assemblies; and accompanying the child to support classes like PE, art and music. Sometimes it is necessary for the paraprofessional to be in close proximity to the child, but at other times monitoring the situation is enough.

When school districts decline to provide a paraprofessional, I encourage parents to ask the IEP team to get creative. Perhaps a parent volunteer would agree to help. Very responsible high school students also do a nice job assisting younger children. The key is consistency. It helps for the child to have a good ongoing relationship with his paraprofessional. Identifying the "trouble spots" and prioritizing them can help the IEP team determine when and where help is needed. Parents always want their child to go as far as she can, but she is probably like so many other children with ND children – consistently inconsistent – and therefore will need help. Keep in mind that the objective is "What is needed for this child to be successful?" The paraprofessional should be a part of the IEP team. Usually the paraprofessional communicates any concerns to the teacher so the teacher can address the concerns with the parents. The paraprofessional and teacher must have a good relationship and effective communication for this to work.

See Acceptance, Brainstorming, Communication Between School and Home, Educating School Staff, Individualized Education Program (IEP)

PARENT JOURNAL

In the Appendix you will find a copy of the Parent Journal, a form to document information about your child with ND. It is important for parents to keep written records of all pertinent information relating to their child's disorders. Document when medications are started and changed, as well as any improvements and side effects. You will forget this information if you don't write it down! When you see the doctor, you have only a certain amount of time to relay your concerns and successes. The written documentation will help you remember and ensure more accurate information. In the journal also document behaviors, changes in symptoms, sleep concerns, school concerns and the child's overall emotional well-being, as medications can impact all of these areas. Include in your parent journal notes from each IEP or 504 Plan meeting and a copy of the IEP or 504 Plan. It is important to note any teacher observations and share those with the doctor. Start a yearly file and keep the journal in it. You will also want to include medical records, including phone contacts with your doctor. Even today I keep a file for Josh to refer to.

See Communication Between School and Home, Individualized Education Program (IEP), Observations at Home, Observations at School, Teacher Journal

PARENT RIGHTS

Parents have protection under the law (IDEA) when they do not agree with the school's recommendations about their child's education. For example, they have the right to challenge decisions about their child's evaluation, about her eligibility for special education services, her placement and related services. If the parents disagree with the school, they have the right to do the following: they can talk with school officials and try to reach an agreement; they can agree to a temporary solution for a specified time; they can ask for mediation; they can file a complaint with their state education agency; or they can request a due process hearing. Before the school provides a child with special education services for the first time, the parents must give their written permission. See Wright's Law under recommended websites in the Resources.

See Due Process

PARENT STRESS

As parents of children with ND you will experience times where you feel you have reached your limit. If you have a spouse or significant other, you must both agree to give each other breaks. If you don't have a family member, find another parent, friend or a mentor you can call for support or in an emergency. Identify situations that are most stressful for you and your child and try to brainstorm strategies to help. I know a mom and dad who are both incredibly patient, and while the dad's strengths are helping his son each night with the homework, the mom's strengths lie in her ability to help their son get off to a good start each day when her child is under stress. You will be surprised at how strong you can be. But you can't do it alone – ask for help.

See Mentoring, Support Groups, Support System

PARENTING A CHILD WITH ND

Parents of children with ND will have moments when they think they are not going to make it. Just take one step at a time. You will learn to get organized and plan for situations. You will learn how to advocate for your child and you will learn that you are not perfect. You will make mistakes. Remember, a child with ND will impact the whole family. Raising children with ND is labor intensive, requires time, attention, and energy, and at times is frustrating and exhausting. It is important for parents to take care of themselves physically and emotionally. It doesn't help anyone if the parent is always exhausted. Worrying about your child will only increase his symptoms. If you go up and down an emotional roller coaster every time your child's symptoms get worse, you will be so exhausted that you will not be able to provide him the support and parenting that he needs.

See Discipline, Extended Family, Grieving, Parent Stress, Siblings

PARENTS AS THE EXPERTS

Parents know their child better than anyone else. What teachers see at school in no way compares to what parents experience at home. Teachers should enlist the help of the parents when having concerns or questions about the child's ND.

See Brainstorming

PARENTS AT SCHOOL

I'll never forget the time I observed a fourth-grade student who had just been diagnosed with TS. I was pretty sure he also had ADHD or at least similar symptoms. After the observation I met the mother outside the school. She was having a very difficult time with her son's diagnosis of TS, and even when I tried to assure her that her child would be OK, she wasn't convinced.

Over the next few weeks I developed a good relationship with the school. One day I heard from the principal, who commented that he and the teacher were concerned about the child's mother spending too much time in the school. Since I had met with the school and had observed the child several times and felt the school staff was very supportive, I decided to meet with the mother again. I found her so full of anxiety over her son that I encouraged her to seek medical attention. In addition, I convinced her to stay away from the school unless they called her. She was smothering her child. She did get help and was placed on medication for her anxiety. Sometimes parents do more harm than good for their child by spending too much time at school or otherwise preoccupying themselves with their child. A parent with high anxiety can, without realizing it, cause her child to become anxious.

Nevertheless, there are times that merit parents being at the school. One of them is when a child is frequently insisting that he be allowed to go home. One family addressed this problem by having the mother or father go to the school and sit with their child until he was able to return to class. Their son learned pretty quickly that he would not be allowed to go home, but in the interim he was receiving assurance by a comforting parent that he would be OK. The parents had to go to the school off and on for a couple of months before their son was able to give up this support. Parents can also be helpful at school if a teacher is having difficulty understanding how to handle certain behavior concerns. Just having the parent sit at the back of the room sometimes helps reinforce positive behaviors with the child if the behavior is a chosen one. If the behavior is related to the ND, the parent may be able to help a teacher brainstorm a positive intervention. It is also important for parents to be involved in PTA, support school parties and accompany their child on field trips. Such involvement allows parents to observe how their child is interacting with other children and ensures their child is having a positive experience.

See Brainstorming, Communication Between School and Home, Grieving

PEDIATRIC AUTOIMMUNE NEUROPSYCHIATRIC DISORDERS ASSOCIATED WITH STREPTOCOCCAL INFECTIONS (PANDAS)

I'll never forget the day a mother called me in a panic. Her child had originally been diagnosed with mild TS, but he suddenly started having more severe symptoms. When she took him to the doctor, the doctor thought the tics were purposeful and merely told the boy to "straighten up." However, since the mom knew her child was not misbehaving, she saw another doctor and learned the child had a strep infection. Indeed, it turned out that he met the criteria for PANDAS, an acronym for Pediatric Autoimmune Neuropsychiatric Disorders Associated with Streptococcal Infections.

A child who has no history of tics may suddenly start ticcing, or may present with complex tics instead of simple tics if he already has a tic disorder. The symptoms appear to be related to strep infections and typically worsen dramatically following streptococcal infections. Parents may be unaware their child has had a strep infection. Parents should notify their child's doctor if tics or an increase in tics suddenly appear.

See Complex Tics, Simple Tics, Tics, Tourette Syndrome

PEER RELATIONS

Children with ND frequently have poor peer relationships due to immaturity and poor social skills. It is very important for our children to have social opportunities. Parents and teachers need to do everything they can to help with this. Often you will be able to identify one or two children that your child can have a good social interaction with. I usually suggest that the child with ND invite just one child at a time to his house to play, for a specified time and for a specific activity. Children with ND can wear down other children rather quickly with their impulsivity and hyperactivity. Plan the activity with your child before the other child arrives. Parents must be available at all times to monitor behaviors. Give your child opportunities for extracurricular activities, but plan what it will take for your child to be successful. At school I suggest teachers identify one or two students the child can interact with in a positive way. I believe children without friends are sad and their sadness can lead to depression. It is important to teach children with ND skills that facilitate friendship development.

When a child is bullied, don't put up with it. Start with teachers and the principal, but don't accept a "boys will be boys" attitude. Children with ND deal with a lot as it is, they don't need to be bullied too.

See Educating Peers, Educating School Staff, Immaturity, Pragmatics, Social Skills, Speech-Language Pathologist

PENCIL TICS

Josh used to have a terrible time concentrating on the teacher's instructions because he had a compulsive need to even up the pencils on his desk. Many children have compulsions to constantly sharpen their pencils, others have a compulsion to break them. To help deal with this problem, I usually suggest that parents supply each of their child's classes with enough pencils to last a month or allow the child to use mechanical pencils. Children who constantly tap pencils might be redirected to tap on a mouse pad that is kept on the child's desk.

See Motor Tics, Tics

PERCEIVING THINGS DIFFERENTLY

Sometimes children with ND do not fully grasp events or situations the same way others do. They seem to process their experiences in a way that keeps them from obtaining complete information. Needless to say, this may cause them problems. These children usually believe their perceptions are correct and can become very frustrated when their misperceptions interfere with their ability to meet the demands placed on them. Social Stories are helpful tools in addressing perception concerns.

See Social Stories

PERFECTIONISM

Children with perfectionistic tendencies often have difficulty at school because their expectations for themselves are so high that unless they feel they can "perform" perfectly, they cannot even get started on an assignment or project. For the same reason they also have a difficult time saying, "I'm finished." Try to identify the problem areas and brainstorm modifications. If handwriting is involved, it may help if they use a word processor because they may insist on trying to make the letters perfect and therefore fail to complete their work. If graphics are part of a project, allow students to use clip art rather than having to draw, for example. In severe cases, consult the doctor and counselor for help with perfectionist tendencies.

See Brainstorming, Computers, Counseling - Individual/Family, Getting Started, Handwriting, Obsessive Compulsive Disorder

PERFORMANCE INCONSISTENCY

See Being Flexible, Consistently Inconsistent, Waxing and Waning

PERSEVERATION

My – oh – my, can children with ND perseverate and perseverate and perseverate! I remember one time Josh was talking about something that I had little interest in or understanding of. I knew by the way he was saying things in different ways that it was one of those times when he needed to get it out "just right" so I listened, but I glanced at the clock to see when he started. Forty-five minutes later he was finally done. I kept that "very interested" facade up until he was finished. Recently I decided to tell him the story and he just laughed and laughed and laughed! Parents may be able to agree with their child on a cue to stop perseveration when out in public. Teachers can do the same in school. Help the child understand that this is only done to spare her some embarrassment.

See "Just Right" Feeling

PERSONAL HYGIENE

Problems with hygiene in children with ND often trace to obsessive and compulsive behaviors as well as sensory sensitivity. Some children spend an inordinate amount of time showering and on personal care. Others may not enjoy bathing or having their face and hair washed. Some actually turn the water on, but never step into the shower. You might try purchasing fancy soaps, deodorants, etc., to entice a child with this aversion. Sometimes depression is associated with personal hygiene, so consult with the child's doctor and counselor.

See Sensory Sensitivity

PERVASIVE DEVELOPMENTAL DISORDER (PDD)

Pervasive development disorder (PDD) is characterized by problems in social development, communication and behavior. Specific symptoms vary widely for each child and generally appear within the first three years of life. There are five types of PDD under the criteria of the *Diagnostic and Statistical Manual of Mental Disorders – 4th Edition, Text Revision* (DSM-IV-TR, 2002): Childhood Disintegrative Disorder, Asperger's Disorder, Autistic Disorder, Rett's Disorder, and Pervasive Developmental Disorder Not Otherwise Specified (PDD-NOS).

PETS

Pets are a wonderful source of nonjudgmental, unconditional love. For children with ND a pet can represent a safe companionship and a sense of belonging in a world that is often difficult for them. At the Joshua Center's annual bowl-a-thon I met a wonderful man who had called the center looking for answers to some of his questions about Tourette Syndrome. I was so thrilled when I received the following story from him by email that I asked permission to reprint it for this book. He says so well what I believe about the importance of pets.

"CAT ... MALE ... BROWN ... 17"

The animal shelter was almost about to close as I drove up. The attendant and I walked along the rows of cages. I was there for a kitten, and there were only three. "If you had come yesterday we had 12," said the attendant. We stopped at cage 17 and observed its pathetic contents. The kitten was a mess, and due to be destroyed the next day. I didn't look further to the gratification of the attendant. The transaction also went fast, "cat ... male ... brown ... 17" was marked off the office blackboard as "save." Thirty bucks lighter – adoption fee, plus neutering and declawing – I drove home with three days to think of names for "cat ... male ... brown ... 17," who would be recuperating from his surgical ordeal. When I went to pick him up, his front paws were bandaged and he threw up in the car on the way home. Home – where the litter box is ... Home – where the milk dish is ... Home – security, love, family. He spent his first night hiding under the sofa.

So my wife and I had adopted a new child, the nest was empty, our kids out. Why not? She named him Spunky and he adapted swiftly to his new realm. Six years passed ... 12 cat years? The drawer reopened, the nightmare came back, the genie re-emerged from the bottle and hell was released. My Tourette's came back. I had quit smoking ... simply quit smoking ... the nicotine, bittersweet suppressant now denied, triggered it after 35 years. I was derailed, went into denial, deep crisis. This was a part of my childhood that I outgrew ... I'm a Veteran! ... I did my stint in the world! – and had hoped to retire, now this ... I'm on a Clonidine patch, laced with Zoloft, I am "mostly" under control, neutered and declawed? But this story is not about Tourette's, something beyond friendship is. As I pen this, Spunky is at my feet, his tail is brushing past me and he is purring. I come home from work and let "it" go. "It" wakes me ..."it" tucks me in at night. Sometimes I have no control over "its" volume. I try ... fail ... suppress ... blow, and Spunky is there. There is no "duck and cover" instinct in him. He can be sitting on my lap and not flinch as a sudden, resounding tic erupts. He will sleep at my feet and be there in the morning. Even during nights when "it" gives me no quarter, Spunky is a "constant." He is there when I shave, supervising the "tic-nicks." No matter how violent and frequent the outburst of my tics might be, he knows there is gentleness, peace and love within me. He knows not to fear what is happening. He comes to me and his big, brown, soft paws find my lap. Spunky senses I mean no harm, I'm like a child in distress and he is needed. He is my angel, he is my companion, he is a true friend, he is "cat ... male ... brown ... 17" and I'm glad I saved him! Spunky is braver than I am, I want to hide under the sofa.

NOTE: While writing this draft and final, I did not tic once!

– J. M. Graff

PHYSICAL EDUCATION (PE)

Physical education (PE) class is often difficult for children with ND. Some children have gross-motor concerns, but usually problems in PE are not related to the actual activities involved, but to the program structure and physical environment. For example, in PE there is more chance for inappropriate interactions (such as inappropriate physical or verbal exchanges) of all children to go unnoticed, especially in the locker rooms, so it is important for the child with ND to be closely supervised. If the child has difficulty dressing out in gym clothes (frequently a sensory issue), he may need to be exempt from changing clothes.

I suggest that children with ND have PE at the end of the day, but if that is not possible, I suggest allowing the child to leave the gym ahead of the other students to get to his other classes on time. Another option is for children with ND to participate in adaptive physical education classes. Unless absolutely necessary, though, children should not be exempt from gym class because they need the physical activity. Exercise is an important part of life. In addition, it is a great stress reducer and, therefore, particularly beneficial for children with ND who frequently have a need to reduce stress! (See information worksheet for PE teacher in the Appendix.)

See Unstructured vs. Structured Environments

PLANES, TRAINS AND AUTOMOBILES

OK, you're finally going to take a family trip, including your child with ND. Once you have ironed out the details, you will decide on the method of transportation. If you are going by car, you must plan for frequent stops. And remember never to let the children take off their seatbelts to sleep.

The train can be a wonderful experience if you don't have far to go. It usually doesn't have much of a dining car, so you will need to plan to carry favorite food and snacks. Think ahead about how you are going to keep your child in his seat.

Only you know when the best time is to tell your child about an upcoming trip. Once you tell her, I suggest giving your child as many details as possible. Talk about where you are going and what you'll do when you get there.

If your child has anxiety about plane or train travel, arrange to visit the airport, bus station or train station before the trip. Read books about transportation. Talk to your doctor about your child's concerns and your own.

If your child's symptoms are noticeable and could be misinterpreted, call the airline, bus company, or railway in advance to inform them. Then, when the trip actually takes place, you will need to re-inform the ticket agents, flight attendants, and possibly other passengers. Take brochures about your child's disorders and carry a medical card at all times.

Plan and pack a travel bag with favorite and comforting items, including snacks. Make or highlight a map showing the planned route and stops along the way. Make a scrapbook of instant photos and souvenir brochures as you proceed on your trip, or buy your child his own instant disposable camera to take some of the pictures.

Hand-held electronic games are great entertainment on the way (remember to take extra batteries). Take a radio and headphones. Purchase children's magazines and distribute at intervals. Pocket "tic-tac-toe" games are well received by children.

If your child takes medications, pack them in your purse. You might also want to bring an extra supply in case your purse or bags are lost. For night travel in the car, dress the child in his pajamas and bring his pillow and favorite blanket. One parent planned instant surprise objects or treats when needed. Also take gum and hard candy, especially if your child has loud, intruding vocal tics.

See Family Reunions, Vacations, Importance Of

POSITIVE REINFORCEMENT

When you think of positive reinforcement, you usually think of some kind of star chart in which the child gains stars as a reward for achievements. It has been my experience that children with ND often argue over whether they should receive four or five stars, or whatever, and as a result, the focus becomes more the argument and not the positive behavior. Instead I recommend that parents and teachers provide reinforcers on an unscheduled basis. When you see the child doing something well, reinforce him. This does not mean that you need to reinforce the child every time he is doing something well, but do it frequently enough so the child knows that good behavior will be rewarded.

See Behavior Modification, Reinforcers

PRAGMATICS

The term "pragmatics" refers to the difference between what is said and what is actually communicated. Often children with ND lack the skills to read others' nonverbal cues or to adequately communicate their own needs. Many do not know how to use language appropriately in social situations, how much distance there should be between two people having a conversation or how to take turns in a conversation. Needless to say, this can have a negative impact on peer relationships. Pragmatics problems have nothing to do with intelligence, but everything to do with communicating. Speech pathologists can provide training in this area as a related service through your child's IEP, including using language for various purposes, changing or adapting language to meet different expectations, practicing rules for conversations, and appropriate use of nonverbal signals in conversations. These are life skills that our children need to be taught.

See Individualized Education Program (IEP), Life Skills, Speech-Language Pathologist

PRAYER

One mother whose son at times experiences extreme anxiety about going to school would hold his hand and pray with him on the drive to school. This simple act proved comforting, giving him added strength and her as well. These are the special times they both will treasure for the rest of their lives. While prayer may not be your choice in situations like this, other family traditions can prove equally beneficial to both children and adults.

PREMONITORY URGES

A premonitory urge is a sensation that immediately precedes an involuntary movement or vocalization. It is an intense feeling just before the release of a tic or compulsion.

PREVENTION

If I've said it once I've said it a hundred times, "If I had known then what I know now," I would have tried to prevent some of the things our family had to go through as a result of my son's ND. I wonder if I could have prevented some of those meltdowns. For example, I would have tried to offer more diversions when I saw my son in the rumbling stage to try and prevent the escalating behavior.

See Parenting a Child with ND, Rage Stage, Rumbling Stage

PREVOCATIONAL/VOCATIONAL EDUCATION

Transition planning is required for all students who have an IEP. Part of the process should include discussing vocational education programs. These programs provide opportunities for students to explore occupations and gain some basic knowledge in several fields while still in high school. Vocational rehabilitation counselors are available to help determine eligibility for job development, job coaching, counseling, training, assistive technology and job placement. Transition coordinators can arrange for students to visit with individuals whose job or career interests them. Students can conduct informational interviews with these individuals or job shadow for careers that seem the most interesting to them.

See Career Development, Transition Planning for Post-High School

PRINCIPALS

Principals can make all the difference in the world! One principal did so much to help a young man with ND. Since the student had trouble getting to school, the principal met him in front of the school when his mother dropped him off. They stayed at the front door until all the other children were inside, and then the principal walked him to his first class. Another principal helped a boy who always wanted to go home when he became overwhelmed. The principal was very supportive, allowing one of the parents to come to the school to be with their son. The principal even sat with them to show support. When a principal has to intervene with a behavioral concern the teacher needs assistance with, one of the most important things she can do is "walk and don't talk." Please do not hold the student accountable for his actions and his words at this time. (See the Principal worksheet in the Appendix.)

See Rage Stage, Recovery Stage, Rumbling Stage, Walk and Don't Talk

PRIVATE SCHOOLS

I have worked with many private schools. One such school initially felt a student with ND would do better in a public school setting where he could receive more services. Instead of transferring the student, the counselor and I identified a supportive individual in the school who would serve as the student's case manager. As a team we created strategies and implemented a plan that made accommodations for the student to help him succeed. There were plenty of tense moments, but the case manager did a wonderful job of consistently communicating with the counselor, and rather than give up on the student they supported him all the way to high school graduation.

I commend education professionals who are willing to be educated to help one child succeed. If the private school staff is unable to work with your child, you may want to consider other education options. But remember that even in a private school setting, the child with ND should have access to special education services from the public schools. Above all, don't force your child to remain in a situation where accommodations are not provided when needed.

See Educating School Staff

PUBERTY

The impact of puberty in all children has been well defined. While it has similar effects on children with ND, puberty also complicates other neurological processes. One of the areas where this is most clearly seen is medication management. You work hard to find a good medication balance only to find that balance upset by growth spurts or other developments as a result of puberty.

Q

QUIET

What you gave up when you had children!

R

RACING THOUGHTS

When Josh's thoughts would race fast, he could not focus on any one thing. His speech would be fast and disjointed, and he could not organize his thoughts to write a sentence, much less a paragraph or a paper for a class. A solution was for me to type while he dictated. Racing thoughts can be a symptom of mania in which the individual's thoughts seem to be speeded up and come tumbling out. The thoughts may all be logical or they may jump from one topic to another without any apparent connection to the listener. Contact your child's doctor any time the thoughts are interfering with her ability to function.

See Mania, Obsessive Compulsive Disorder

RAGE OUTSIDE THE HOME

Sometimes you may suddenly have to deal with a rage from your child away from home. When this happens, you will need to get your child to a safe place. This may be your car, a restroom, or taking her for a walk. It is important always to be aware of your surroundings so you can make a quick decision when needed. If you are with others, give explicit instructions as to what you expect from them if you need to remove your child to a safe place. You might want to carry with you some Power Putty, a hand-held computer game or something else your child can do with her hands while she is trying to calm down. Just sit and don't talk. Head home when you feel doing so will be safe. Talk as little as possible, keeping the tone of your voice low and calm.

See After School, Rage Stage, Rumbling Stage, Walk and Don't Talk

RAGE STAGE

In *Asperger Syndrome and Difficult Moments: Practical Solutions for Tantrums, Rage, and Meltdowns*, Myles and Southwick (1999) identify the three stages of a meltdown. The rage stage is the second stage of the rage cycle. If the child's anger is not diffused during the first stage, the rumbling stage, a tantrum, rage or meltdown may occur. Behaviors at this stage may include: screaming, biting, hitting, kicking, destroying property and self-injury. The Joshua Center staff believes that a meltdown is caused by a large chemical shift in the brain that causes a drastic increase in emotional activity. We believe there is less ability to think and the child at this time has no control. Meltdowns are not purposeful, and once this stage begins, it often must run its course. It usually takes 10-20 minutes. The goal of the adults during this time is to prevent harm to the child, to others and to property. You cannot correct or teach a child during a meltdown. All involved must agree on the plan they have previously developed to handle such situations. The rage stage will dissipate faster if there is minimal stimulus. Say as little as possible and encourage other children and unneeded adults to leave the area. Younger children in a tantrum, rage or meltdown may be held securely to protect the child and others. Older children should be escorted to a home base or other safe area, if possible. Remember, the rage stage will be over in a short time, although it will seem like hours.

See Home Base, Recovery Stage, Rumbling Stage, Siblings

READING ACCOMMODATIONS

Many children with ND have reading deficits, some middle school students reading at only a second- or third-grade level. I once worked with a seventh-grade boy whose reading tested at the second-grade level. Nevertheless, the principal did not want to continue to provide special education services when the student entered middle school, reportedly feeling sure the boy could perform at a seventh-grade level. It is no wonder that we began to see behavior problems. The child with ND is frustrated and wants to do well in school, but cannot. How can you expect a seventh-grader to read a seventh-grade textbook if he can only read at the second-grade level?

Often children with reading problems need to have someone read to them or have the material read to them on tape. This may be the teacher, paraprofessional, another student, etc. Some children with ND have reading concerns due to interfering neurological symptoms such as racing thoughts, ticcing, or having to read the same line over and over due to OCD.

For children who have a reading disability, I recommend that they read aloud at their independent reading level each day for practice. One of the best things parents can do is to get their child a library card and take her to the library often. Talk to the librarian prior to visiting to line up assistance. Whatever your child's interest is at the moment is a great topic to select for reading material. Let your child choose books at her current reading level or lower. Purchase magazines on favorite subjects. Reading should be exciting. Join a book club and start ordering books at an easy level. The more the child reads, the better her reading skills will get. Read to her often. She can increase her vocabulary if you read books that she is not able to read. Ask questions to check for understanding. No child is ever too old to reap the benefits of being read to.

I am convinced that children with ND need to use assistive technology as part of their educational programming, not just as rewards as is often the case. Many interactive stories on CD offer highlighted text to reinforce reading and have just enough interactive graphics to engage the child, but not too many to distract him. My grandson belongs to a CD book club and I have seen it do wonders for him. Look also for textbooks on disk or tape. Remember that any accommodations needed in reading should to be added to the IEP.

See Books on Tape, Individualized Education Program (IEP), Library, Racing Thoughts, Reading, Tics and Compulsions

READING, TICS AND COMPULSIONS

At one point Josh could not read anything because, due to his OCD, he would have to reread a line one hundred times before he could go on. Some children have to repeat certain letters or words over and over again before they can continue. Just imagine how difficult reading a passage can be when you have to open and close a book several times before you can even start reading. Needless to say, comprehension suffers greatly too. This is one reason why so many children with ND need someone to read textbooks to them. Books on tape are helpful too.

See Books on Tape, Paraprofessionals

RECESS BEHAVIOR

I strongly believe that recess should never be taken away as part of a discipline system for children with a ND as they need this time to release their symptoms. However, these children often have difficulty with sensory overload as a result of being around too many people and too many noises, which frequently shows up on the playground where peer interactions tend to be less supervised by an adult. Allowing the child with ND to play with only one or two other children at one time may be helpful. So often problems at recess start when the teacher is lining the children up to go to or return from recess. Allowing the child to be at the front of the line accompanied by the recess attendant or teacher may help. In addition, giving the child something to carry that requires two hands prevents her from touching other students and helps build self-esteem, as almost all children love to help. Transition from one lesson or activity to another can be a nightmare, so giving incremental warnings to end an activity or starting a new one may help. In some cases it becomes necessary to write in the IEP or 504 Plan that the child needs a personal recess attendant who will supervise her during transition to and from recess and during the actual recess time.

See Individualized Education Program (IEP), Recess - Educating Monitors, Section 504 Plan, Transition to and From Recess

RECESS, EDUCATING MONITORS

In many schools teachers take turns monitoring recess. To make sure everybody knows what to expect, the child's behavior plan should include details on how to handle everything from lining up to what activities need accommodations. Consistency is the key. Every teacher should have a copy of the child's behavior plan and a Recess Monitor worksheet (see Appendix) should be placed in the substitute folder.

See Behavior Plan, Recess Behavior

RECOVERY STAGE

When the child has calmed down after a behavioral outburst, usually after anywhere from a few minutes to an hour, you enter the recovery stage – it often takes the parents a lot longer to recover than the child! Some children sincerely apologize after a meltdown and continue as if nothing happened, others are so worn out that they have to sleep. Sometimes the child apologizes while the parent is still trying to recover, assessing the damage (broken door, holes in walls, broken dishes, etc.) and not in the mood to forgive. But parents must pull themselves together because the things that are said by parents out of frustration during these times could haunt them for the rest of their lives. This is a good time for parents to take a "walk and don't talk," if only in their minds. Even though it is not easy, parents need to do whatever they can to help restore dignity to the household.

See Drives, Prayer, Rage Stage, Recovery Stage, Rumbling Stage, Walk and Don't Talk

REFERRALS TO SCHOOL OFFICE

When a student is referred to the office for escalating, goofy or inappropriate behavior, he should not have to sit out in the open for hours because the school personnel do not know what to do with him. This is a stressful time, and just sitting there could increase the child's stress, not reduce it.

I usually suggest to elementary and middle school principals that they have a sorting tray with age-appropriate items (examples for elementary age include: buttons, toy animals, keys; and for middle-school age: money, cards, pencils) to give to the child, saying, "Hey, I need some help with this. Would you please sort these items for me? I'll be back in a few minutes." A 100-piece puzzle that the child could put together is another option. These activities will help the child settle down. A few minutes later the principal will be able to talk to the child about the episode that sent the child to the office in the first place. Once the talk is over, the child could be sent for a drink of water before returning to the classroom. Don't have a child with handwriting problems, do a think sheet – a widespread punishment for behavioral problems in school. Many of these children have processing and handwriting problems, and thinking and writing at the same time is very hard for them. That is why talking to them is more helpful.

See Consequences, Discipline, Handwriting

REHABILITATION ACT OF 1973

This law was created to ensure affirmative action in employment and nondiscrimination due to a handicapping condition. "No otherwise qualified individual with a disability in the United States, as defined in section 706(20) of this title, shall, solely by reason of his or her disability, be excluded from the participation in, be denied the benefits of, or be subjected to discrimination under any program or activity receiving federal financial assistance or under any program or activity conducted by any executive agency or by the United States Postal Service."

See Section 504 of the Rehabilitation Act

REINFORCERS

Reinforcers are more effective than punishments in motivating children with ND, and positive attention from adults is particularly reinforcing. Try to pay attention to desired behaviors rather than undesired behaviors. Identify the child's favorite activities to reward him for completing less enjoyable activities. Children with ND usually enjoy helping their teachers in school, so when a child completes his class assignments, teachers could let him help erase the chalkboard or hand out papers as a reinforcer. At home playing with friends or helping to wash the car might be good reinforcers for completing regular chores or homework.

RELIGIOUS ORGANIZATIONS

I have had the opportunity to educate many members of religious organizations about individuals with neurological disorders. If a child attends religious education classes or is involved in a church-affiliated youth program, it becomes important to build a support system at the church. Parents should start with the individuals who work closely with their child and bring them together for an informal meeting. In the Appendix, I have included an information sheet for the parent and child to complete and share with members of religious organizations. If the child experiences tantrums, rage or meltdowns, you must be clear on how such situations are to be handled. Similarly, if your child requires close supervision, you need to identify individuals with whom you and your child feel comfortable when you are not available. Small-group settings are usually more successful than large ones.

REPEATING ACTIONS AND WORDS

Some children with ND have repetitive symptoms such as having to move an arm out to the side several times or repeating words or a certain phrase over and over. There was a time when Josh would have to shoot the basketball a certain number of times from a certain angle before we could leave in the car and at other times he would repeat words he heard on the TV. Sometimes what we call tics may be compulsions: an organized, ritualistic expression of certain actions. Some call these symptoms compulsions, others refer to them as tics. The distinction between the two only makes a difference when doctors are treating the symptoms with medication. Regardless, when having these symptoms the child appears to experience a great deal of internal discomfort. Often doctors start by prescribing medication for one (compulsion or tic) and observe if the movement stops. If not, they try something else. It is often a process of trial and error.

See Checking, Complex Tics, Compulsions, "Just Right" Feeling, Obsessive Compulsive Disorder, Rituals

RESIDENTIAL PLACEMENT

Oh, how I remember the day when Jack, our family counselor, attended a "meeting" with me at the psychiatric treatment center where Josh had been for a month. One by one, the "experts" told us how Josh belonged in a residential treatment center. When Jack walked out with me to the parking lot, I was devastated but got renewed hope when he said, "You don't have to do that. There are other options." Thank God I had Jack. I know now for sure, and knew from my gut feeling then, that residential placement would not have been appropriate for Josh. Many professionals have a great deal of experience working with behavior disorders but lack experience with ND. When children with ND are placed in situations, such as residential placements, with students who have behavior disorders, they are like sponges and easily end up manifesting the behaviors of children with behavior disorders. I have known a few children with ND who also have serious behavior problems that are not associated with their disorders. When these children continually hurt you physically, steal and are a danger to others, parents may temporarily have to place them out of the home.

See Counseling - Individual/Family, Parenting a Child with ND, Support Groups

RESOURCE ROOM

Many children with ND receive services in a resource room, where a special education teacher helps them with a variety of activities, including academics, organization, social skills, and test taking. The resource room can also provide a quiet place for a child to have a break. This is often the place where the child with ND begins and ends his day. That is, the resource teacher helps get the child organized for the day and checks to make sure he has everything in order to go home in the afternoon. This is a good time to teach the child organization skills.

See Accommodations, Individualized Education Program (IEP), Self-Contained Special Education Classroom

RESPONSIBILITY

Children with ND have difficulty following directions. Many have auditory or visual processing problems. In addition, they are often immature compared to their same-age peers. When addressing responsibility issues with children with ND, you must keep all of these areas of concern in mind. First make a list of the types of responsibility you want the child to take ownership for. Next prioritize the list. After that pick one or two tasks at a time, and teach, practice and allow the child to master those before adding any more. Some things, such as medication compliance, should not be the child's responsibility. Don't expect your child to automatically assume responsibility; he will need to be taught. In addition, the list may need to be developed into a visual support and placed in a highly visible location. Remember, one step at a time.

See Auditory Processing Disorder, Immaturity, Medication Compliance, Visual Processing Disorders, Visual Supports

RESTRAINT

If the adults involved in working with children with ND have been trained properly, restraint should not be necessary. But there may be times when a child and others around him require protection from hurting himself or others. Restraint should be used only if all other avenues have been tried such as following the behavior intervention plan, sending the child on a break to cool down or "walking and not talking."

I remember an episode when a principal and a teacher who taught students with behavior disorders held a middle-school-aged boy for about 40 minutes. While waiting for his mother to come get him, one had his hands; the other had his feet. The child had calmed down after a few minutes, but I guess they were afraid he would start up again if they released him. They even had another individual videotape the situation! It broke my heart.

See Diversion, Educating School Staff, Home Base, Rage Stage, Recovery Stage, Rumbling Stage

RITUALS

Rituals are compulsions that have to be performed in a certain way – that is, repetitive behaviors in response to an obsession. Some children may have to switch lights on and off several times when entering a room; others have to perform tasks in a certain order when taking a bath or shower. If the process is interrupted, they have to start all over. The ritual might be performed to prevent something from happening or to reduce stress and anxiety. Although the anxiety is reduced once the ritual has been performed, eventually the thought recurs and the child has to engage in the ritual again. Rituals can change like tics, or a child may have just one for quite a while. Sometimes parents are unaware of their child's rituals if they are not obvious, but they may interfere with a child getting a task done such as having to count to 100 by 10s before starting. Medication and therapy may reduce rituals.

See Cognitive Behavioral Therapy, Compulsions

RUMBLING STAGE

Some children who have ND become intensely angry. These episodes are called rages or meltdowns. Myles and Southwick (1999) describe the cycle of these episodes. During the first stage, the rumbling stage, the child may not be aware that he is experiencing difficulties that could escalate to a meltdown. Signs of a rumbling stage may include: biting nails or lips; raising or lowering voice; tensing muscles; foot tapping; grimacing; increasing physical movements; lowering head; appearing to shut down; and showing overall discontentment. Events that may trigger this stage include: fear of failure; interruptions; oversensitization; overstimulation; being ordered to do something; fear of losing control; being asked to do multiple things at once; belittling; or protecting an irrational thought, obsession or compulsion.

During the rumbling stage, the child progressively becomes more and more upset and his self-control diminishes. Unless this progression is broken, the child is likely to have a full meltdown, also called a rage attack. The length of time a child remains in the rumbling stage before a full meltdown can vary, and based on my experience, the length of this stage increases with maturity. It is important for parents and teachers to identify the behavioral patterns that indicate the child is headed toward an outburst of intense anger. Techniques parents may use to divert the growing anger in the rumbling stage include: redirecting to another activity, changing the subject to one of high interest for the child or taking a walk with the child. A good counselor may be able to help children learn how to "read" their own approaching meltdown and how to avert it.

See Home Base, Rage Stage, Recovery Stage, Walk and Don't Talk

S

SAFE ROOM

See Home Base

SCHOOL ASSEMBLIES

I have known children with ND who were denied attendance at school assemblies and other special activities by school staff because they were concerned about inappropriate behaviors the child may exhibit. Special programs are a part of the child's education and should be encouraged with proper supervision and planning. Seating a child with ND between "model" students may be the only intervention necessary. Or it may help to leave seats directly in front of and behind the student vacant to reduce or eliminate negative social interaction. Placing the child in close proximity to an adult often helps. Due to sensory issues I suggest placing the child close to the aisle in case she needs to leave. If the assembly setting proves to be more than the child can handle, he may be allowed to watch from the hall.

See Panic Attacks, Sensory Integration Issues, Sensory Sensitivity, Social Stories, Visual Supports

SCHOOL – BEGINNING OF YEAR

Parents need to start preparing for the school year early. If your child has sensory-defensive clothing concerns, purchase tagless and seamless clothes at the nearest "Sensory Defensive Surplus Store" and if you want your child to get organized, you must model and teach organizational behavior. Purchase your child's school supplies and mark everything. Start establishing school time routines two weeks before the starting date of school, including bedtime schedules, morning routine and nightly story time. If your child is starting a new school, take her several times for a visit. Ask for and expect weekly communication every Friday and stay on top of it because this is the most important thing you will do to ensure your child's success at school. Help your child lay out clothes and organize his backpack or book bag before going to bed each evening. Plan with your child how homework will be accomplished. Try to identify situations that have posed the greatest difficulty in the past and anticipate solutions before they become problems again. Prepare packets of information for your child's teachers including copies of the current IEP or 504 Plan; information about the disorders; teacher worksheets (see Appendix); medication information and alternate phone numbers.

See Backpacks and Book Bags, Organizational Skills, Sensory Integration Issues, Sensory Sensitivity, Structure and Routine

SCHOOL COUNSELOR

The school counselor can be a great help to parents and children. When there is a crisis involving your child, this individual will be expected to help. Therefore, this is a person you want to educate. Create a folder and include the

counselor worksheet at the end of this book. If the counselor sees your child on a weekly basis, he will be in an excellent position to detect any changes in mood, behaviors, tics, peer relations, etc. The school counselor can help your child with peer concerns, self-advocacy skills, and brainstorm strategies for interfering symptoms. However, do not expect the school counselor to replace good individual therapy. The school counselor is responsible for all the children in the school and is not able to provide intense cognitive behavioral therapy.

See Cognitive Behavioral Therapy, Educating School Staff, School - Beginning of Year

SCHOOL – END OF YEAR

It seems like children with ND start shutting down in April. By that time of the year, they have gone about as far as they can go. Symptoms increase and behavior deteriorates. These children do not want to fall apart and cause trouble. Many of their symptoms are out of their control. As a result, many children receive an incredible number of detentions or out-of-school suspensions (or worse) during this time. If teachers are made aware that this is a difficult time, accommodations can be planned, such as modified assignments, reduced homework or no homework, and extra support can be built in, such as the school counselor touching base with the child more frequently. Some may need to be placed on homebound instruction. Children who are placed on homebound instruction should be notified and included in any end-of-year school activities to give them closure.

I knew a little boy in kindergarten who had a wonderful teacher who was very supportive of his ND. On the last day the boy was denied participation in the annual field day. Why? Because the PE teacher had placed his name on the behavior list because he had occasionally spent time running in the gym to release his energy. This was a positive activity the school staff had developed to help children with ND. It backfired! At the end of the year the PE teacher simply associated the boy being in the gym as "bad behavior." They all apologized, but it was too late.

See Homebound Instruction, Shutting Down

SCHOOL NURSE

The school nurse may be one of the most important persons in the school to parents and their child with ND. Work cooperatively with this individual. In particular, it is important to communicate on a regular basis the following: medications the child is taking; medication changes and side effects to look for; increases in symptoms; and any specific fears or anxieties. Also, share the times when your child did not get off to a good start in the morning. The school nurse is a VIP in the success of your child's day. Complete the Information for the School Nurse worksheet (Appendix) and give it to the nurse along with the worksheets on medication changes. It is always a good idea to include the school nurse as a member of the IEP or 504 Plan team.

See Communication Between School and Home

SCHOOL PHOBIA

School phobia is a sense of general anxiety that is based on neurological dysfunction and not related to any clear, logical or understandable social reason. Sometimes the child will be able to tell why he is afraid to go to school, but often he cannot. I remember vividly Josh experiencing school phobia. He would try so hard to get to school and when he made it, he often called with such a great anxiety that I would have to return to the school to bring him home. He described it as a feeling of being paralyzed. During these periods no matter how hard he tried to go to school, he rarely made it. Neuroleptic medications can sometimes cause these symptoms, so share your concerns with her doctor if your child experiences a lot of anxiety after starting a new medication. Counseling helps.

See Calling Home, Counseling - Individual/Family, Fears, Neuroleptics, The "Feeling"

SCHOOL PSYCHOLOGIST

The school psychologist is the individual who assesses children for intelligence, academic achievement, learning style and emotional functioning. The information gathered in this manner may be used to develop an individualized educational plan. The school psychologist will consult with your child's principal and all his teachers to share information regarding the child's specific neurological disorders.

SCHOOL REPORTS AND PROJECTS

I'll never forget a time when I went to observe a young man who was a freshman in high school. I just happened to be there the day class reports were due. When the teacher asked for the reports, this poor student didn't have a clue what the teacher was talking about. The young man did not get the assignment information written in his planner so he had forgotten about it completely.

This is why good communication between parents and teachers is so important. Reports can be overwhelming to children with ND. The very first day the child knows about a project is the day to start planning and get organized. The parents and/or the child's teacher need to break the report down into manageable parts and prioritize each part. Note the due date both on the family calendar and in the child's assignment notebook. For each day leading up to the due date, one of the small parts should be noted on the calendar and assignment notebook. Gather supplies in advance of starting.

If research outside the home is necessary, plan when and where you will take the child to do it. Assist and monitor Internet research because it is easy for students to get on inappropriate websites. Finally, be prepared if your child needs you to type as he dictates information to you.

See Assignment Notebook/Planner, Executive Functions, Time Management, Weekly Reports

SCHOOL – RETURNING TO

It is often difficult for children with ND to return to school after having been away for even a short time. One young man became very concerned about falling behind in his classes and reuniting with his classmates if absent from school for more than a week. In general, he was afraid to return to school. His family counselor offered to drive him to school and accompany him inside to see if he was able to stay. The young man was assured that if he couldn't stay, his counselor would take him home. After walking down the hall with the counselor, the young man still didn't think he could stay. The counselor was disappointed but knew the student had tried his best. To his great relief, a few minutes later the young man said he was going to class. Sometimes you have to go to unusual means to break the cycle. He trusted the counselor enough to allow him to help.

See School Phobia

SCHOOL RULES

Schools set up rules – one size fits all! We make exceptions all the time for children who have physical disabilities, for example, but if the child with ND looks like everybody else, the assumption often is that she should be able to follow the rules just like everybody else. Children with ND need structure and flexibility. They will inevitably break some of these rules, and when that happens they need to be held accountable, but educators must understand the child's specific disorder and apply the rules appropriately. For example, some children with ND have personal hygiene rituals that may cause them to be late for class. Also, children with TS who blurt out inappropriate language should not be punished because the school has a zero tolerance for bad language.

See Being Flexible, Structure and Routine

SCHOOL SUPPLIES

I recommend that at the beginning of each school year parents supply their child's classroom with the necessary pencils, papers, notebooks, etc. I also recommend that textbooks remain in each class and that a set remain at home for the year. Far too often children with ND receive detentions for not bringing their supplies to class. This is unacceptable. Extra sets of books and materials are accommodations and help tremendously by preventing valuable time from being lost while retrieving supplies from the locker.

See Accommodations, Books Left at Home, Books Left in Locker

SCOUTING

Many children with ND have been very successful in the Scouting program. Since children with ND often have few friends at school, Scouting can be a great opportunity for them to experience positive social experiences and success while earning badges. Good leadership will allow all children to succeed. Visit with prospective leaders and educate them on your child's ND, focusing on his special needs. I recommend that a parent stay with the child as a volunteer to assist with the program and to be ready to intervene when their child needs help. In addition, the other children and their parents should also be educated.

See Educating Peers, Extracurricular Activities

SECTION 504 OF THE REHABILITATION ACT OF 1973

One of the requirements of Section 504 of the Rehabilitation Act of 1973, a federal civil rights law, is that school district buildings and programs be accessible to individuals with disabilities. It protects individuals from discrimination under federal grants. The Office of Civil Rights of the U.S. Department of Education is responsible for its enforcement. Section 504 does not furnish federal funds, but covers recipients of federal funds.

SECTION 504 PLAN

Section 504 of the Rehabilitation Act of 1973 is a federal statute that protects individuals with disabilities from discrimination in programs and activities that receive federal funds, including public education. A Section 504 Plan is an instructional services plan designed to assist students with special needs who are in a general education setting. A 504 Plan is not an IEP, which is required for special education students. When a student moves from a special education to a general education placement, she may be placed under a 504 Plan. However, this does not always mean that the IEP goes away. A student may be considered for a 504 Plan if she has a physical or emotional disability or has an impairment (i.e., ADHD) that restricts one or more major life activities. Major life activities include learning, walking, seeing, hearing, speaking, breathing, reading, writing, performing math calculations, working, caring for oneself and performing manual tasks. Teachers, support staff, a parent/legal guardian, physician or therapist can refer a student for a 504 Plan. A meeting is held, a plan is developed with parents and school staff and a review date is set. Under Section 504, the child with a disability may receive accommodations and modifications that are not available to children who do not have disabilities.

See Individualized Education Program (IEP)

SELF-CONTAINED SPECIAL EDUCATION CLASSROOM

There are two types of special education programs – instructional and resource. In instructional programs students receive special education services for 50 percent or more of the school day, and in resource programs they receive special education services for less than 50 percent of the school day. Some children benefit from an instructional or a self-contained special education setting with fewer children than in a general education classroom. This is particularly true if the child has many sensory issues, interfering symptoms or behaviors, needs one-on-one assistance or a more controlled environment. In my opinion children with ND do best in classes of about six.

I observed a self-contained special education classroom one time that I thought was wonderful. The teacher treated her class like an ordinary class; she just had fewer children. The children received direct instruction just like in general education classes and the room was set up like a general education classroom. So often when I visit special education classrooms, I have found that the children are expected to stay in their seats and do their work. I find this appalling because the students are in a special education setting because they need help. When you have a great special education teacher, you are half way there. I worked with a boy who for one year preferred placement in the special education classroom. He knew he needed this additional help and realized he had problems with noise and crowd-ed rooms. By staying in the special education classroom he received individual help with homework assignments and was able to go home and spend more pos-itive time with his parents because his homework was completed.

See Classroom Environment, Observations at School, Resource Room

SELF-CONTROL

When children with ND are not under stress, they tend to think and feel the same as other children, but when they are under stress and are out of control they are not thinking because they do not have that control. Most children are able to put a thought barrier between their thoughts and actions, but for children with ND it seems that if a thought crosses the brain, it's out the mouth or out the fist. From our experience at the Joshua Center, it seems that as the children mature they have better self-control. After observing these kids at camp, the staff came to realize that until children are about 14 they don't have much ability to control their behavior.

See Impulse Control, Neurotransmitter, Rage Stage

SELF-ESTEEM

It has been interesting to watch my grandson versus my son grow up with ND. While Josh was not diagnosed until 13, I knew at six months that my grandson had TS, OCD or a similar disability. Josh's self-esteem was fractured by all the misunderstandings we had to go through until he was diagnosed and required years of counseling to change. But my grandson knows he has TS and OCD and accepts this as "no big deal." In addition, his mother and I are more relaxed over the diagnoses, he has an "expert" doctor and nurse, and he has the opportunity to participate in programs geared to his special needs.

Many children with ND who have been teased a lot because of their symptoms have a poor self-image. A mother tells me one of her daughters thought she was "stupid" in all areas of her life because she had learning problems in school. Such thoughts can follow us into adulthood. All adults involved with children with special needs must recognize the impact they have on a child's life. It is critical for a child to feel a sense of self-acceptance. This self-acceptance comes from feeling accepted by parents and other key adults in his life. We must all encourage children's strengths and potential.

See Counseling - Individual/Family

SELF-INJURY

Some children with ND have self-injurious symptoms. For example, in middle school a wonderful young man "had to" somersault so much that he ended up with bruises on his back the size of fists. He would somersault at school, in parking lots and in fast-food restaurants. After being seen by a specialist, a hot tub was prescribed for treating his severe bruises and to help him relax. He was highly medicated for about three months to try to break the cycle. He stayed home from school and just about everywhere else for a few months, but the hot tub and medication helped his back heal.

In other instances of self-injurious behavior, some children cut their skin until it bleeds. This cutting is sometimes the child's effort to escape the "feeling." One girl would pop her hipbone out of the socket. If self-injurious behaviors occur, parents absolutely need to contact the child's doctor.

See Obsessive Compulsive Disorder, Skin Picking, The "Feeling"

SENSE OF HUMOR

The first year I attended the National Tourette Syndrome Association conference, I met Susan Conners, a wonderful lady who diagnosed herself with TS at 36 while watching an episode of "Quincy." She was the keynote speaker at the conference, and the one thing that impacted me the most was her sense of humor. She told of many "trying" experiences that she and other family members had gone through before learning about TS, but she was still able to laugh. You won't make it if you don't have a sense of humor. Many times in my life I just had to sit down and laugh to keep my sanity. Identify one person who will understand your experiences and share frequently.

See Socks and Underwear

SENSORY INTEGRATION ISSUES

For children with sensory integration difficulties the brain does not integrate sensory information properly. Sensations of touch, movement, and gravity are considered to be the most primary sensations of the body because they are needed for smooth motor control. It is imperative that children with these issues undergo occupational therapy evaluation. This is just as important as an academic assessment. Your child's school should include an evaluation by an occupational therapist familiar with sensory integration when doing an assessment. Check to see if your insurance provider covers this service.

See Occupational Therapist

SENSORY SENSITIVITY

Children with ND are often sensitive to touch – from clothing and touching by others. For example, many children misinterpret a friendly tap as an intentional hit because of sensory problems. Indeed, children who are extremely sensitive to touch may spend a great deal of the day trying to avoid being touched altogether. Tags, seams, elastic, tight clothes and certain textures can cause problems. In situations like this, the child can wear socks inside out to avoid the seams or wear sandals! Many children with ND are very sensitive to odors. At the grocery store they are not able to go near detergents or fresh fish. You can't imagine how all the sounds of a classroom can impact a child's learning. Most of us filter out these sounds, but squeaky chairs, tapping feet and rustling papers can be terribly hard for these children. One child became nauseated when around noisy fluorescent lights whereas many children with ND often want to wear sunglasses in bright areas. I have known children whose eye blinking tics increased dramatically in bright lights and visually stimulating environments. Supermarkets, department stores, sports arenas may all be stimulating visually. This is probably why I hear so many stories of meltdowns occurring in these environments. Children can also be overly sensitive to movement. Those who seem to move all the time are undersensitive and children who are overly sensitive to movement might be afraid to ride their bikes.

See Occupational Therapist, Sensory Integration Issues, Socks and Underwear

SEROTONIN

Serotonin, one of the brain's neurotransmitters believed to be involved in OCD, communicates with brain cells by way of other brain nerve cells.

SHOPPING

I never liked to take Josh shopping unless I had no other choice. Even when the shopping spree was for him, it wasn't fun. I always ended up spending much more than I anticipated because I was worn out and unable to say no. Finding clothes that felt "just right" was almost impossible. Although Josh never had a meltdown in a store, I have known many children who have. Children who are impulsive and obsessive often have a great deal of trouble accepting no for an answer. When they get stuck on having to have something right now and don't get it, they are headed for trouble.

When planning a trip to a grocery or other store, parents should tell their child exactly what they are planning to do. As much as possible, determine ahead of time the amount of time it will take. Also decide ahead of time if the child will be allowed to purchase anything for himself. Some grocery stores now have special shopping carts for children. Giving them a cart and a list seems to help keep them focused. However, you might have to check for unsolicited items at the checkout! Reinforce appropriate behaviors.

If, despite all the best laid plans, the child becomes out of control, leave as quickly as possible. If you need assistance, ask for help from the store manager, explaining that your child has an ND. Try to keep calm and ignore the inappropriate behavior. This is no time to get into a power struggle. Once at home, call a friend who understands to help you relieve your stress from the experience. Not until the child is calm should you and the child discuss the situation. Inform the child that his inappropriate behavior will not be tolerated in public places. Be sure and listen to the child's version, listening for cues as to what set him off. You might learn something to be avoided the next time you try to go shopping.

See Diversion, Obsessive Compulsive Disorder, Overstimulation, Rage Stage, Reinforcers, Rumbling Stage, Socks and Underwear, Stuck Thinking

SHOWERS

Many children with ND hate taking showers. Some have to mentally prepare themselves to take a shower because the feel of the water makes them very uncomfortable. If told to get in the shower or tub without any warning, others might resist, not because they don't want to comply but because they haven't had enough time to prepare themselves. For these children taking a shower or bath is not a pleasant experience. I know a boy who not only didn't like taking a shower but also had difficulty getting into a swimming pool. At camp we worked with him and did succeed in getting him in the pool up to his knees. A good counselor may be able to help the child develop strategies for showering. I also encourage consulting with an occupational therapist.

See Counseling - Individual/Family, Occupational Therapist, Sensory Sensitivity

SHUTTING DOWN

When some children are overwhelmed by stress or fatigue, or are overstimulated, they "shut down." At such times, they may refuse to continue an activity, stare into space, put their hands over their ears, engage in self-relaxing movement behavior or try to sleep. Some may interpret this as chosen behavior or as being lazy. But shutting down may be a coping mechanism serving the same purpose for the child as a fuse does for an overloaded electrical circuit. That is, without shutting down the child might explode. Usually the best way to handle shutting-down behavior is to divert to another activity or take a break. Perhaps a quiet walk might help the child feel less overwhelmed. A few children may learn that they can utilize shutting-down behavior as a means of avoiding certain tasks. When doing so, the child is trying to manipulate the situation. Perhaps the parent will agree that a short break is in order, but it is important to return to the activity that the child is trying to avoid by his manipulation. Only by knowing your child well will you be able to distinguish between shutting down and manipulation and act accordingly.

See Depression, Getting Started, Manipulating Behavior, Rage Stage, School - End of Year, Sleeping at School

SIBLINGS

Having a brother or sister with special needs is not always easy. Siblings often feel that they are ignored or that more is expected of them compared to their brother or sister with ND. Acknowledge to the siblings that the child with the disorders does take extra time and energy, but assure them that even though you are not able to divide your time equally, you will divide it fairly. Equality and fairness are not the same. While some parents think it is not fair to treat one child differently than the other, the key is to treat each child in a manner that provides him or her with the greatest possibility of success. Try to give each child the care and attention he or she needs even if it is not the same amount. Just as in school, some special accommodations may be required for each child in the family.

Another issue facing some siblings is the fear that they will develop the disorder. Help them develop empathy but do not expect them always to respond with understanding. Do not burden siblings with too much responsibility or too many expectations. Like parents, siblings often become overwhelmed and scared, feeling as if the problems surrounding the child with ND are never-ending. Don't get angry if they worry about how their friends will respond. Get them away from the situation, go for a drive and talk about what is going on in their lives or schedule a time when you can share a hobby with them. Take them and their friends out. Recognize their feelings and let them know how important they are to you.

I remember the times when Josh was having a meltdown and Sarah would try to intervene because she didn't like the way he was treating me. Rather than helping, her reaction made the situation more difficult because I was then dealing with two children. Have an agreement with siblings that when the child with ND is in the rage stage, you can take care of it and that the best thing they can do is to go to their room and shut the door and wait until you come to them. When your child with ND is going through a time of raging, do not leave him home alone with other siblings, as things could escalate – it is unfair to put a sibling in this position.

On a brighter note, nothing is more rewarding than seeing your children getting along when for years you were sure only one would make it to adulthood! It does get better! (I'm not sure I would have believed that 10 years ago!)

See Parenting a Child with ND, Rage Stage

SIMPLE TICS

A simple tic involves only a single body part. Examples of simple tics are eye blinks, shoulder shrugs and facial twitches.

See Tics

SKIN PICKING

Skin picking, a form of self-mutilation, is a pretty common symptom among children with a diagnosis of OCD. Many children pick until they bleed. Some have an uncontrollable urge to pick, while others may begin picking at a perceived imperfection including acne, scars, scabs, bites, bumps, moles, pimples or freckles. Picking may also be used as a way to relieve depression. Whatever the reason, it is neurological in origin. Sometimes the child will try to hide his picking from others with clothing. I have known kids to wear long sleeves in the summer not only to hide the sores, but to hide their embarrassment. Treatment for compulsive skin picking may include the use of medications, behavioral therapy and/or cognitive behavior therapy.

See Cognitive Behavior Therapy, Obsessive Compulsive Disorder, Self-Injury

SLEEPING AT HOME

I always said that if ever I opened a school for students with ND, I would start the "day" at 10:00 P.M. and send them home at 6:00 A.M.! So many children with ND have difficulty getting ready for bed, getting to bed and falling asleep that they frequently wake up during the night or don't fall asleep at all. And if they do fall asleep, it's almost impossible to wake them in the morning. Sometimes racing thoughts or excessive energy interferes with the ability to fall asleep as can certain medications.

Medication dosages may need to be adjusted, so it is a good idea to inform the doctor of sleep concerns. A good counselor can also help. Some children were helped when their counselor taught them how to visualize their favorite "quiet" place. Others have been successful listening to soft music, while yet others have used a sound machine with sounds of the sea or the forest to calm down. I know several children who can only fall asleep listening to the TV. When Josh had sleep problems, I would take him on a two-hour drive each night as it helped calm his thoughts and therefore enabled him to fall asleep.

A consistent bedtime routine is a must if your child has sleep problems. Allow extra time to prepare for bed when a child has several bedtime rituals. You will need to decide whether you should set the child's bedtime by the clock or by how tired he is. Often children have difficulty transitioning from an activity to bed. You might try five-minute warnings. You must determine if the late bedtime adversely affects the morning routine. If it does, then you might want to endure the bedtime hassle rather than have a difficult time in the morning getting your child off to school. Medications can also affect sleep.

Parents who insist on a strict bedtime for a child who is not ready are sometimes in for a fight. Allowing your child to stay up one hour later than the normal time may give her body a little more time to wind down and she may be able to fall asleep more quickly.

See Bedtime Behavior, Drives, Medication Side Effects, Rituals, Sleeping at School

SLEEPING AT SCHOOL

Frequently children with ND have trouble waking up in the morning, either due to a sleep disorder, a side effect of a medication or depression. If a child falls asleep in class, accommodations need to be considered. For example, I recommend that the teacher wake him and send him to get a drink. In more serious cases the child may need to start his day later – a class or subject could be eliminated or provided through homebound instruction. Sometimes scheduling a high-interest class first thing in the morning helps the student get started. While many children with ND do better in the mornings, children who have severe sleep concerns may need their "core" subjects scheduled in the afternoon. Always enlist the help of the child in making changes. He will have ideas. Finally, parents should communicate sleep concerns to their doctor.

See Accommodations, Communication Between School and Home, Medication Side Effects, Sleeping at Home

SOCIAL SKILLS

Many children with ND have great difficulty making and keeping friends and easily become victims of taunting and teasing. Reasons for their difficulties in these areas include their immaturity and their inability to recognize nonverbal clues. Teachers can encourage a child's special interests or strengths during class time as a way to increase her acceptance and self-esteem. A good way to increase peer acceptance, whether at home, school or in extracurricular activities, is to give the child a leadership position. Parents and teachers should take every opportunity to teach appropriate social behavior. Identify a few areas where your child is having difficulty and practice those over and over. Another option is to enroll your child in a social skills class – check with your doctor or teachers for recommendations.

See Board Games, Bullying, Extracurricular Activities, Hidden Curriculum, Immaturity, Peer Relations, Self-Esteem

SOCIAL STORIES

Social Stories were developed by Carol Gray as a way to describe a situation in terms of relevant cues and common responses (Gray, 2002; Gray & Garand, 1993). A Social Story gives the child information about a situation and provides guidance on ways to respond. Professionals or parents write Social Stories to describe social situations that the child with ND finds difficult. Every Social Story has a reassuring, accepting quality, positively and matter of factly describing a specific event (Gray, 2002; Gray & Garand, 1993). For example, a Social Story might be created to help a child learn how to meet a new friend.

See Hidden Curriculum

SOCKS AND UNDERWEAR

Comfort wear! I could paper my entire house with underwear and socks that were not worn due to one or more of the following: itchy; rough seams; lumpy seams; seams over toes; seams at end of toes; rough texture; too thin; too heavy; tags; rough elastic; heels; too short; too long; too tight; too lose; and too clean – but never "too dirty." How many times have parents caught their child going through the dirty laundry for the "perfect" socks? (I read this to my nine-year-old grandson who has TS, OCD and ADHD. His comment was, "Hmm, I've been wearing these socks for three days.")

See Sense of Humor, Sensory Sensitivity

SPEAKING IN PICTURES

Many children with ND are visual learners. That is, they learn best by seeing and doing. As a result, directions should be both oral and written. To make written instructions more memorable, include pictures. Another way to help children with ND is by drawing stick figures similar to cartoons to draw the situation. Temple Grandin (1995) has written a wonderful book, *Talking in Pictures*, that describes this process well.

See Social Stories, Visual Supports

SPECIAL EDUCATION

Congress enacted the Education for All Handicapped Children Act (Public Law 94-142) and the Individuals with Disabilities Education Act (amended in 1997) to support states and local school districts in meeting the individual needs of and protecting the rights of infants, toddlers, children and youth with disabilities and their families. The goal was to implement effective programs and services for early intervention, special education and related services. Meeting the unique needs of students with disabilities is the job of special education. This includes not only instruction in the classroom but instruction in physical education, homebound instruction, and instruction in hospitals and institutions when applicable. For example, children with ND may need homebound instruction when symptoms are severe enough to interfere with learning at school or they may need an alternative physical education program.

See Individuals with Disabilities Education Act, Learning Disabilities, Section 504 Plan, Special Education Placement

SPECIAL EDUCATION PLACEMENT

Many parents are resistant to having their child labeled as needing special education assistance. While avoiding such a label can be a good thing, one must balance that against the increased services the school may be able to provide if an IEP is developed. Special education placement does not or should not mean the child is going to be in a self-contained special education classroom all day. It may open up the availability of individualized instruction, speech-language therapy, occupational therapy or other services. Good communication with the special education staff is a must.

See Communication Between School and Home, Individualized Education Program (IEP), Weekly Reports

SPEECH-LANGUAGE PATHOLOGIST

The speech-language pathologist evaluates, diagnoses and treats a child for receptive or expressive language difficulties, as well as problems with articulation, auditory processing, pragmatics, verbal comprehension, expressive and receptive language and word retrieval. The therapist also works with the student who is having difficulty organizing and expressing ideas in writing due to organizational problems. Treatment can include: helping individuals who cannot make speech sounds, or cannot make them clearly; helping individuals who have fluency problems, such as stuttering; and working with individuals who have problems understanding and producing language skills. In addition, the speech-language pathologist works closely with the IEP team.

See Auditory Processing Disorder, Individualized Education Program Team

SPELLING MODIFICATIONS

Many children with ND have spelling concerns. To help, teachers may require fewer spelling words to be learned each week. Once the child performs better with fewer words, words can be added. If the child is a visual learner and has trouble with spelling words, let him type them in a special font on the computer or draw them in colors. When reviewing spelling words, have the child spell the words he does know first to build confidence. Make word cards and place them in strategic locations throughout the house (parents can purchase magnetic words or make them themselves and place on the refrigerator, bedroom door, etc.). When children with ND complete assignments in class, spelling errors should not be counted against them; however, all homework and out-of-class reports and projects should be free of spelling errors as required for all other students. Children with ND should be allowed to use spell checkers.

SPITTING

Some children have spitting tics. When that happens, the child's doctor needs to be consulted for possible medication management. Since spitting tics can be a health and safety issue, the child's doctor, a counselor knowledgeable about ND, school administrators and parents need to help the child develop a strategy to cover up the tic or replace it with another more appropriate tic. If the child is spitting in the lunchroom, the school needs to make another place available for him to eat.

See Brainstorming, Complex Tics, Lunchroom Concerns, Tics, Tourette Syndrome

SPORTS AND DISABILITIES

My friend Fred Engh, president and CEO of National Alliance for Youth Sports, gave me permission to reprint this passage from his book, *Why Johnny Hates Sports: Why Organized Youth Sports Are Failing Our Children and What We Can Do About It* (1999, pp. 110-114).

"Children and adults with disabilities are much more visible in today's society than they have been at any other time in history. Inclusion has emerged as an important concept in the education of children with special needs, but few administrators recognize and understand this point. We have seen the need for administrators to support inclusive policies regarding girls in sports, and we find a similar need when it comes to children with disabilities. Including kids with disabilities in activities with their peers who are not disabled is a guiding principle of the Americans with Disabilities Act (ADA), which applies to 43 million people. This 1990 Federal law provides an opportunity to welcome all children into youth sports. The ADA is an important piece of broad-sweeping civil rights legislation that insures the rights of people with disabilities to be included in all aspects of community life, enjoy the full benefits of participation, and be served in the least restrictive setting. Youth league administrators must remember that kids with disabilities are, first and foremost, children. These youngsters have the same dreams and desires as others do. The only difference is that they happen to have a condition that may affect some of their abilities and skills, but that doesn't mean that they shouldn't be able to reap the benefits that sports provide. So their participation in the youth sports arena should be fully supported by everyone involved, not because of any law, but because it's the right thing to do. The adults should be removing roadblocks to participation, not putting them in. Many youth leagues have policies and mission statements that at least touch on the goal of helping children learn and develop skills for that particular sport, among other areas. Administrators must realize that all children have a right to learn and develop these skills to the best of their ability. Pitcher Jim Abbott is living out his dream. He plays baseball with only one "good" arm, but he plays at the Major League level. In fact, one year, he pitched a no-hitter for the New York Yankees. Abbott is wonderful proof that with the opportunity, anyone can excel, regardless of the limitations adults may perceive a child to have. Why should a child with speech impairment, a learning disorder, or a physical ailment be denied one of life's greatest treasures – the right to participate in sports? And why do many administrators cruelly continue to step on these youngsters' dreams by turning them away season after season? It's because winning championships and trophies are the main goals in the minds of many administrators, even though in the process, some youngsters are excluded. It's time administrators began to put aside their petty prejudices, ignore their fears of the unknown, become better informed on these issues, and educate the coaches and parents throughout the league who have a responsibility, as decent human beings, to welcome all children to the world of youth sports."

See Extracurricular Activities

STAYING IN SEAT

Due to some neurological symptoms, not all children, especially those with ADHD, will be able to comply with the rule of staying in their seat. Instead of trying to "make" the child stay in her seat, a much more effective strategy is to ask, "What accommodations does he need to complete class assignments?" These students may need preferential seating arrangements or be allowed to get up and move when necessary.

See Accommodations, Attention Deficit Hyperactivity Disorder (ADHD), Impulse Control

STEALING

I have known quite a few children who had problems with stealing. Often I think it relates to impulsivity – they see something and think they have to have it right away. Some children with OCD say they are driven to steal. Others hoard things in their room, usually items they take from within their own home. Regardless of the reason, stealing cannot be tolerated. There must be consequences, as stealing has a tendency to escalate to bigger items until the police are involved in a juvenile action. Parents should get their child counseling immediately if stealing begins to be a problem to prevent it from getting worse.

See Consequences, Counseling - Individual/Family, Hoarding, Impulse Control, Legal System, Obsessive Compulsive Disorder

STEPPARENTS

The parental team needs to agree on the basic causes of behavior and how to handle discipline and child rearing. These matters are difficult at times for birth parents, and the stepparent status can make decisions regarding discipline and child-rearing even more difficult. Not only do the parents have strong feelings, so do the children. It is not uncommon for any child to feel that he may have been the cause of a divorce, and when the child has a neurological difficulty that complicates his behaviors, he is more likely to feel this responsibility. As a result, he may secretly resent the stepparent and harbor wishes of a reunification of the birth parents.

The key factor is that all these concerns elevate the child's stress level, and until a workable solution has been reached, tics and behavioral problems may increase. The way the birth parents and the stepparents work these matters out is highly individualistic and must be left to their own discretion. Some decide that only the birth parents are involved in behavioral discipline. This is often the case with adolescents and older children. Conversely, the younger the child is at the time of the formulation of the mixed family, the more important it will be for both the natural parents and the stepparent to take on a more equal role.

See Acceptance, Educating Parents

STIMULANT MEDICATIONS

Like most parents, I do not like giving children medications, but if a child with ND has difficulty functioning in school, medications may help. Since the areas of the brain thought to be involved in planning, foresight, and inhibiting actions are underaroused in individuals with ADHD, for example, stimulant medications may work by increasing neural activity to more normal levels. More research is needed, however, to firmly establish the mechanisms of the stimulants. Among the symptoms of children with ND, I have found attentional problems to have the greatest impact on their education. One thing that stands out in the children I observe is that they seem to be getting into trouble right around or just after lunch. After some investigation I have learned that some stimulant medications for ADHD are given right after lunch. If the child takes his medication at 7:00 A.M. and eats lunch at noon, that is a span of five hours, which may be too long before taking the second dose, and as a result, the rebound effect sets in. Rebound occurs when the behavior deteriorates worse than if the child had not been on medications. Since many children cannot go for more than four hours without the second dose, the prescription bottle must be specific. The parents and the child's doctor must decide on the exact time to dispense the medication. Newer medications have a longer-lasting effect, which may be an option. A word of caution: *Do not under any circumstance adjust medications without the consent of the child's doctor.*

See Communication Between School and Home, Documentation, Medication Management at School, Parent Journal, Teacher Journal

STOMACH DISTRESS

If your child frequently complains of stomach distress, contact the doctor. Some medications for ND can cause an upset stomach. Some children with TS have internal tics that can cause stomach disorders. It's also not uncommon for children with ND to have allergies that may contribute to stomachaches. Finally, high anxiety can contribute to stomach problems.

If your child maintains that she cannot go to school due to a stomachache, generally, give a clear message that she is going to school. It's hard sometimes, but I have learned that the more they stay home, the harder it is for them to return to school. It's very hard as a parent watching your child suffer. Some days it seems like every decision is a monumental one. Document the time of day your child complains about stomachaches. Discuss with your doctor medication possibilities to help give your child some relief. Some parents supply the school nurse with a box of crackers, Sprite or 7-UP to give to the child to help soothe an upset stomach. Young children may not be able to tell you what is causing their anxiety, so you will need to listen for clues as they share information about daily situations. Try to be consistent in handling these complaints. The child needs to know that life does go on in spite of her discomfort.

See Allergies, Documentation, Internal Tics, Medication Side Effects, Overprotecting, School Phobia, School - Returning To

STORMS

Does your child ever act like a storm cloud with lightening coming out of it and you as the lightening rod? Even though you don't like it, you know that you are about to be the "ground" for all your child's pent-up anger. I first heard the word "storm" given to this type of behavior from Marilyn P. Dornbush and Sheryl K. Pruitt, authors of *Teaching the Tiger, A Handbook for Individuals Involved in the Education of Students with Attention Deficit Hyperactivity Disorder, Tourette Syndrome or Obsessive-Compulsive Disorder* (1995). Brenda Myles and Jack Southwick (1999) refer to it as tantrums, rage, and meltdowns.

See Diversion, Meltdowns, Rage Stage, Recovery Stage, Rumbling Stage

STRESS

One theory, and the staff's belief at the Joshua Center, is that when under stress, children who have ND have fewer of certain key neurotransmitters in the "thinking centers" of their brain. Four common causes of stress are: (a) threats to sense of self-esteem, (b) a feeling of not getting one's needs met, (c) excitement and (d) fatigue. Overstimulization also produces almost the same body reaction as stress. Overstimulization for children with ND may include: sensitivity to light, sound, smell, touch; too many people; too small or too large a room, etc. When not under stress, the child with ND may think and feel about the same as other children, but when under stress she may have more difficulty thinking and be more emotionally reactive.

See Auditory Processing Disorder, Overstimulation, Visual Distractions, Visual Processing Disorders

STRUCTURE AND ROUTINE

Children with ND need consistency in structure and daily routines. Doing homework at the same time each day, eating meals at a scheduled time and having specific morning routines are a few examples of consistency with structure and routine. Since these children do not adapt well to change, parents and teachers must learn how to help the child transition from one activity to another, including planning for a change in routine. For instance, if the father helps the child with nightly homework and is going on a business trip for a few days, how will that impact your child? Can some of the homework be completed ahead of schedule? If the mother needs to return to the work force to help the family financially and the child is used to her being home after school, what other arrangements will need to be made to provide that after-school support? Similarly, when class schedules are adjusted to accommodate school assemblies, children with ND may have a difficult time.

See After School, Changes in Schedule and Routine, Homework Strategies, Morning Routine

STUCK THINKING

Stuck thinking is a symptom of obsessions, which is pretty common among children with ND. In such cases, the thought seems to control the person, rather than the person controlling the thought. Thoughts are unwanted and persistent and often interfere with daily life. Common "stuck thoughts" include: fear of germs or disease, fairness vs. unfairness, hurting or being hurt by others, and sin and religion. Children sometimes spend hours, days and even weeks paralyzed by their thoughts. Frequently the child is aware that the obsession is not logical, but that knowledge doesn't help. The best thing to do is try to redirect the child to an enjoyable activity. If a child gets stuck on a thought of violence to self or others, contact the child's doctor and counselor. Medication may help and some counseling techniques are also effective.

See Counseling - Individual/Family, Obsessive Compulsive Disorder

STUDY CARREL

A study carrel is a three-sided partition that either is connected to or placed on top of a desk to help reduce distractions while a student is studying. Children with ND who have used study carrels have reported that they are able to do more work in class when using study carrels. If study carrels are going to be used, I suggest that they be available for the whole class. Have at least two in the room and refer to them as the classroom office, available to all students as needed. The child should be consulted first to make sure using a carrel or moving to the carrel in front of his peers won't cause him stress. One teacher who couldn't take the noises of a boy with TS placed him in a study carrel with his back to the wall. Not only did he feel humiliated, he wasn't able to see the rest of the class or the teacher for instruction. A study carrel should be a helpful, not harmful strategy. It should never be used as a punishment.

See Classroom Distractions, Classroom Environment, Classroom Seating Arrangements

STUDY SKILLS

By the time the child enters middle school, the demands for studying will increase. Parents and teachers must teach and model good study skills. First teach organization – this means every detail from the student's notebook to the study area at home. Assess what works best for the child. In the child's planner, short- and long-term assignments, daily work and prospective tests must be identified. Purchase a calendar for homework only and list the due dates of all projects. Use the calendar to monitor that projects are completed and turned in. Remember: Completed and turned in are two separate tasks. Make a list of projects and break them down into manageable steps. For upcoming tests it's best to review a little each night. Estimate how much time is needed to complete the project for your child to be successful. For instance, many children with ND have difficulty completing their library books. How many chapters are there? How long are the chapters? When is the best time for your child to read? With whom does she complete this activity? Does she need to have the book read to her? What is involved in writing the book report? Document how long it actually took to complete an assignment, project, etc., so you can use this information to plan for the next time. Also, such information is valuable at IEP meetings when accommodations are discussed.

Some things will need to be memorized, and this can be difficult for children with ND. Identify the child's strengths. Helpful strategies include mnemonic devices such as rhymes, acronyms and other tricks that help us remember things. Some children find music association helpful. For visual learners "a picture is worth a thousand words," so creating a mental picture or drawing one will help them remember and understand difficult material. To help retention, the SQ3R formula is effective (Survey, Question, Read, Recite, Review) for handling lengthy reading assignments for history, social studies, etc. Using this technique the student: surveys or scans the assignment noting important information; asks himself questions about what information may be important; reads the assignment carefully; recites the information read; and reviews it when completed.

Build a routine because you will be doing this for many years. Make sure your child has all his supplies and replenish them often, because when your child is "ready," you don't want to break his focus just because he is out of paper! Have a list on the refrigerator that you and your child can check when supplies are low. When writing a paper, use the mapping method. Start with a word in the center of the paper and add details radiating out from the central subject. This method can be used when studying for tests also.

See Organizational Skills, School Supplies

SUBSTITUTE TEACHERS

A lot of children with ND have had horrible experiences with substitute teachers. First of all, they do not adapt to change very well, so stress associated with change can lead to an increase in anxiety and symptoms. I worked with one boy in elementary school whose substitute was so annoyed that he would not stop burping (a tic) that she had him stand and burp in front of his classmates even after the other students informed her that he had TS. Unless substitutes receive training and proper information, they cannot help. The child's teacher should place all relevant information in the substitute folder. In extreme cases, the best thing may be to keep the child home if the parents know in advance the teacher is going to be gone. (See worksheet for substitute teachers in the Appendix.)

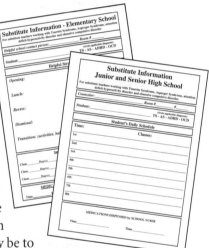

SUMMER TIME

Summer provides an opportunity to give children a break from routine classroom learning experiences and promote learning in settings with less structure. Check with parents who have had a child in the grade your child is entering to see what subjects will be explored. Summer is a good time to consider what the child needs to learn to help her succeed the next school year. Take her to the library regularly. Work on math skills if that is a deficit. Write stories, make a newspaper or write a book. If you make these activities fun, your child will enjoy returning to school. Some doctors recommend medication vacations, but keep in mind that sometimes medications do not work the same after you stop and then go back on. Two weeks before school start preparing your child to return to school. Get him back into the "early to bed, early to rise" routine.

SUPPLEMENTARY AIDS AND SERVICES

Supplementary aids and services are those aids, services and other supports that are provided in regular education classes or other education-related settings to help children with disabilities to be educated with their nondisabled peers to the maximum extent appropriate.

See Individualized Education Program (IEP)

SUPPORT GROUPS

Getting involved in the local chapter of the Tourette Syndrome Association was the smartest thing I did once Josh was diagnosed. At support group meetings parents share concerns, hopes, learn from each other and validate their parenting. If there is not a chapter in your area for your child's disorder, start one. It will save your life. Contact the national association for help. Don't try to do this alone.

SUPPORT SYSTEM

Parents need to count on other individuals when things get tough. It helps to talk to other parents having similar concerns. It also helps to identify one person in the extended family who will "be there."

See Extended Family, Parenting a Child with ND, Support Groups

SWEARING

When under stress children with ND are less able to put a thought barrier between their impulses and their actions. For example, if an impulse to swear enters their mind, it is usually out of their mouth. Some children have trouble thinking things through to arrive at an adaptive response. They may know they are mad but have trouble thinking what to do next. All they can think of is to strike out at something. Since they are slow at developing language skills, they are likely to swear or talk trash. Parents need to stay cool and recognize the trash talk as just that – trash. However, this does not mean you merely accept such talk. If possible, teach the child alternative words to use and encourage the child to keep practicing until the new words become automatic.

See Coprolalia

T

TAKING CARE OF IT

The symptoms of children with ND can cause relationships to become damaged. This story does a wonderful job of explaining how parents can help their child take responsibility for repairing a relationship when symptoms are involved. A mother writes, "In the beginning we knew our son couldn't help the things he was doing. There was still a lot we did not know. We were still reeling from the extreme sadness and fear of what was to come. Wanting to shield and protect him we always gave him the benefit of the doubt. I still believe that is very important. One day another important piece dawned on me. I was sitting in the living room with my son, who was then in fifth grade, and his older sister. He saw a dime on the sofa table and put it in his mouth. His sister was upset because it was her dime and it was now contaminated. He immediately began saying, 'I can't help it, I had to put it in my mouth.' That's when it came to me. I said to him, 'I know that was an obsession and you couldn't help it, but you're the one who needs to take care of it. You can either wash the dime or give her one of your dimes and you need to let it be her choice.' Of course, she wanted the fresh dime. When I told him this would help his relationship with his sister and others, he felt empowered. Here was something he could control and take charge of. So much of his life at that time seemed out of his hands and he often felt helpless. Learning to take care of things had a very positive impact on him. We were there to help him figure out ways to take care of things and as time went on he needed less and less help."

TALENTS

If your child has a special talent, do everything you can to encourage him. If you cannot identify one special thing that the child is exceptional at, make it your challenge to help her develop some interests. If things get rough for your child, she is going to need to have these interests, talents and hobbies to rely on. For example, as she becomes older and it becomes more clear that her maturity level is lagging behind her peers, she may go through a time where she does not have many friends to interact with.

TALKING LOUDLY

Talking loudly seems to be a symptom of ND. I haven't come up with anything that helps other than food. It does seem to work for a while! Most people can monitor their own internal states while simultaneously attending to what's going on around them – also called operational thought. From experience in working with hundreds of children, the Joshua Center staff believes that until children with ND turn 14-16 they don't develop operational thinking. They can only think of one thing at a time, so if they are listening to what is going on around them, they are unable to focus on how loud they are talking. For some children, loud voices can signal that a meltdown is coming.

See Nonverbal Learning Disabilities, Rage Stage, Rumbling Stage

TALKING NON-STOP

If the child has been diagnosed with ADHD, it is a given that he will talk all the time. Sometimes letting the child suck on hard candy or chew gum will give you a chance to "think." I remember when Josh was six or seven I offered him a quarter if he could be quiet for one minute. His comment, "Good try, mom."

Talking to oneself and repeating words may be a tic. Sometimes children tell me they work better when they talk to themselves. Social skills classes can help.

Giving the child frequent breaks can also help. Having an agreed-upon cue at school to let the child know he needs to be quiet may help, but don't expect it to last. The children often do not see the impact their talking has on others. These children should not be constantly punished for a symptom that is neurological.

See Repeating Actions and Words, Social Skills, Speech-Language Pathologist, Vocal Tics

TARDINESS

Many children with ND are either late for school or late to individual classes during the day. When that happens, it is necessary to evaluate what is going on. Are the symptoms, such as rituals and tics, so severe that they prevent the child from getting out the door at the right time in the morning? Are medications preventing the child from a good night's sleep? Is the child more of a night person? Some schools have allowed children with ND to start their day later because no matter how hard the school staff tried, the student was always late. It helps to schedule a class that the child shows a keen interest in during first hour. For children who are late to most of their classes, arrange to have someone observe them between classes to see what is taking them so long. Don't penalize a child with ND for being late to class; instead, develop a plan to help him get to class on time such as assigning a paraprofessional to either accompany him or be available during these times.

See Accommodations, Brainstorming

TARDIVE DYSKINESIA

Tardive dyskinesia may be a side effect of long-term use of neuroleptic drugs. Repetitive, involuntary, purposeless movements characterize tardive dyskinesia. Facial symptoms may include grimacing, tongue protrusion, lip smacking, puckering and pursing, and rapid eye blinking. Other symptoms may include rapid movements of the trunk, legs, arms and fingers. The fingers may look like the child is playing a guitar.

See Neuroleptics

TEACHER COMMUNICATION WITH STUDENT

The best thing a teacher can do for a child with ND is to build a solid relationship with her. If the student knows the teacher is supportive, it can make all the difference in the world. If a teacher is concerned about a symptom he has observed, in a private setting with the child ask him to clarify the observation.

For example, the teacher may say, "I am trying to learn about Tourette Syndrome (or whatever the diagnosis is). I observed you tapping the desk behind you several times, could you explain why you did that? Did you feel you had to do this? Was it something you couldn't hold back? Were you angry with the student sitting back there? Or were you just being ornery?" The children are usually very honest. If the problem was caused by chosen behavior, the standard consequence should apply. If it was caused by the disorder, teachers should be creative and brainstorm with the student ways to address it. For example, together they may come up with an agreed-upon cue to be used to signal that the child needs to take a break to reduce certain symptoms.

At the end of an IEP meeting it is helpful to invite the child to come and share the plan. When the child hears from the teachers personally that they are there to help, it often relieves a lot of anxiety. Sometimes it is the little things we do that make the biggest difference.

See Documentation, Individualized Education Program (IEP), Teacher Journal

TEACHER JOURNAL

When communicating with parents of children with ND, teachers need to provide documentation of changes seen in the child and observations they are concerned about. The Teacher Journal (see Appendix) was developed to help teachers make such documentations. It is important to include the date, the specific concern, the time of day that the concern is exhibited and any other observations that might be helpful to the parents and possibly the child's doctor. Teachers do not need to write a book. Merely record such things as: changes in symptoms, behavior or moods; attention to task; and incomplete assignments. Are symptoms interfering with learning or increasing? How is the child with ND interacting with peers? Is she having trouble keeping up? What's going well? Any changes when medications are changed or adjusted? (Doctors rely on this type of communication to guide them in medication management.) Teachers should keep the original documentation, but send the information to parents in the Weekly Report. The teacher's input is instrumental to the child's success.

See Communication Between School and Home, Documentation, Weekly Reports

TEAMWORK

It really does take a village to raise a child with ND. You need the support of the extended family, teachers, other parents of children with neurological disorders, counselors and the community at large. Many times the children are able to articulate ideas on how others can help them. It is important to identify the areas of support the child and family need and then determine who can best meet them. For instance, I know a family who calls a neighbor their child is close to when the child begins to rage. This individual helps to calm the child down better than anyone else. Perhaps a grandparent can take the child with ND for an afternoon or overnight so that the parents can spend some quality time with a sibling.

See Educating Neighbors, Educating School Staff, Extended Family, Support Groups

TEASING

Teasing is NOT a normal rite of passage. I knew a boy in fifth grade who went to his principal begging for help with a bully in his class. The principal tried to shrug it off until the child with ND convinced her that he didn't know how much longer he could restrain himself. No child should be harassed like that and for an educator to handle the situation in this manner is appalling. Because the symptoms of ND are often unnoticed by the casual observer, in this case the principal, many take the disability lightly. Parents should listen to their child in a nonjudgmental way and watch for behavior changes. It is important to see the problem from the child's point of view. Assure your child that reporting teasing and bullying is not tattling. Document each time your child shares an incident.

See Bullying, Documentation, Educating School Staff, Parent Journal, Principals

TEST MODIFICATIONS

For most children with ND test taking is challenging. To help them succeed, they should be consulted about strategies that work for them. Modifications may include: test taking in alternative locations with few distractions; alternate testing formats such as oral presentations, projects or take-home, open-book exams; extended time; taking only one test per day as exams often cause the children a great deal of test anxiety; avoiding fill-in-the-blank type tests because many children with ND have word retrieval problems; allowing the use of computers; or providing a scribe. Giving tests orally can also be very helpful because so many students with ND have processing problems. Have someone read the questions to the child and allow the child to dictate the answers. Assessment of the child's knowledge of the information will be more accurate that way. Most of the time I am against "timed" tests because they tend to increase children's anxiety, but some children with ND do fine with them, so talk to the child about how he is most comfortable with test taking.

See Timed Tests

TESTS, NATIONAL AND STATE

According to the Reauthorization of the Individuals with Disabilities Education Act and Section 504 of the Rehabilitation Act, students with ND are entitled to take national and state tests with modifications. Examinations, including the ACT and SAT assessment for college entrance, may be administered with modified time limits and given in private. Parents and students should talk to the school counselor for more information about national and state testing accommodations for ND.

See ACT and SAT Accommodations, Timed Tests

TESTS, ORAL VS. WRITTEN

Children with ND often have handwriting problems. If they concentrate on writing legibly, they frequently cannot complete a test because time runs out. In addition, the child may have neurological symptoms that interfere with written work, such as tics, having to write and rewrite words, counting letters or words as the student writes them, and erasing. When administering tests, teachers need to remember to accommodate such deficits. For example, oral testing allows the child to demonstrate knowledge without the stress of written performance.

See Handwriting, Test Modifications

THE "FEELING"

Many children report a discomforting state, which they term "the feeling." Some children experience "the feeling" as being charged with "electrical energy." Others have described it as a state of internal confusion or rage. One child responded that it felt as if the whole world was in fast-forward and he was in slow motion. However it is described, the universal condition is one of great discomfort and anxiety. Usually children develop some mechanism that helps "the feeling" go away. Some sleep, others display meltdowns, and for some "the feeling" only seems to go away when they induce self-pain, such as picking themselves or sticking themselves with paper clips. It is important to share this information with the child's doctor. Also, it is somewhat comforting to children to share this symptom. The family counselor can help the child develop strategies to deal with it.

See Counseling - Individual/Family

THIRST

Many of the medications that are prescribed to children with ND cause excessive thirst, so please don't deny these children a drink of water. Some children need to have a bottle of water on their desk at all times.

See Medication Side Effects

TICS

Tics are involuntary, rapid, repetitive motor or vocal movements of individual muscle groups. When tics are observed, it is a good idea to take the child to a doctor knowledgeable about neurological disorders. Tics can increase in frequency and severity and change over time. They may last for a few weeks to a month or disappear suddenly. New tics will replace old ones. Josh's tics changed about every three months. Tics often look or sound like nervous habits, allergy symptoms, or intentional misbehavior. If the tic can be tolerated, the best course of action is to ignore it. When the child indicates that the tics are interfering with his life, then medications may be considered.

See Complex Tics, Doctors, Documentation, Simple Tics, Tourette Syndrome, Waxing and Waning

TIC SUBSTITUTION

For many children with inappropriate vocal or motor tics, tic substitution is difficult because the tic often has to feel "just right" – sometimes it needs to be expressed in a certain way or involve a certain person. Tics have a tendency to go through a cycle. A specific tic may be gone in three months but others may last longer. For tics that are uncomfortable or inappropriate, it is worth having a counselor work with the child to see if one tic may be substituted for another. For example, children who have a spitting tic can often get the same relief from spitting into a tissue. Children who have inappropriate vocal tics can often change the word slightly to avoid offending others. With kicking tics the child will need to learn to perhaps tap his foot instead, and for kissing and licking tics, perhaps kiss or lick the back of his hand. Children who have inappropriate touching tics may need to brainstorm with parents and the counselor on alternate ways to touch.

See Inappropriate Tics, Tics, Touching Tics, Tourette Syndrome

TIC SUPPRESSION

Tics can be suppressed when the child is totally engaged in an activity, but they will have to be expressed at some point. Tic suppression in this manner is not usually stressful, but when the child is suppressing tics so others won't notice, it can be extremely stressful, and often the child is so engaged in suppressing the tics that he is not able to concentrate on anything else.

See Tics, Tourette Syndrome

TIMED TESTS

Children with ND often do poorly on timed tests. One girl became so anxious when having to take tests that had time limits that she marked any circle on the answer sheet just to get finished. She said it didn't help to remain in the general education classroom setting to take the tests even without time limits because her anxiety level was so high from knowing that her peers were finishing far ahead of her. For these reasons she needed to be in a quieter setting with fewer children. When she was allowed to take tests in the special education classroom, she was able to complete them in the time allotted even though her IEP gave her extra time. She also took her ACT test in the special education classroom. During her first few years of college she received testing accommodations but during her last two years she was able to stay in the class to take them.

See Individualized Education Program (IEP), Tests, National and State

TIME MANAGEMENT

Children with ND need to learn how to manage their time so they can have some control over their lives. Teach them to make lists and prioritize them. Teach them to break down large assignments and projects and have them work on only one part at a time. Hang a large calendar in the child's room to record dates of field trips, extracurricular activities and appointments as well as assignment due dates. Teach him how to alternate work tasks with play tasks to help prevent him from feeling overwhelmed. In school suggest that teachers write due dates in the upper right-hand corners of worksheets. Also, showing children with ND how to plan by including step-by-step details, such as the time it takes to collect supplies for a project, can be very helpful.

See Checklists, Homework, Stressless, Organizational Skills, Study Skills

TOUCHING TICS

Some children have no control of their tics, much as they would like to. When the recipient of a touching tic is uncomfortable, he needs to let the child with ND know, saying something like, "Please don't tic on me." Children who are recipients of tics should be encouraged to seek the help of an adult when needed. Many children who have a touching tic (usually older teens) may be able to ask if they can tic on another person before they "have to" touch them. Nobody should feel they have to accept a tic if they are uncomfortable with it.

A counselor who has experience with tic disorders may be able to work with the child to replace an intrusive tic with one that is not as invasive. For example, children who have severe intruding tics should teach themselves or let a counselor teach them how to tic only within an allowable space. I remember a child who could not keep his hands off a certain child at school. A circle was drawn on the floor to designate his space, and he was not allowed to go outside the circle without the teacher's permission. The circle was large enough to provide him some freedom for movement.

Many of the problems in school regarding tics involve touching tics in the halls. For younger children, this may be alleviated by giving the child something to carry with both hands, having her walk with both hands in her pockets or allowing her to walk in front of the line. In middle and high school the student may be released a little early or after the other students have passed.

See Breaks, Difficulty with Tics, Inappropriate Tics, Tic Substitution, Tourette Syndrome

TOURETTE SYNDROME (TS)

Tourette Syndrome (TS) is a neurological disorder characterized by involuntary, repetitive, rapid motor and vocal movements called tics. Doctors diagnose TS by observing the symptoms and evaluating the history of their onset. A medical test is not available to assist in the diagnosis. To receive a diagnosis of TS a person must exhibit both multiple motor tics and one or more vocal tics for a period of at least one year, not necessarily at the same time, and these tics must have occurred before age 21. TS is four times more prevalent in boys than girls and knows no racial, ethnic, or social boundaries. According to the *Diagnostic and Statistical Manual of Mental Disorders – 4th Edition, Text Revision* (DSM-IV-TR, 2002), the incidence of TS is about 4-5 per 10,000, but those of us at the Joshua Center believe it is far more widespread, perhaps one in several hundred. The natural course of TS varies from person to person. Although TS symptoms range from very mild to quite severe, the majority, of cases fall into the mild category. Most symptoms improve with maturity, and individuals can expect a normal life span. Tics periodically change in number, frequency, type and location. They can wax and wane in severity and sometimes disappear for weeks and months at a time, reemerging in the same or a different form. Tics, classified as simple and complex, range from simple eye blinking and throat clearing to more complex symptoms of jumping and uttering words out of context. Only 15 percent of individuals with TS have coprolalia, the uttering of obscenities and ethnic slurs. The first symptoms of TS are usually facial tics – commonly eye blinking (motor tic), while the initial vocal tic might be throat clearing or sniffing. The majority of people with TS are not significantly bothered by their tics or behavioral symptoms. In addition, most people with TS can exercise some control over their tics, but suppression may simply postpone more severe outbursts of symptoms. Eventually all tics must be expressed. While tension and stress can increase tic expression, concentration on an absorbing task may actually decrease the expression of tics. The majority of people with TS does not require medication, but may need simply to have information about the disorder. When tics or behavioral symptoms interfere with functioning, medications may be prescribed. A doctor knowledgeable about TS must monitor medications carefully. Therapy with a counselor knowledgeable about TS can often help.

See Complex Tics, Coprolalia, Counseling - Individual/Family, Motor Tics, Simple Tics, Tics, Touching Tics, Vocal Tics, Waxing and Waning

TRANSIENT TIC DISORDER

Many children experience a transient tic at some point during their childhood. The tics occur many times a day, nearly every day for at least 4 weeks, but for no longer than a year. They are not usually associated with behaviors or school problems.

See Changes in Tics, Tourette Syndrome

TRANSITION FROM ONE ACTIVITY OR LESSON TO ANOTHER

Children with ND often have great difficulty transitioning from one activity or lesson to another. This is true for home as well as school. Accept it, plan for it. Sometimes racing thoughts are involved. Allowing the child to complete the racing thought cycle is often necessary before starting something new. Developing routines for transitioning – whether bedtime, homework, changing classes, taking showers, etc. – will help. Remember to give only one-step directions. Sometimes setting time limits or using a timer helps.

Providing a structured routine both at school and at home requires planning. Parents should prepare their child for upcoming events, as unexpected changes in routine may cause children with ND to become anxious. It is helpful to inform the child of a change in a quiet setting so he can process the information without a lot of auditory and visual stimuli. The child may need some extra time to prepare. Respect this as part of the neurological disorder.

At the beginning of the year teachers should explain to the child with ND that they will help him as much as possible, but there may be unplanned events that could change the schedule. If the child starts to feel anxious, send him on an errand or to get a drink or send him to his designated home base to release. Prepare the child for the scheduled events such as fire drills, tornado drills, etc. It may be necessary to enlist the help of another supportive adult in the school to work with the child at these times.

In school, transition takes place many times a day with lessons, activities, classes, etc. At these times you may want to give the child as much notice as possible, with several warnings. Teachers might need to start with a 30-minute warning and work down to 5-minute and 1-minute warnings. Remember, the objective is a smooth transition. I have recommended to some teachers that they use timers to help remind the child of a change in routine.

Frequently, children in middle school have problems getting to class on time. Allow the child with ND to leave class a few minutes early to go to her next class. Consider having a responsible peer accompany her.

Combination locks frequently cause problems because fine-motor problems or OCD-like behaviors cause the child to have to go past a number a certain number of times or open and shut the locker a certain number of times before he can finally use the locker. For these reasons it is important that the school allows a complete set of books to remain at home during the school year. The IEP or 504 Plan can be written to make these accommodations.

One word of advice: Many children with ND cannot handle prior knowledge of upcoming events. They will obsess over an event and not be able to focus on anything else, driving you nuts until the actual event takes place. Teachers should talk to parents about how to handle upcoming events.

See Acceptance, Brainstorming, Home Base, Individualized Education Program (IEP), Locker Concerns, Racing Thoughts, Section 504 Plan, Structure and Routine

TRANSITION PLANNING FOR POST-HIGH SCHOOL

It is never too early to begin transition planning for a child with ND. Special education law (IDEA '98) states that school districts must start transition planning for children who have an IEP by age 14 or ninth grade, whichever comes first. The planning team will help parents and students identify skills needed for these plans to become a reality. Planning should encompass all areas of living, including postsecondary education, living arrangements, employment, as well as recreation and community life. While the schools should initiate and oversee transition planning, parents must be prepared to keep the process going to ensure their child receives all the services he is entitled to. Now is also the time to help your child to begin advocating for himself.

One of the goals of transition planning is to gain independence. A well-written transition plan should reflect the needs and wants of the student, listing every step the child needs to take in order to make good decisions, develop goals and carry out successful plans. In particular, the transition plan should address the following areas: social, time management and communication skills, employment goals, lifestyle preferences, educational needs, classroom accommodations, experiences needed, community involvement, and independent living skills needed. Transition planning is critical to post-high school success, so I encourage parents to stay on top of this planning phase.

See Advocacy, High School Diploma, Independence, Prevocational/Vocational Education

TRANSITION TO AND FROM RECESS

The last year I taught school before I quit to start the Joshua Center, I had an adorable little boy with ADHD in my class. I learned quickly to have him at the front of the line with me when lining up for recess so he would not get into trouble. Also I usually gave him something to carry outside, like the balls, so his hands couldn't get him into trouble. He was a talker, but I didn't punish him for it. Instead, I allowed him to tell me what his plans were for recess and had him report to me before going on to the next activity. I tried to keep fairly close to his chosen activity, but still far enough away to provide him some space. And, of course, I was watching all the children at the same time. When it got close to the time to go inside, I gave him 5-minute interval warnings. Two minutes before the bell rang, I sent him inside. If I didn't send him in first, he could not handle the commotion of all the other children lining up. It took him a little longer to "unwind," so this gave him a couple of extra minutes to do so.

See Transition From One Activity or Lesson to Another

TRICHOTILLOMANIA

Trichotillomania, a symptom of obsessive compulsive disorder, is the repetitive, uncontrollable pulling of one's body hair. Common symptoms are pulling scalp hair, eyelashes, and eyebrows. Treatments may include the use of medications and/or habit reversal training. Habit reversal is basically an approach by which individuals become more aware of behaviors and surroundings associated with hair pulling and develop an alternative competing response that replaces hair pulling.

See Obsessive Compulsive Disorder

TROUBLE AT SCHOOL

When a child returns home all upset over a situation that happened at school, parents must listen to everything he has to say without overreacting. If you are upset with what you hear, it is sometimes a good idea to talk to another parent before you confront the teacher or principal. Ask detailed questions and assure your child that you will talk to the school staff about his concerns, but do not rant and rave in front of him. Never talk negatively about school staff in front of your child. I have seen far too many parents jeopardize home-school relationships that way. Remember, children with ND often have processing problems and may not have all the information. Sit down with the school staff and brainstorm how to prevent future problems. Remember, no one person has all the answers.

See Brainstorming, Communication Between School and Home

TUNNEL VISION

Many children with ND seem to see things from only one perspective – their own! It's kind of like the "my way or no way" attitude, or stuck thinking. I have watched Josh over the years and while he seems to still be that way when he is focused on doing, or talking about, one particular thing, when he is not stuck (when the brain chemicals are calm) on anything in particular, he is able to see another perspective. I have watched this get better as he has matured into his late twenties. For example, when he was younger I was never able to interject a thought when he was talking to me, but now I can – and he is able to listen.

See Stuck Thinking

TV

Many children need to watch TV alone in their own rooms because they cannot filter out other sounds, including the slightest talking. For the rest of the family this is often a good solution too. Many times when Josh and I would be watching a program, he would constantly be asking, "Why?" or "What's going on?" or "What did they say?" so I would miss the next line and lose all continuity. It was not fun! For some children with ND watching the TV helps them fall asleep.

U

UNDERACHIEVING

If a child is failing or is underachieving, the adults need to change their teaching to help him be successful. I don't believe a child should have to try and change to fit the mold of the "typical" child. The adults involved with the child, including parents, teachers, school administrators and coaches, should brainstorm what they can do to help the child succeed. Does he need one-on-one help? Does he need assistance with organization? Does he need testing accommodations? A written document such as an IEP or a 504 Plan does not guarantee success. It's the adults who need to change the way they do things in order for the child to be successful.

UNDERSTANDING

Those of us who do not have ND will never truly understand what it is like. We can only try to learn as much as possible. For the most part I find that children with ND do a better job of explaining what is happening to them than anyone else. At about age 14 the kids are pretty good at describing how a tic feels, what racing thoughts are like, and explaining why they have to do things a certain way.

See Acceptance

UNDIVIDED ATTENTION

I'll never forget Josh standing with me at the top of our split-entry stairs trying to get my undivided attention. He was trying to get me to understand something and I was trying to intervene and offer some motherly advice. Josh finally stopped and said, "Mom, I'm just trying to get something out in a certain way. I need to get the thought out without interruption." I think of this conversation often. I now look very interested when he starts talking in this way. Knowing that he has to get something said in a certain way, I keep my mouth shut. Even when he calls me from out of town, I often must remember to let him talk, to finish his thoughts. Mom has come a long way!

At school this is very hard. I suggest the teacher and child privately discuss strategies to handle such situations. Sometimes teachers can help by sending the child on an errand or they can have an agreement with the child to give him a few minutes of undivided attention at some time during the class.

See Acceptance

UNKNOWN

Almost inevitably your child will do things for reasons that are unknown to you. One parent shares the story of not understanding why her teenage son was not using the skin care products she had purchased to wash his face. When he told her he did not have time, her response was, "But it only takes a couple of minutes." He then went on to explain that it takes 20 minutes for him to wash his face because of his OCD – he would have to make sure he had an even amount of the skin care product all over his face. He would rather put up with the blemishes than go through that each day. Listen to your children. There is often more going on than you realize.

See Obsessive Compulsive Disorder

UNSTRUCTURED VS. STRUCTURED ENVIRONMENTS

Children with ND do so much better with structure and routine. For example, a disorganized classroom can overload children and cause them to engage in inappropriate behaviors. It takes planning to set up a tightly structured environment, but the time spent planning is worth it. If possible, a student with ND should be matched with a teacher who has a structured classroom, but who is also flexible enough to make adjustments for the child. Some unstructured times to be especially concerned about include passing periods in hallways, lunchroom, and sometimes the physical education locker room.

See Being Flexible, Classroom Environment, Lunchroom Concerns, Physical Education (PE), Structure and Routine

V

VACATIONS, IMPORTANCE OF

When my children were young, the three of us rarely took trips – we couldn't afford them, and Josh was so involved with baseball that I felt it was important for him to be at all his games. We did manage a few trips to visit my brother a couple of hours away. I wish now that Josh had more life experiences such as vacations to draw upon. This is one area I see missing from many children with ND who are now young adults. Because they often have poor social skills and poor peer relations, they are left out of opportunities to learn the appropriate skills. It starts with recess, extracurricular activities, etc. All of these experiences are built over a lifetime as we learn to relate to new experiences. My suggestion is to not eliminate these opportunities for life skills, but to plunge ahead. But plan every minute. Even day trips or one-night overnight trip can be beneficial.

See Planes, Trains and Automobiles

VIDEOTAPING

One of the best ways to communicate to a doctor or a parent a true picture of a concern – whether it is a tic, obsession or a behavior – is to "catch" it on video. For example, parents may bring a video clip of a child's movements so the doctor can have a clear understanding of what is taking place. The same is true of symptoms in school. If a teacher or parent does not have knowledge of the disorders, sharing a clip of the symptoms with someone who does allows the adults to brainstorm strategies. I suggest placing the video camera in a strategic location days before actually doing the taping. In some classrooms teachers have placed it on top of a filing cabinet. Videotaping is not to be used for any type of punishment; it is to be used to gather information to help the child. Over the years I have seen many parents and teachers have difficulty describing a concern.

VISUAL DISTRACTIONS

The fewer visual distractions the better for children with ND. This is especially true when doing homework or trying to go to sleep. Having the child face a blank wall when doing homework or trying to fall asleep may help. If a child has difficulty getting to sleep at night, the parents should take a look at his room to see if it is too stimulating. Soft, warm colors may help him relax more. Too many posters on the walls might be too stimulating. Too many visual and auditory distractions can also cause behaviors to erupt in public places. This includes grocery stores and department stores where even the bright lights bother a lot of these kids.

See Auditory Processing Disorder, Classroom Environment, Shopping, Visual Distractions, Visual Processing Disorders

VISUAL PROCESSING DISORDERS

A visual processing disorder impacts the child's ability to make sense of information taken in through the eyes. This has nothing to do with the child's vision. It has everything to do with how visual information is interpreted or processed by the brain. The printed page, including worksheets and textbooks, can be overwhelming. Consequently, I often suggest books on tape or a reader to read textbooks to the child. In math it helps if teachers copy one math problem per paper. In general, the lines on writing paper can be darkened and worksheets can be modified to limit the amount of information that is given per sheet.

See Academic Assessment, Learning Disabilities

VISUAL SUPPORTS

Visual supports provide children with ND a tool to understand their world. Pictures help them process information. These tools help children follow rules, complete directions, sequence events, transition from one activity to another, and make choices. As with social situations, children with ND often need something visual to get a clear picture of what you are trying to teach. Giving simple visual directions can often help them "stop and think" when doing an assignment. With a three-step direction for a worksheet, a visual might include a

Step 1:
Write name
on paper.

Step 2:
Cover
everything
except the
first problem.

Step 3:
Raise hand
when first problem
is finished.

sheet with Step 1. Write name on paper (with a picture of the child); Step 2. Cover everything except the first problem (with picture of covered sheet or blanket to represent "to cover"); and Step 3. Raise hand when first problem is finished (picture of a hand). To help you create visual supports for your child, I highly recommend the book *Making Visual Supports Work in the Home and Community: Strategies for Individuals with Autism and Asperger Syndrome* (Savner & Myles, 2000).

VOCAL TICS

Simple vocal tics may include clearing the throat, noisy breathing, sniffing, humming, burping, coughing, puffing expirations, spitting, laughing, making "pft" noises and snorting, just to name a few. Complex vocal tics may include repeating words and phrases, stuttering, barely audible muttering to loud talking, repeating one's own words, repeating others' words or statements, talking to oneself and making animal sounds. Most of the time it is best to ignore these tics. When they are very loud and occurring frequently, medication may help. Sucking on cough drops, hard candy or chewing gum helps some children. Asking a child to stop his tics will only prolong and intensify the expression later. Although they can often be suppressed for a short while, the tics must be expressed eventually. Suppressing tics requires concentration and increases anxiety, and when a child expresses tics that have been suppressed for a long time, he often must express more of them and for a longer period.

See Difficulty with Tics, Motor Tics, Tics, Tourette Syndrome

VO-TECH CLASS

Vo-tech class should be treated like all other classes. The vo-tech instructors should receive the same training and information as all the student's other teachers about special concerns. If the child has an IEP or 504 Plan, it is important for the vo-tech instructor to attend all meetings and communicate with parents on a weekly basis the same as regular education teachers.

See Communication Between School and Home, Educating School Staff, Individualized Education Program (IEP), Prevocational/Vocational Education, Section 504 Plan, Weekly Reports

W

WALK AND DON'T TALK

This is by far the most important thing I have learned from Josh and all the other children I have worked with. It can be the most difficult for parents, siblings, teachers, principals and the list goes on. The idea is that when the child is having a difficult time or is in the middle of the rumbling stage of the rage cycle, try the "walk and don't talk" strategy. During the rumbling stage, the child is not thinking logically. So anything that is said will be wrong or misinterpreted. Let the child talk and don't react; don't overreact. He must be able to say whatever he wants without fear of discipline. In the meantime, the adult must be quiet, calm, just listen and not be confrontational. Rational discussion will take place after the child has calmed down. Once the adults have mastered this skill, they are home free – almost!

See Rage Stage, Recovery Stage, Rumbling Stage

WANDERING

I frequently suggest that children with ND be allowed to take a break and go for a walk to release excess energy, interfering symptoms and anxiety. However, they should know their boundaries and be held accountable to them. Breaks may need to be supervised. To ensure the child returns from the break at the agreed-upon time, I suggest the child wear a watch. If the child does not comply, there should be a consequence. Most of the time the children comply with the rules. When allowing a child to walk, the entire staff needs to know it is an accommodation. In this way they can help monitor the child and not overreact when they see him in the halls.

See Behavior Plan, Consequences, Drives, Educating School Staff, Home Base

WAXING AND WANING

Tics change in frequency, severity and location. The term "waxing" refers to the increase and worsening of tics, while "waning" refers to a decrease of symptoms. The cycle repeats itself. This characteristic of tics can be difficult to understand. It seems that Josh would get a new tic about every three months. I used to think they could not get worse, but they did. Some of them can be very annoying – like non-stop sniffing! Sometimes they may disappear for a while, but sooner or later another one shows up.

See Changes in Tics, Tics, Tourette Syndrome

WEBSITES

Many helpful websites address ND. Several of them have online newsletters. See *Internet Resources* in the Appendix.

WEEKLY REPORTS

Weekly Reports are the one of the most important accommodations the school can provide to ensure a child's success. A Weekly Report is a written document that teachers complete each Friday and send home to parents. It includes the date, subject and class instructor and all pertinent information relating to the child's ability to succeed in class. Teachers need to share not only interfering symptoms and concerns but also any incomplete assignments. By receiving the form each Friday, the parents will have the weekend to address the concerns. Weekly communication is crucial to the success of children with ND. If children are left to fail due to uncommunicated information, it is very difficult for them to catch up. (See the Weekly Report worksheet in the Appendix.)

See Communication Between School and Home

WORDS, THE POWER OF

The words we use have a profound effect on how children with ND view themselves. If a child is described as a "troublemaker," for example, there is a good chance he will integrate the word and its meaning into his sense of self and will indeed be a "troublemaker." Further, when adults use the word "troublemaker" to describe a child, others will adopt this view and unconsciously assume this is a part of the child's identity. Adults and other children will look for and assume there will be trouble.

Working with children who have been diagnosed with labels or words such as TS or ADHD creates a challenge for all of us to look beyond those labels. These words become a part of the vocabulary used by the teachers, doctors, counselors, parents and the children, themselves. This unconsciously brings into thought the idea that there is something "wrong" with the child or that the child is the "problem." When the adults and the social world that surrounds the child refer to him as "the one with Tourettes" or "my ADD kid," he integrates the words and their meanings into his being. He sees himself as abnormal. Each person is much more than what can be seen from the outside. Every child has many things he can do well. The language of strengths focuses on the abilities versus the disabilities. Learn to use phrases that build self-esteem, such as "Thank you for helping" or "That was a very nice thing you did." Look for strengths and build your conversations around them. Children with ND see themselves the same way we do ... as resilient, talented, special, capable ... and they will become all those things!

WORKING INDEPENDENTLY

Most children with ND have attention problems, so expecting them to work independently is often unrealistic. Don't just assume they are lazy. To show children with ND how to become independent, you might try pairing them with another child who is "disorder free," responsible and compatible. Creating a visual organization sheet to accompany assignments, chores, etc., can help the child complete the steps needed to accomplish a task. Modeling each step and having the child role-play the demonstration also helps.

See Getting Started, Visual Supports

WORKING IN SMALL GROUPS

From my experience children with ND often do better in small groups. Large groups tend to be overwhelming and often cause them to shut down, because

they are too stimulating auditorily and visually, thus interfering with the child's ability to process information. Also, many children with ND experience a sense of claustrophobia or panic in larger groups. With fewer distractions in a small-group setting it is easier for the child to get started on an activity, assignment or job. Pairing a child with ND with a child who is supportive and interacts appropriately with others will allow the child with ND to learn how to work in a cooperative situation. However, even when placed in good cooperative situations, the child will still require close monitoring and instruction.

See Auditory Processing Disorder, Claustrophobia, Getting Started, Panic Attacks, Shutting Down, Visual Processing Disorders

WORKSHEETS

Many children with ND experience anxiety over having to complete worksheets. Just trying to start a worksheet can be a nightmare. Often worksheets are too visually stimulating. As a result, some students rush through a worksheet writing down anything that comes to mind just to get it done. Others simply write their name on the paper and don't even begin to work on it, choosing not to complete it rather than attempting and risking failure.

Breaking down assignments into smaller segments by covering up everything but one word, problem, etc., will help. Also, teachers should model each part of the worksheet before assigning it. Students who need more than simple modifications might benefit from giving worksheet information orally to demonstrate their knowledge more accurately. When worksheets are sent home, it is a big help to parents when the required date of completion is written in the upper right-hand corner.

See Accommodations, Modifications, Self-Esteem, Shutting Down

WORRYING

Parents of children with ND often worry about their child's future, sometimes the next hour! Parents must educate themselves by reading and attending support group meetings and conferences when available, as other parents who are experiencing similar concerns often have the best information. Identifying a good doctor, counselor and education staff also helps reduce worry. Parents must have someone they can call when things get rough.

It is not just parents who worry. Some children with ND worry that something bad is going to happen or that something won't be perfect. If the child is worrying excessively, I suggest getting her counseling and calling the child's doctor. Parents should assure the child that they will always be there for her and give her opportunities to ask questions. Talking through a specific concern with pictures, puppets, or reading books together can help. One boy who obsessed a great deal was able to give his obsessive thought a name and destroy it that way. Sometimes medication can help tremendously.

See Counseling - Individual/Family, Parenting a Child with ND, Obsessive Compulsive Disorder, Support Groups

WRITTEN EXPRESSION

The writing skills of children with ND are often below what is typical considering the student's age, intelligence and education, and these skills can cause problems with academic success. Written expression is a complex task that requires integrating several things at once. For example, the child has to remember her ideas while trying to pay attention, spell correctly, organize her thoughts, attend to details and write down the letters correctly. Symptoms associated with a written expression disorder include inadequately formed sentences and paragraphs; excessive grammatical, punctuation and spelling errors; and extremely poor handwriting. These symptoms often show up around fourth or fifth grade when writing requirements increase.

Children need to practice writing stories, but it should be fun. If you start out slowly, they will feel success. I love the "What is it?" stories. The children describe in three sentences something "red and under my bed" or "something in the refrigerator," etc. When the story is complete, they read the sentences aloud and have their peers guess what it is. Peers are given three chances to guess. This exercise can be done both at home and at school. The key is to make writing fun. Adults can help with grammar, spelling, etc. Using computers also helps tremendously by giving children with written expression problems a chance to express their creativity without all the stress of handwriting. In addition, they can use spell check and grammar check.

See Computers, Handwriting

WRITTEN WORK, REFUSAL TO DO

When the teacher relates that the child refuses to write, parents should not automatically assume it is a chosen behavior. It is difficult for many children with ND to write for extended periods of time due to fine-motor deficits and interfering symptoms. In addition, instructions on worksheets and textbooks can be so overwhelming that the kids shut down. They don't know how to explain it, but they know they cannot get started. To help, teachers and parents need to break the page down into manageable steps, covering all but one sentence at a time; read the directions with the child; check for understanding, telling the student to raise her hand after completing the first step so it can be checked before going on to the next one; and give frequent breaks. If the assignment involves writing a paper or a story, allow students to use the computer or to dictate to someone.

See Enabling, Getting Started, Handwriting, Shutting Down, Tests, Oral vs. Written

X

XOXOXO

Hugs and kisses will go a long way in helping your child with ND! Sending encouraging cards through the mail or placing notes in their room will give children encouragement to keep plugging along.

Y

YOUNG ADULTS

When I think about children with ND becoming young adults, I think about the baggage some have traveled with. According to Gary Gaffney, M.D., a child psychiatrist from the University of Iowa Hospitals, children with ND have an emotional maturity that lags behind their peers and does not catch up until about 25. It sometimes makes for a difficult trip. The parents' job is not over just because their child has received a high school diploma. Parents are just getting started. While they don't have to worry about incomplete assignments, teachers who don't understand or IEPs any longer, they still have to be there for support and to teach life skills that were missed along the way.

If I could start over, I would develop an Individual Life Skills Plan. There were so many skills Josh did not learn because he did not have the opportunities to participate in the same life experiences as his peers. Don't expect individuals with ND to be able to enter adulthood without support. I'm not talking about money as much as I'm talking about encouragement. Develop a plan. Is your child planning on attending college? Is your child mature enough to attend college away from home? Is there a junior college closeby? Whatever you do, don't throw 18 years away by sending them out on their own without support. In a few more years you will be able to sit back and enjoy the progress your young adult has made, knowing that you were there during those post-high school years to offer support. Keep the lines of communication open, encourage independence, and expect your child to show some responsibility. But be there when she needs direction. It's worked for me!

See Career Development, College Accommodations

Z

Zzzzzzzzzzzzzzzzzzzzzzzzzzzzzzzzz.........

What you think you'll get to do when your children are raised!

Resources

Professional Organizations

American Speech Language Hearing Association
10801 Rockville Pike
Rockville, MD 20852
www.asha.org

The Asperger Syndrome Coalition of the U.S.
P. O. Box 351268
Jacksonville, FL 32235-1268
www.asperger.org

The Autism Society of America
7910 Woodmont Ave.
Bethesda, MD 20814-3067
www.autism-society.org

**Children and Adults with Attention
Deficit Hyperactivity Disorder (CHADD)**
8181 Professional Place, Suite 201
Landover, MD 20785
www.CHADD.org

Council for Exceptional Children (CEC)
1110 North Glebe Road, Suite 300
Arlington, VA 22201
www.cec.sped.org

Council for Learning Disabilities
P.O. Box 40303
Overland Park, KS 66204
www.cldinternational.org

Division for Children with Learning Disabilities
c/o The Council for Exceptional Children (CEC)
1110 North Glebe Road, Suite 300
Arlington, VA 22201
www.cec.sped.org

Learning Disabilities Association of America
4156 Library Rd.
Pittsburgh, PA 15234-1349
www.ldanatl.org

Maap Services, Inc.
(More Advanced Individuals with Autism,
Asperger's Syndrome, and Pervasive Developmental Disorder)
P. O. Box 524
Crown Point, IN 46307
www.maapservices.org

**The National Information Center for Children
and Youth with Disabilities (NICHCY)**
P. O. Box 1492
Washington, DC 20013
www.nichcy.org

The Obsessive-Compulsive Foundation, Inc.
337 Notch Hill Rd.
North Branford, CT 06471
www.ocfoundation.org

Tourette Syndrome Association, Inc.
42-40 Bell Blvd.
Bayside, NY 11361
www.tsa-usa.org

Tourette Syndrome Foundation of Canada
194 Jarvis Street, Suite 206
Toronto, Ontario, M5B 2B7
www.tourette.ca

Books on Tape

Recording for the Blind & Dyslexic
20 Roszel Road
Princeton, NJ 08540
www.rfbd.org

Talking Tapes/Textbooks on Tape
16 Sunnen Drive, Suite 162
St. Louis, MO 63143-3800
www.talkingtapes.org

Internet Resources

www.abcteach.com
This site lists resources for teaching the basics along with theme teaching, games and puzzles, report writing, shapes, comprehension, and fun activities. Of interest to both educators and parents.

www.act.org
The website has information for ACT assessment.

www.alphasmart.com
The AlphaSmart is a portable and affordable computer companion (Macintosh and PC compatible) that is a great tool for children to use in the classroom.

www.AmicusforChildren.org
This website educates, supports, and empowers the families of children. The mission of Amicus is to unite caring professionals with families in need, to work in partnership in order to enhance the lives of the children who depend on us. Amicus has a key interest in assisting, educating, and providing resources for the parents/guardians of children with special needs.

www.aplusmath.com
This website has math facts flashcards.

www.aspennj.org
This website belongs to a regionally based organization located in New Jersey, ASPEN (AS Educational Network). They provide educational, supportive, and advocacy services to families and individuals affected with AS and other related disorders.

www.ccoder.com/GainingFace
This very informative website provides a free demo of a computer program designed to help students learn to recognize facial expressions

www.collegeboard.org
This website provides information for SAT assessment.

www.difflearn.com
The Different Roads to Learning website provides information on books/manuals, flashcards, sequencing, scheduling products, software, videos, puzzles, handwriting, sorting and manipulating and step-by-step books. There are also over 20 related links for educators and families.

www.do2learn.com
This website provides free picture cards and print activities for autism and LD; almost the same as the Mayer-Johnson pictures but a lot cheaper. This is a great site for teachers and parents to get ideas on fun activities.

www.ebuddies.org

e-Buddies is an email friendship program for people with and without cognitive disabilities (age 12 & up). They match people on age, gender, and common interests.

www.ed.gov/pubs/parents/Math/funmath.html

This is a good website to help your child learn math.

www.funbrain.com

This website makes learning math fun with a baseball theme (choose +, -, x and divide).

www.gigglepotz.com

This site provides teachers with free resources for the classroom. Check out the special education and autism section!

www.gomilpitas.com/homeschooling

THE starting place for exploring homeschooling resources.

www.harcourtschool.com

This website teaches multiplication using a mystery theme.

www.help4teachers.com

Dr. Kathie Nunley's website for educators bears the same name as her book, *The Layered Curriculum*. It is designed to help teachers focus on student-centered education, even when their classroom is full of diverse learners. The site offers a free newsletter, free samples of lesson plans, free articles and instructions on building a "layered curriculum," free access to research and strategies, a Parents Corner and a Discussion Forum.

www.home-school.com

Site for the latest homeschooling news, articles, organizations and Homeschooling Mall.

www.home2school.com

This is a wonderful interactive site where parents can refresh their memory on long-forgotten skills and find reading books for their children by grade level and interest.

www.hwtears.com

Handwriting Without Tears is a great handwriting program developed by Jan Olson, an occupational therapist.

www.latitudes.org

This site provides information about alternative treatments of neurological disorders, including a newsletter.

www.LDOnLine
An excellent website on learning disabilities for parents, teachers and other professionals with an email newsletter.

www.math.com
This website provides help for more advanced math.

www.nays.org
The National Alliance For Youth Sports is a non-profit organization dedicated to improving out-of-school sports for youth.

www.nichy.org/pubs/newsdig/nd20txt.html
This website responds to the informational needs of parents who have just learned that their child has special needs, as well as those who have lived with this reality for some time but who need new information or renewed support.

www.npin.org
The National Parent Information Network is a website that works in coordination with the ERIC System and ERIC Clearing Houses to provide parents and educators with easy access to a variety of information and helpful links pertaining to disabilities and special education. Discussion lists and virtual libraries can be accessed for free. This site is easy to manipulate, and full of beneficial information and helpful links.

www.pbis.org/english/index.html
This great site maintained by the federal government contains links to information sources, training sites, and products. For teachers and parents.

www.pbskids.org
This is a wonderful interactive site for children with lots of education help.

www.readingrockets.org
This is a great site to get help for young, struggling readers.

www.reedmartin.com
Reed Martin, J.D., is an attorney who specializes in special education law and is recognized as one of the nation's leading experts in this area.

www.schwablearning.org
A wonderful website on learning disabilities with a great email newsletter.

www.sensoryresources.com
Lots of information on conferences that would benefit parents and professionals working with students with autism and sensory needs.

www.senteacher.org/main/print.php

If you use worksheets, this website will be a great resource for you. There are lots of printable worksheets, flashcards, handwriting exercises, etc.

www.skill.org.uk/I-sheets/Isheet17.html

This page offers suggestions for support services and accommodations for students with various disabilities in higher education.

www.sinetwork.org

The Sensory Integration Resource Center provides resources for families, educators, therapists, physicians and kids. The site provides sensory integration research information, FAQs, resources and related books and media.

www.strategicstudies.com/ssboard/index.html

This site is a bulletin board where educators share ideas on working with students with Asperger Syndrome and other disabilities.

www.surfnetkids.com

Surfing the Net with Kids provides multiplication drills and worksheets.

www.syvum.com

This site offers wonderful math activities for kids of all ages.

www.tourettesyndrome.net

This website of Dr. Leslie Packer, a psychologist and parent of a child with neurological disorders, includes information on Tourette Syndrome, attention deficit hyperactivity disorder, obsessive compulsive disorder, rage attacks and mood disorders. There are many links.

www.udel.edu/bkirby/asperger

This informative website is a great starting point for those who are interested in Asperger Syndrome.

www.weightedwearables.com

Weighted Wearables offers quality weighted adaptive products that facilitate proprioceptive feedback, increase postural stability and attention span, and organize arousal levels for learning. Products include weighted vests, pillows, blankets and and more. These attractive-looking products are suited for children and adults with various sensory integrative needs.

www.wrightslaw.com

An excellent website for information about advocacy for children with disabilities, including articles, cases, and newsletters about special education law.

References

American Psychiatric Association. (2002). *Diagnostic and statistical manual of mental disorders* (4th ed., text revision.). Washington, DC: American Psychiatric Press.

Bieber, J. (Producer). (1994). *How difficult can this be? The F.A.T. city workshop with Richard Lavoie.* Washington, DC: Public Broadcasting Service.

Bieber, J. (Producer). (1994). *Learning disabilities and discipline: When the chips are down with Richard Lavoie.* Washington, DC: Public Broadcasting Service.

Bieber, J. (Producer). (1994). *Learning disabilities and social skills with Richard Lavoie: Last one picked … first one picked on.* Washington, DC: Public Broadcasting Service.

Dornbush, M. O., & Pruitt, S. K. (1995). *Teaching the tiger: A handbook for individuals involved in education of students with attention deficit disorders, tourette syndrome or obsessive compulsive disorder.* Duarte, CA: Hope Press.

Engh, F. (1999). *Why Johnny hates sports.* Garden City Park, NY: Avery Publishing Group.

Fisher, T. (1998). Oppositional behavior of TJ. *Tourette Digest, 1*(4), 7-8

Graff, J. M. (2001). "Cat … male … brown … 17." *Joshua Center Digest, 4*(4), 33. Grandview, MO.

Grandin, T. (1995). *Thinking in pictures and other reports from my life with autism.* New York: Doubleday.

Gray, C. (2002). *The new social story book: Illustrated edition.* Arlington, TX: Future Horizons, Inc.

Gray, C., & Garand, J. (1993). Social stories: Improving responses of students with autism with accurate social information. *Focus on Autistic Behavior, 8*(1), 1-10.

Greene, R. W. (2001). *The explosive child: A new approach to understanding and parenting easily frustrated, chronically inflexible children.* New York: Quill.

Myles, B. S., & Adreon, D. (2001). *Asperger syndrome and adolescence: Practical solutions for school success.* Shawnee Mission, KS: Autism Asperger Publishing Company.

Myles, B. S., & Simpson, R. L. (2001). Understanding the hidden curriculum: An essential social skill for children and youth with Asperger Syndrome. *Intervention in School and Clinic, 36*(5), 279-286.

Myles, B. S., & Southwick, J. (1999). *Asperger syndrome and difficult moments: Practical solutions for tantrums, rage, and meltdowns.* Shawnee Mission, KS: Autism Asperger Publishing Company.

Perry, P., & Gaffney, G. (1996). *Pediatric psychopharmacology: Tourette's syndrome, pediatric child psychiatry case studies and tests.* Clinical Psychopharmacology Seminar, Iowa City Hospitals, Iowa City, IA.

Savner, J. L., & Myles, B. S. (1999). *Making visual supports work in the home and community: Strategies for individuals with autism and asperger syndrome.* Shawnee Mission, KS: Autism Asperger Publishing Company.

Tobin, G. (1998). The power of our words. *Tourette Digest, 1*(4), 28-29. Grandview, MO.

Wood, R. (1999). *Dysinhibition syndrome: How to handle anger and rage in your child and spouse.* Duarte, CA: Hope Press.

Recommended Reading

In addition to the sources cited in the book and listed in the reference list above, parents and educators alike may find the following books and materials of interest.

Barkley, R. A., & Benton, C. M. (1998). *Your defiant child: 8 steps to better behavior.* New York: Guilford Press.

Budman, C., & Bruun, R. D. (1999). *Tourette Syndrome and repeated anger generated episodes.* New York: Tourette Syndrome Association.

Chansky, T. E. (2000). *Freeing your child from obsessive-compulsive disorder.* New York: Crown Publ.

Comings, D. E. (1990). *Tourette Syndrome and human behavior.* Duarte, CA: Hope Press.

Debbaudt, D. (2001). *Autism, advocates, and law enforcement professionals.* London: Jessica Kingsley Publ.

Durand, V. M. (1997). *Sleep better!: A guide to improving sleep for children with special needs.* Baltimore: Paul H. Brookes Publ.

Foa, E. B., & Kozak, M. J. (1996). Psychological treatment for obsessive-compulsive disorder. In M. R. Mavissakalian & R. F. Prien (Eds.), *Long-term treatments of anxiety disorders* (pp. 285-309). Washington, DC: American Psychiatric Press, Inc.

Gagnon, E., & Myles, B. S. (1999). *This is asperger syndrome.* Shawnee Mission, KS: Autism Asperger Publishing Company.

Ives, M. (2001). *What is asperger syndrome, and how will it affect me? – A guide for young people.* Shawnee Mission, KS: Autism Asperger Publishing Company.

Kranowitz, C. S. (1998). *The out-of-sync child: Recognizing and coping with sensory integration dysfunction.* New York: Perigee.

Merrell, K. W. (2001). *Helping students overcome depression and anxiety: A practical guide.* New York: Guilford.

Myles, B. S., Cook, T., Miller, N., Rinner, L., & Robbins, L. A. (2000). *Asperger syndrome and sensory issues: Practical solutions for making sense of the world.* Shawnee Mission, KS: Autism Asperger Publishing Company.

Savner, J. L., & Myles, B. S. (2000). *Visual supports in the classroom.* Shawnee Mission, KS: Autism Asperger Publishing Company. [Video]

Appendix

Worksheets

Helpful Information
for My Activity Leader

For leaders working with children with Tourette Syndrome, Asperger Syndrome, attention deficit hyperactivity disorder and obsessive compulsive disorder

Name:_____ **(I have the following)**
TS - AS - ADHD - OCD

Person at activity I am comfortable talking to when needed:
_____

Basic Information About Tourette Syndrome, Asperger Syndrome, Obsessive Compulsive Disorder and Attention Deficit Disorder

What Is Tourette Syndrome?

Tourette Syndrome (TS) is a neurological disorder characterized by tics - involuntary, rapid, sudden movements or vocalizations that occur repeatedly in the same way. To receive a diagnosis of TS, a person must exhibit both multiple motor and one or more vocal tics in a period of a year, not necessarily at the same time. Tics usually start in the head area, as young as 3 or 4 years old, and progress down the torso as one matures. Tics are experienced as irresistible and (as the urge to sneeze) eventually must be expressed. Tics increase as a result of tension or stress, and decrease with relaxation or concentration on an absorbing task.

What Is Asperger Syndrome?

Asperger Syndrome (AS) is a neurological disorder. Characteristics of AS are: above-average intelligence, concrete thinking, inflexibility, communication deficits, problem-solving concerns, social deficits, behavioral issues, repetitive and stereotyped patterns of behavior and interests.

What Is Obsessive Compulsive Disorder?

Obsessions consist of repetitive unwanted or bothersome thoughts. Compulsions and ritualistic behaviors involve thinking that something must be done over and over and/or in a certain way.

What Is Attention Deficit Hyperactivity Disorder?

Attention deficit hyperactivity disorder with or without hyperactivity (ADHD) occurs in about 90% of persons with TS. Indications of ADHD may include: difficulty with concentration; failing to finish what is started; not listening; being easily distracted; often acting before thinking; shifting constantly from one activity to another; needing a great deal of supervision; general fidgeting; and difficulty with impulse control.

MEDICATIONS I TAKE AND HOW THEY MAKE ME FEEL

Medication _____ **I feel** _____

Medication _____ **I feel** _____

SYMPTOMS THAT INTERFERE WITH EXTRACURRICULAR ACTIVITIES AND SUGGESTIONS FOR DEALING WITH THEM

BEHAVIOR MANAGEMENT STRATEGIES

Additional Information

Helpful Information
for My Art Teacher
For art teachers having students with Tourette Syndrome, Asperger Syndrome, attention deficit hyperactivity disorder and obsessive compulsive disorder

Name:_____ **(I have the following)**
TS - AS - ADHD - OCD

Person at school I am comfortable talking to when needed:
_____

Basic Information About Tourette Syndrome, Asperger Syndrome, Obsessive Compulsive Disorder and Attention Deficit Disorder

What Is Tourette Syndrome?
Tourette Syndrome (TS) is a neurological disorder characterized by tics - involuntary, rapid, sudden movements or vocalizations that occur repeatedly in the same way. To receive a diagnosis of TS, a person must exhibit both multiple motor and one or more vocal tics in a period of a year, not necessarily at the same time. Tics usually start in the head area, as young as 3 or 4 years old, and progress down the torso as one matures. Tics are experienced as irresistible and (as the urge to sneeze) eventually must be expressed. Tics increase as a result of tension or stress, and decrease with relaxation or concentration on an absorbing task.

What Is Asperger Syndrome?
Asperger Syndrome (AS) is a neurological disorder. Characteristics of AS are: above-average intelligence, concrete thinking, inflexibility, communication deficits, problem-solving concerns, social deficits, behavioral issues, repetitive and stereotyped patterns of behavior and interests.

What Is Obsessive Compulsive Disorder?
Obsessions consist of repetitive unwanted or bothersome thoughts. Compulsions and ritualistic behaviors involving thinking that something must be done over and over and/or in a certain way.

What Is Attention Deficit Hyperactivity Disorder?
Attention deficit hyperactivity disorder with or without hyperactivity (ADHD) occurs in about 90% of persons with TS. Indications of ADHD may include: difficulty with concentration; failing to finish what is started; not listening; being easily distracted; often acting before thinking; shifting constantly from one activity to another; needing a great deal of supervision; general fidgeting; and difficulty with impulse control.

MEDICATIONS I TAKE AND HOW THEY MAKE ME FEEL

Medication _____ **I feel** _____

Medication _____ **I feel** _____

SYMPTOMS THAT INTERFERE WITH ART AND SUGGESTIONS FOR DEALING WITH THEM

BEHAVIOR MANAGEMENT STRATEGIES

Additional Information

Helpful Information for the Assistant Principal

For assistant principals working with students with Tourette Syndrome, Asperger Syndrome, attention deficit hyperactivity disorder and obsessive compulsive disorder

---

Name:_____

(I have the following)

TS - AS - ADHD - OCD

Person at school I am comfortable talking to when needed:

_____

Basic Information About Tourette Syndrome, Asperger Syndrome, Obsessive Compulsive Disorder and Attention Deficit Disorder

---

What Is Tourette Syndrome?

Tourette Syndrome (TS) is a neurological disorder characterized by tics - involuntary, rapid, sudden movements or vocalizations that occur repeatedly in the same way. To receive a diagnosis of TS, a person must exhibit both multiple motor and one or more vocal tics in a period of a year, not necessarily at the same time. Tics usually start in the head area, as young as 3 or 4 years old, and progress down the torso as one matures. Tics are experienced as irresistible and (as the urge to sneeze) eventually must be expressed. Tics increase as a result of tension or stress, and decrease with relaxation or concentration on an absorbing task.

What Is Asperger Syndrome?

Asperger Syndrome (AS) is a neurological disorder. Characteristics of AS are: above-average intelligence, concrete thinking, inflexibility, communication deficits, problem-solving concerns, social deficits, behavioral issues, repetitive and stereotyped patterns of behavior and interests.

What Is Obsessive Compulsive Disorder?

Obsessions consist of repetitive unwanted or bothersome thoughts. Compulsions and ritualistic behaviors involve thinking that something must be done over and over and/or in a certain way.

What Is Attention Deficit Hyperactivity Disorder?

Attention deficit hyperactivity disorder with or without hyperactivity (ADHD) occurs in about 90% of persons with TS. Indications of ADHD may include: difficulty with concentration; failing to finish what is started; not listening; being easily distracted; often acting before thinking; shifting constantly from one activity to another; needing a great deal of supervision; general fidgeting; and difficulty with impulse control.

<u>MEDICATIONS I TAKE AND HOW THEY MAKE ME FEEL</u>

Medication _____ **I feel** _____

Medication _____ **I feel** _____

SYMPTOMS THAT I AM HAVING NOW
AND THINGS THAT YOU CAN DO TO HELP ME

My ADHD causes me to

If I am getting really anxious, fidgety or out of control, here are some strategies you can use to help me gain control:

Information for the Bus Driver

For all bus drivers transporting students with Tourette Syndrome, Asperger Syndrome, attention deficit hyperactivity disorder and obsessive compulsive disorder

School:_____Bus #_____

Student_____ (circle applicable diagnosis)
TS - AS - ADHD - OCD

Address Home_____ Phone #_____

Parent/Guardian_____ Work #_____

Basic Information About Tourette Syndrome, Asperger Syndrome, Obsessive Compulsive Disorder and Attention Deficit Disorder

What Is Tourette Syndrome?

Tourette Syndrome (TS) is a neurological disorder characterized by tics — involuntary, rapid, sudden movements or vocalizations that occur repeatedly in the same way. To receive a diagnosis of TS, a person must exhibit both multiple motor and one or more vocal tics in a period of a year, not necessarily at the same time. Tics usually start in the head area, as young as 3 or 4 years old, and progress down the torso as one matures. Tics are experienced as irresistible and (as the urge to sneeze) eventually must be expressed. Tics increase as a result of tension or stress, and decrease with relaxation or concentration on an absorbing task.

What Is Asperger Syndrome?

Asperger Syndrome (AS) is a neurological disorder. Characteristics of AS are: above-average intelligence, concrete thinking, inflexibility, communication deficits, problem-solving concerns, social deficits, behavioral issues, repetitive and stereotyped patterns of behavior and interests.

What Is Obsessive Compulsive Disorder?

Obsessions consist of repetitive unwanted or bothersome thoughts. Compulsions and ritualistic behaviors involve thinking that something must be done over and over and/or in a certain way.

What Is Attention Deficit Hyperactivity Disorder?

Attention deficit hyperactivity disorder with or without hyperactivity (ADHD) occurs in about 90% of persons with TS. Indications of ADHD may include: difficulty with concentration; failing to finish what is started; not listening; being easily distracted; often acting before thinking; shifting constantly from one activity to another; needing a great deal of supervision; general fidgeting; and difficulty with impulse control.

SYMPTOMS THAT MAY INTERFERE WITH BUS BEHAVIOR AND SUGGESTIONS FOR DEALING WITH THEM

1. Impulsivity, loud ticcing, inappropriate touching of others. Seat the student close to the front, possibly placing in seat by himself, leaving seats in front and behind student vacant or place a responsible student in seat in front of and behind student with these disorders.

2. Clear rules, and consequences for breaking those rules, should be established on day 1. Other students should be disciplined for teasing students with disabilities. Enforcement of those rules will guarantee your year will be successful.

3. Students with these disorders ALWAYS react without thinking. This is neurological so don't overreact to everything they say.

4. The more support the student receives from the bus driver, the better the ride will be for all.

5. Before overreacting to student's behavior, contact school counselor, teacher, or designated person for clarification. You cannot be expected to know everything about these disorders. Documentation of questionable behavior will help others to address concerns.

6. If possible, arrange bus route to pick up and deliver student with these disorders early in the ride.

Additional information specific to this child:

Helpful Information
for My Coach

For coaches working with kids with Tourette Syndrome, Asperger Syndrome, attention deficit hyperactivity disorder and obsessive compulsive disorder

Name:_____ **(I have the following)**
TS - AS - ADHD - OCD

Person at games/practice I am comfortable talking to when needed:
_____

Basic Information About Tourette Syndrome, Asperger Syndrome, Obsessive Compulsive Disorder and Attention Deficit Disorder

What Is Tourette Syndrome?

Tourette Syndrome (TS) is a neurological disorder characterized by tics - involuntary, rapid, sudden movements or vocalizations that occur repeatedly in the same way. To receive a diagnosis of TS, a person must exhibit both multiple motor and one or more vocal tics in a period of a year, not necessarily at the same time. Tics usually start in the head area, as young as 3 or 4 years old, and progress down the torso as one matures. Tics are experienced as irresistible and (as the urge to sneeze) eventually must be expressed. Tics increase as a result of tension or stress, and decrease with relaxation or concentration on an absorbing task.

What Is Asperger Syndrome?

Asperger Syndrome (AS) is a neurological disorder. Characteristics of AS are: above-average intelligence, concrete thinking, inflexibility, communication deficits, problem-solving concerns, social deficits, behavioral issues, repetitive and stereotyped patterns of behavior and interests.

What Is Obsessive Compulsive Disorder?

Obsessions consist of repetitive unwanted or bothersome thoughts. Compulsions and ritualistic behaviors involve thinking that something must be done over and over and/or in a certain way.

What Is Attention Deficit Hyperactivity Disorder?

Attention deficit hyperactivity disorder with or without hyperactivity (ADHD) occurs in about 90% of persons with TS. Indications of ADHD may include: difficulty with concentration; failing to finish what is started; not listening; being easily distracted; often acting before thinking; shifting constantly from one activity to another; needing a great deal of supervision; general fidgeting; and difficulty with impulse control.

MEDICATIONS I TAKE AND HOW THEY MAKE ME FEEL

Medication _____ **I feel** _____

Medication _____ **I feel** _____

SYMPTOMS THAT MAY INTERFERE WITH SPORTS ACTIVITIES AND SUGGESTIONS FOR DEALING WITH THEM

BEHAVIOR MANAGEMENT STRATEGIES

Additional Information

CONCERNS FOR THE STUDENT WITH TOURETTE SYNDROME, ASPERGER SYNDROME, ADHD, & OCD

The Concerns Checklist is to be completed by parents and all individuals working with the child with neurological disorders. It is to be shared with the child's parents, doctor, counselor and teachers or other disorder-specific expert to assess problems areas and strategize solutions.

Student_____ Date_____

Individual completing checklist _____

WRITTEN WORK

____Rarely completes written assignments
____Spends too much time on board work
____Handwriting consistently poor
____Inconsistent handwriting
____Very slow with written work
____Frequently able to start assignment but shuts down after a few minutes
____Unable to perform tasks that require both visual and motor skills
____Unable to follow a three-step direction
____Messy papers due to frequent erasing
____Does not get assignments written down
____Turns assignments in late or not at all
____Refuses to do written work

CLASSROOM BEHAVIOR

____Compared to other students in class, he/she is behind academically
____Fails to abide by behavior modifications
____Refuses to try suggested modifications
____Constantly out of seat
____Constantly talking to a neighbor
____Constantly talking to himself
____Frequently out of seat to touch another student
____Frequently tapping pencil
____Frequently dropping something on floor, distracting others
____Asks to leave classroom more than 3 times each hour
____Amount of time student is out of classroom interferes with his/her learning
____Fails to return to class even with an agreed-upon time limit
____Problems in restroom during allowed break
____Problems in hall during student's break
____Frequently interrupts teacher/another student
____Frequently blurts out inappropriate responses
____Frequently blurts out racial slurs
____Frequently blurts out obscenities
____Obscenities or racial slurs directed at one person

____Frequently touches staff/peers inappropriately
____Frequently complains of headaches
____Inappropriate touching directed at one individual
____Frequently requests to leave after entering classroom
____Frequently fidgets with items in/on desk
____Easily distracted by noise in hall
____Easily distracted by auditory stimuli in classroom
____Easily distracted by visual stimuli
____Has difficulty working in small-group setting
____Frequently argues with teachers
____Frequently complains of stomachaches
____Frequently forgets to take meds at school
____Frequently asks to use restroom
____Consistently speaks with a loud tone
____"In face" when talking to another person
____Frequently falls asleep in class
____Frequently requests to go to nurse's office
____Falls asleep in nurse's office
____Frequently insists on calling home—Give time_____
____A certain time each day seems to be more difficult—Give time_____
____Frequently losing classroom privileges for not following rules
____Moods cycle throughout day
____Frequently loses recess for incomplete assignments
____Rushes through tests
____Inconsistent grades
____Appears to have an "I don't care" attitude
____Frequently says "That's stupid" to a teacher direction
____Frequently says "I don't have to"
____Frequently lies
____Appears to "shut down" at certain times
____Intrudes on others
____"Acts before thinks" behavior
____Frequently appears to be manipulating a situation or person to get attention

____Perseverates on a subject or thought, unable to let go
____Does opposite of what he/she has been told
____Frequently becomes emotional
____Has difficulty listening and writing concurrently
____Frequently appears to be "daydreaming"
____Difficulty staying focused on task at hand
____Has to say something until it's "just right"
____Has difficulty accepting help from adults/peers
____Even when provided a quiet setting, continues to have difficulty: tics, attention, written work
____Appears claustrophobic
____Appears to panic (time:_____ ; location:_____)
____Frequently sent to office for inappropriate behavior (time:_____; class:_____)

ORGANIZATION

____Frequently "forgets" to bring books to class
____Notebook is completely disorganized
____Frequently is out of supplies
____Frequently "forgets" assignment in locker

TRANSITION CONCERNS

____Frequently late to class
____Has difficulty transitioning from one lesson to another
____Has difficulty stopping an activity when instructed to do so
____Has difficulty changing classes
____Uses inappropriate touching
____Uses inappropriate language
____Uses inappropriate conversations
____Engages in frequent full body tics
____Spends too much time at locker
____Spends too much time in restroom
____Frequently fights with other students
____Constantly talking
____Frequently strays from group

RECESS CONCERNS

____Has difficulty interacting appropriately
____Plays by himself
____Wanders
____Has difficulty keeping hands off other students
____Very aggressive
____Shows disrespect for recess monitor
____Cries frequently
____Complains of not feeling well
____Uses inappropriate language

LUNCH CONCERNS

____Other students intolerant of him/her
____Eats inappropriately
____Spends too much time eating
____Refuses to eat
____Unable to eat in allotted time due to high incidence of tics
____Frequently takes other students' food
____Frequently teased by other students
____Unable to finish due to many distractions

CONCERNS AT HOME

____Frequently has great difficulty sleeping at night
____Frequently unable to read without repeating words
____Frequently unable to write without motor tics with hands
____Unable to complete homework in time allotted
____Frequently unable to sustain attention for more than a few minutes at a time
____Cries frequently
____Frequently distressed over school situations
____Irritable
____Frequently has difficulty changing tasks
____Mood frequently cycles throughout day
____Recently began having complex full body tics
____Unable to participate in community activities due to severity of tics
____Frequently arrives home without assignments written down
____Assignments are not legibile
____Frequently arrives at home without necessary materials, including books
____Frequently, after spending hours studying for a test, still unable to answer questions when quizzed
____Unable to follow a one-step direction
____Requires both verbal and visual clues with homework
____Frequently suffers from "school phobia"
____Has difficulty handling a small room
____Frequently able to start an assignment, but unable to complete because of an increase in tics
____Has "explosive tics" returning home from school due to tic suppression while at school
____Requires full assistance doing homework
____Frequently spends a great deal of time fulfilling obsessive-compulsive behaviors
____Collects useless items
____Has excessive concerns (dirt, germs, responsible for something terrible happening)

Information for the Dentist

Information about individuals with Tourette Syndrome, Asperger Syndrome, attention deficit hyperactivity disorder and obsessive compulsive disorder

*Name:*_____

*Primary Care Physician:*_____*Phone #:*_____

TS - AS - ADHD - OCD

Parent/Guardian:_____ Work #_____

Basic Information About Tourette Syndrome, Asperger Syndrome, Obsessive Compulsive Disorder and Attention Deficit Disorder

What Is Tourette Syndrome?

Tourette Syndrome (TS) is a neurological disorder characterized by tics - involuntary, rapid, sudden movements or vocalizations that occur repeatedly in the same way. To receive a diagnosis of TS, a person must exhibit both multiple motor and one or more vocal tics in a period of a year, not necessarily at the same time. Tics usually start in the head area, as young as 3 or 4 years old, and progress down the torso as one matures. Tics are experienced as irresistible and (as the urge to sneeze) eventually must be expressed. Tics increase as a result of tension or stress, and decrease with relaxation or concentration on an absorbing task.

What Is Asperger Syndrome?

Asperger Syndrome (AS) is a neurological disorder. Characteristics of AS are: above-average intelligence, concrete thinking, inflexibility, communication deficits, problem-solving concerns, social deficits, behavioral issues, repetitive and stereotyped patterns of behavior and interests.

What Is Obsessive Compulsive Disorder?

Obsessions consist of repetitive unwanted or bothersome thoughts. Compulsions and ritualistic behaviors involve thinking that something must be done over and over and/or in a certain way.

What Is Attention Deficit Hyperactivity Disorder?

Attention deficit hyperactivity disorder with or without hyperactivity (ADHD) occurs in about 90% of persons with TS. Indications of ADHD may include: difficulty with concentration; failing to finish what is started; not listening; being easily distracted; often acting before thinking; shifting constantly from one activity to another; needing a great deal of supervision; general fidgeting; and difficulty with impulse control.

SYMPTOMS THAT MAY INTERFERE WITH DENTAL PROCEDURES
SUGGESTIONS FOR DEALING WITH THEM

1. Impulsivity, loud ticcing, inappropriate touching of others. Sometimes individuals with neurological disorders need to release tics, compulsions, or other symptoms. They may need frequent breaks to release symptoms.

2. Don't overreact to a child with ND.

3. The more support the individual receives from the dental staff, the better the visit will be.

4. It is important that all medications considered for the patient be approved by the individual's primary physician.

5. A limited amount of time in the waiting room will keep the stress level of the patient to a minimum.

Medications I am presently taking

Additional information specific to this patient

Helpful Information
for My Elementary Teacher
For elementary teachers having students with Tourette Syndrome, Asperger Syndrome, attention deficit hyperactivity disorder and obsessive compulsive disorder

Name:_____   **(I have the following)**
TS - AS - ADHD - OCD

Person at school I am comfortable talking to when needed:
_____

Helpful Strategies

Opening:

Lunch:

Recess:

Dismissal:

Transition: (activities, hallway, lessons)

MEDICATIONS I TAKE AND HOW THEY MAKE ME FEEL

Medication _____ I feel _____

Medication _____ I feel _____

SYMPTOMS THAT I AM HAVING NOW
AND THINGS YOU CAN DO TO HELP ME

My ADHD causes me to

If I am getting really anxious, fidgety or out of control, here are some strategies you can use to help me gain control:

Helpful Information for My Family

Name:_____ | **(I have the following)**
 TS - AS - ADHD - OCD

Person in my family I am comfortable talking to when needed:

_____

Basic Information About Tourette Syndrome, Asperger Syndrome, Obsessive Compulsive Disorder and Attention Deficit Disorder

What Is Tourette Syndrome?

Tourette Syndrome (TS) is a neurological disorder characterized by tics - involuntary, rapid, sudden movements or vocalizations that occur repeatedly in the same way. To receive a diagnosis of TS, a person must exhibit both multiple motor and one or more vocal tics in a period of a year, not necessarily at the same time. Tics usually start in the head area, as young as 3 or 4 years old, and progress down the torso as one matures. Tics are experienced as irresistible and (as the urge to sneeze) eventually must be expressed. Tics increase as a result of tension or stress, and decrease with relaxation or concentration on an absorbing task.

What Is Asperger Syndrome?

Asperger Syndrome (AS) is a neurological disorder. Characteristics of AS are: above-average intelligence, concrete thinking, inflexibility, communication deficits, problem-solving concerns, social deficits, behavioral issues, repetitive and stereotyped patterns of behavior and interests.

What Is Obsessive Compulsive Disorder?

Obsessions consist of repetitive unwanted or bothersome thoughts. Compulsions and ritualistic behaviors involve thinking that something must be done over and over and/or in a certain way.

What Is Attention Deficit Hyperactivity Disorder?

Attention deficit hyperactivity disorder with or without hyperactivity (ADHD) occurs in about 90% of persons with TS. Indications of ADHD may include: difficulty with concentration; failing to finish what is started; not listening; being easily distracted; often acting before thinking; shifting constantly from one activity to another; needing a great deal of supervision; general fidgeting; and difficulty with impulse control.

MEDICATIONS I TAKE AND HOW THEY MAKE ME FEEL

Medication _____ **I feel** _____

Medication _____ **I feel** _____

MY SYMPTOMS THAT I AM HAVING NOW
AND THINGS THAT YOU CAN DO TO HELP ME

My ADHD causes me to

If I am getting really anxious, fidgety or out of control, here are some strategies you can use to help me gain control:

Helpful Information
for My Friends at Church

For leaders working with children with Tourette Syndrome, Asperger Syndrome, attention deficit hyperactivity disorder and obsessive compulsive disorder

Name:_____

(I have the following)
TS - AS - ADHD - OCD

Person at church I am comfortable talking to when needed:

_____

Basic Information About Tourette Syndrome, Asperger Syndrome, Obsessive Compulsive Disorder and Attention Deficit Disorder

What Is Tourette Syndrome?

Tourette Syndrome (TS) is a neurological disorder characterized by tics - involuntary, rapid, sudden movements or vocalizations that occur repeatedly in the same way. To receive a diagnosis of TS, a person must exhibit both multiple motor and one or more vocal tics in a period of a year, not necessarily at the same time. Tics usually start in the head area, as young as 3 or 4 years old, and progress down the torso as one matures. Tics are experienced as irresistible and (as the urge to sneeze) eventually must be expressed. Tics increase as a result of tension or stress, and decrease with relaxation or concentration on an absorbing task.

What Is Asperger Syndrome?

Asperger Syndrome (AS) is a neurological disorder. Characteristics of AS are: above-average intelligence, concrete thinking, inflexibility, communication deficits, problem-solving concerns, social deficits, behavioral issues, repetitive and stereotyped patterns of behavior and interests.

What Is Obsessive Compulsive Disorder?

Obsessions consist of repetitive unwanted or bothersome thoughts. Compulsions and ritualistic behaviors involving thinking that something must be done over and over and/or in a certain way.

What Is Attention Deficit Hyperactivity Disorder?

Attention deficit hyperactivity disorder with or without hyperactivity (ADHD) occurs in about 90% of persons with TS. Indications of ADHD may include: difficulty with concentration; failing to finish what is started; not listening; being easily distracted; often acting before thinking; shifting constantly from one activity to another; needing a great deal of supervision; general fidgeting; and difficulty with impulse control.

<u>MEDICATIONS I TAKE AND HOW THEY MAKE ME FEEL</u>

Medication _____ **I feel** _____

Medication _____ **I feel** _____

SYMPTOMS THAT INTERFERE WITH CHURCH ACTIVITIES AND SUGGESTIONS FOR DEALING WITH THEM

BEHAVIOR MANAGEMENT STRATEGIES

Additional Information

Helpful Information
for My High School Teacher

For high school teachers working with students with Tourette Syndrome, Asperger Syndrome, attention deficit hyperactivity disorder and obsessive compulsive disorder

Name:_____

(I have the following)
TS - AS - ADHD - OCD

Person at school I am comfortable talking to when needed:

_____

Basic Information About Tourette Syndrome, Asperger Syndrome, Obsessive Compulsive Disorder and Attention Deficit Disorder

What Is Tourette Syndrome?

Tourette Syndrome (TS) is a neurological disorder characterized by tics - involuntary, rapid, sudden movements or vocalizations that occur repeatedly in the same way. To receive a diagnosis of TS, a person must exhibit both multiple motor and one or more vocal tics in a period of a year, not necessarily at the same time. Tics usually start in the head area, as young as 3 or 4 years old, and progress down the torso as one matures. Tics are experienced as irresistible and (as the urge to sneeze) eventually must be expressed. Tics increase as a result of tension or stress, and decrease with relaxation or concentration on an absorbing task.

What Is Asperger Syndrome?

Asperger Syndrome (AS) is a neurological disorder. Characteristics of AS are: above-average intelligence, concrete thinking, inflexibility, communication deficits, problem-solving concerns, social deficits, behavioral issues, repetitive and stereotyped patterns of behavior and interests.

What Is Obsessive Compulsive Disorder?

Obsessions consist of repetitive unwanted or bothersome thoughts. Compulsions and ritualistic behaviors involve a person thinking that something must be done over and over and/or in a certain way.

What Is Attention Deficit Hyperactivity Disorder?

Attention deficit hyperactivity disorder with or without hyperactivity (ADHD) occurs in about 90% of persons with TS. Indications of ADHD may include: difficulty with concentration; failing to finish what is started; not listening; being easily distracted; often acting before thinking; shifting constantly from one activity to another; needing a great deal of supervision; general fidgeting; and difficulty with impulse control.

MEDICATIONS I TAKE AND HOW THEY MAKE ME FEEL

Medication _____ I feel _____

Medication _____ I feel _____

SYMPTOMS THAT INTERFERE WITH THIS CLASS AND SUGGESTIONS FOR DEALING WITH THEM

BEHAVIOR MANAGEMENT STRATEGIES

Additional Information

🍎 Class Schedule for Homework Backup Plan

Semester/Year _____School Address_____ School Phone _____

Homework Information Line _____School Contact Person _____

1st Hour/Subject   _____Day _____ Teacher _____ Room _____Plan____

2nd Hour/Subject   _____Day _____ Teacher _____ Room _____Plan____

3rd Hour/Subject   _____Day _____ Teacher _____ Room _____Plan____

4th Hour/Subject   _____Day _____ Teacher _____ Room _____Plan____

5th Hour/Subject   _____Day _____ Teacher _____ Room _____Plan____

6th Hour/Subject   _____Day _____ Teacher _____ Room _____Plan____

7th Hour/Subject   _____Day _____ Teacher _____ Room _____Plan____

8th Hour/Subject   _____Day _____ Teacher _____ Room _____Plan____

After School Activities   _____

_____

Classmates

1st Hour/Subject   _____Name_____ Address_____ Phone_____

2nd Hour/Subject   _____Name_____ Address_____ Phone_____

3rd Hour/Subject   _____Name_____ Address_____ Phone_____

4th Hour/Subject   _____Name_____ Address_____ Phone_____

5th Hour/Subject   _____Name_____ Address_____ Phone_____

6th Hour/Subject   _____Name_____ Address_____ Phone_____

7th Hour/Subject   _____Name_____ Address_____ Phone_____

8th Hour/Subject   _____Name_____ Address_____ Phone_____

Medication Changes

For school nurses responsible for students with Tourette Syndrome, Asperger Syndrome, attention deficit hyperactivity disorder and obsessive compulsive disorder

Student:_____ **(I have the following)**
TS - AS - ADHD - OCD

Name of Medication: **Medication prescribed for:**

Medication: _____**TS - AS - ADHD - OCD**
               Taken at school   yes_____   no_____

Possible side effects: _____

_____

Medication: _____**TS - AS - ADHD - OCD**
               Taken at school   yes_____   no_____

Possible side effects: _____

_____

Medication: _____**TS - AS - ADHD - OCD**
               Taken at school   yes_____   no_____

Possible side effects: _____

_____

Medications

For school nurses responsible for students with Tourette Syndrome, Asperger Syndrome, attention deficit hyperactivity disorder and obsessive compulsive disorder

Student:_____
(I have the following)
TS - AS - ADHD - OCD

Name of Medication: **Medication prescribed for:**

Medication: _____**TS - AS - ADHD - OCD**
          Taken at school   yes_____   no_____

*Possible side effects:*_____

_____

Medication: _____**TS - AS - ADHD - OCD**
          Taken at school   yes_____   no_____

*Possible side effects:*_____

_____

Medication: _____**TS - AS - ADHD - OCD**
          Taken at school   yes_____   no_____

*Possible side effects:*_____

_____

Helpful Information
for My Middle School Teacher

For middle school teachers working with students with Tourette Syndrome, Asperger Syndrome, attention deficit hyperactivity disorder and obsessive compulsive disorder

---

Name:_____

(I have the following)
TS - AS - ADHD - OCD

Person at school I am comfortable talking to when needed:

_____

Basic Information About Tourette Syndrome, Asperger Syndrome, Obsessive Compulsive Disorder and Attention Deficit Disorder

---

What Is Tourette Syndrome?

Tourette Syndrome (TS) is a neurological disorder characterized by tics - involuntary, rapid, sudden movements or vocalizations that occur repeatedly in the same way. To receive a diagnosis of TS, a person must exhibit both multiple motor and one or more vocal tics in a period of a year, not necessarily at the same time. Tics usually start in the head area, as young as 3 or 4 years old, and progress down the torso as one matures. Tics are experienced as irresistible and (as the urge to sneeze) eventually must be expressed. Tics increase as a result of tension or stress, and decrease with relaxation or concentration on an absorbing task.

What Is Asperger Syndrome?

Asperger Syndrome (AS) is a neurological disorder. Characteristics of AS are: above-average intelligence, concrete thinking, inflexibility, communication deficits, problem-solving concerns, social deficits, behavioral issues, repetitive and stereotyped patterns of behavior and interests.

What Is Obsessive Compulsive Disorder?

Obsessions consist of repetitive unwanted or bothersome thoughts. Compulsions and ritualistic behaviors involve thinking that something must be done over and over and/or in a certain way.

What Is Attention Deficit Hyperactivity Disorder?

Attention deficit hyperactivity disorder with or without hyperactivity (ADHD) occurs in about 90% of persons with TS. Indications of ADHD may include: difficulty with concentration; failing to finish what is started; not listening; being easily distracted; often acting before thinking; shifting constantly from one activity to another; needing a great deal of supervision; general fidgeting; and difficulty with impulse control.

MEDICATIONS I TAKE AND HOW THEY MAKE ME FEEL

Medication _____ **I feel** _____

Medication _____ **I feel** _____

SYMPTOMS THAT INTERFERE WITH THIS CLASS AND SUGGESTIONS FOR DEALING WITH THEM

BEHAVIOR MANAGEMENT STRATEGIES

Additional Information

MODIFICATIONS FOR STUDENTS WITH TOURETTE SYNDROME, ASPERGER SYNDROME, ATTENTION DEFICIT HYPERACTIVITY DISORDER AND OBSESSIVE COMPULSIVE DISORDER

A diagnosis of TS, AS, ADHD and OCD requires that some modifications be made in the classroom setting due to the neurological origin of the disorders. The following is a listing of commonly used modifications for students with ND.

MATERIAL PRESENTATION

Break assignments into segments of shorter tasks

Introduce one concept at a time, with as few words as possible, checking for understanding and having student repeat the directions for a task

Provide a model of end-product of directions (completed math problem, finished quiz, etc.)

Introduce an overview of long-term assignments (written and verbal) so student knows what will be expected and when it will be due—make a visual for classroom and a checklist for student

Break long-term assignments into small, sequential steps, with daily monitoring and frequent grading

Alert student's attention to key points with such phrases as: "This is important. Listen carefully."

Number and sequence the steps in a task

Explain learning expectations to student before beginning lesson

Allow student to obtain and retain information by utilizing a tape recorder, computer, calculator and/or dictation

Highlight important concepts to be learned in text

Provide outlines, study guides and copies of overhead presentations to reduce frustration with visual-motor integration and encourage concentration on lesson

Shorten assignments based on mastery of key concepts

Provide incentives for beginning and completing material

Check that all homework assignments are written down correctly, providing assistance when needed

Separate assignment sheets from behavior reports

Provide written and verbal directions with visuals when possible

Give alternative assignments rather than long written assignments

Modify expectations based on student's needs

CLASSROOM ENVIRONMENT

Provide use of study carrel if student is comfortable with it—do not use as punishment

Seat student in area free from distractions, allowing ample space for motor tics

Allow student's input on seating arrangement

Eliminate all unnecessary materials from student's desk to reduce distractions

Use checklists to help student get organized

Provide opportunities for movement

Keep an extra supply of pencils, books, etc., in classroom

Provide a duplicate set of books to remain at home during the school year

Many persons with neurological disorders have feelings of claustrophobia, so small rooms may cause more ticcing and stress

Allow student frequent breaks from classroom to release symptoms, frustration and excess energy (drinks, restroom trips, errand runner, etc.)

Provide a quiet place for student when tics are severe

Have an agreed-upon cue for student to leave classroom

Develop individualized rules for student, if necessary, to accommodate severe impairments

Provide flexible classroom structure according to student's needs

Provide a quiet classroom during intense learning times

Reduce visual distractions in classroom

Seat student away from windows or doorway

TIME MANAGEMENT/TRANSITIONS

Alert student with several reminders, several minutes apart, before changing from one activity to another (classroom changes, lesson changes, recess, lunch, etc.)

Provide additional time to complete a task

Allow extra time to turn in homework without penalty

Since many children with TS and OCD expend a large amount of energy suppressing tics at school, a reduction in the amount of homework by as much as 50% may be necessary

Reduce amount of work (odd numbers vs. all problems)

Space short work periods with breaks

Alternate quiet and active times, allowing for transition time

MATH

Allow use of calculator without penalty

Require fewer problems to attain passing grade

Provide a table of math facts for reference

Provide fewer problems on worksheet

Read and explain story problems, breaking into smaller steps

Use graph paper or notebook paper turned sideways to keep problems in columns

Use computer when at all possible

Allow student to dictate to a paraprofessionals or another student

Allow student to "talk" through problems

Use quality software for homework to remediate deficits

MODIFICATIONS (cont.)

GRADING AND TESTS

Provide a quiet setting for test taking, allowing test to be read to student if necessary and allowing for oral responses

Exempt (or accommodate) student from district/state tests

Divide tests into smaller sections

Grade spelling separately from content

Use typed tests, not cursive

Allow as much time as needed to take tests

Provide movement and breaks during tests

Provide partial grade based on individual progress or effort

Permit student to retake tests until passed

Mark only correct answers

Permit student to rework missed problems for better grade

Change percentage of work required for passing grade

Avoid all timed tests

BEHAVIOR

Avoid confrontations during transition times by allowing student to leave a couple of minutes early or to walk with teacher at front of line (place a responsible student behind this student)

Seat a responsible peer next to student to help stay on task

Modify school rules that may discriminate against a child with a neurological disorder

Amend consequences for rule violations (reward forgetful student for remembering to bring pencils to class, rather than punishing the failure to remember)

Develop an individualized behavior plan for the classroom that is consistent with the student's ability. Most classroom behavior modification plans were not intended for use with students with attention problems, neurological disorders or learning disabilities

Arrange for student to voluntarily leave classroom and report to designated "safe place" when under high stress

Ignore behaviors that are not seriously disruptive

Develop interventions for behaviors that are annoying but not deliberate (i.e., provide a small piece of foam rubber for desk of student who continually taps a pencil on desktop)

Be aware of behavioral changes that relate to medication or length of school day; modify expectations

Develop a system or code word to let a student know when behavior is not appropriate

Do not place students in ISS because it's too restraining

READING

Allow student to sit in comfortable position

Allow student to use marker to follow along

Allow recorded textbooks or reader

Allow student to read aloud to himself, to another student or into a tape recorder

Have student read comprehension questions before reading passage

Encourage student to use headphones to block out auditory distractions

Break reading assignments into smaller segments

Allow parent to read to student at home when symptoms interfere

ORGANIZATION

Establish daily routine and attempt to maintain it

Make clear rules and be consistent enforcing them

Provide notebook with organized sections such as: zip-lock bag for assignments due, extra pencils and supplies; class schedule; assignment sheet; color-coded dividers to match books; three-hole punch to fit notebook

Avoid cluttered, crowded worksheets by utilizing techniques such as:

> BLOCKING-Block assignments into smaller segments
> CUTTING/FOLDING-Cut or fold worksheets into fourths, sixths or eighths and place one problem in each square
> COLOR-CODING, HIGHLIGHTING OR UNDERLINING-Emphasize important information in which the student needs to focus

Hand out written assignments with expected dates of completion written on one corner

Use visual checklist for homework completion

HANDWRITING

Provide a computer for student

Use worksheets that require minimal writing

Provide a designated notetaker, a copy of another student's notes or teacher's notes (do not expect a poor notetaker or a student with no friends to make arrangements with another student for notes)

When using videotapes, provide printed outline

Provide printed copy of assignments or blackboard directions

Do not return handwritten work to be recopied

Avoid large amounts of written work (both in class and homework)

Encourage student to select method of writing that is most comfortable (cursive or manuscript)

Set realistic and mutually agreed-upon expectations for neatness

Let student type, record or give answers orally instead of writing

Avoid pressures of speed and accuracy

Reduce amounts of board work copying and textbook copying; provide student with written information

Grade on content, not handwriting

Allow parent to write for student at home

Helpful Information
for My Music Teacher
For music teachers having students with Tourette Syndrome, Asperger Syndrome, attention deficit hyperactivity disorder and obsessive compulsive disorder

Name:_____ (I have the following)
TS - AS - ADHD - OCD

Person at school I am comfortable talking to when needed:
_____

Basic Information About Tourette Syndrome, Asperger Syndrome, Obsessive Compulsive Disorder and Attention Deficit Disorder

What Is Tourette Syndrome?

Tourette Syndrome (TS) is a neurological disorder characterized by tics - involuntary, rapid, sudden movements or vocalizations that occur repeatedly in the same way. To receive a diagnosis of TS, a person must exhibit both multiple motor and one or more vocal tics in a period of a year, not necessarily at the same time. Tics usually start in the head area, as young as 3 or 4 years old, and progress down the torso as one matures. Tics are experienced as irresistible and (as the urge to sneeze) eventually must be expressed. Tics increase as a result of tension or stress, and decrease with relaxation or concentration on an absorbing task.

What Is Asperger Syndrome?

Asperger Syndrome (AS) is a neurological disorder. Characteristics of AS are: above-average intelligence, concrete thinking, inflexibility, communication deficits, problem-solving concerns, social deficits, behavioral issues, repetitive and stereotyped patterns of behavior and interests.

What Is Obsessive Compulsive Disorder?

Obsessions consist of repetitive unwanted or bothersome thoughts. Compulsions and ritualistic behaviors involve thinking that something must be done over and over and/or in a certain way.

What Is Attention Deficit Hyperactivity Disorder?

Attention deficit hyperactivity disorder with or without hyperactivity (ADHD) occurs in about 90% of persons with TS. Indications of ADHD may include: difficulty with concentration; failing to finish what is started; not listening; being easily distracted; often acting before thinking; shifting constantly from one activity to another; needing a great deal of supervision; general fidgeting; and difficulty with impulse control.

MEDICATIONS I TAKE AND HOW THEY MAKE ME FEEL

Medication _____ **I feel** _____

Medication _____ **I feel** _____

SYMPTOMS THAT INTERFERE WITH MUSIC AND SUGGESTIONS FOR DEALING WITH THEM

BEHAVIOR MANAGEMENT STRATEGIES

Additional Information

Helpful Information
for My Neighborhood Friends

For neighbors of children with tourette syndrome, Asperger Syndrome, attention deficit hyperactivity disorder and obsessive compulsive disorder

---

Name:_____

(I have the following)
TS - AS - ADHD

Person in the neighborhood I am comfortable talking to when needed:
_____

Basic Information About Tourette Syndrome, Asperger Syndrome, Obsessive Compulsive Disorder and Attention Deficit Disorder

---

What Is Tourette Syndrome?

Tourette Syndrome (TS) is a neurological disorder characterized by tics - involuntary, rapid, sudden movements or vocalizations that occur repeatedly in the same way. To receive a diagnosis of TS, a person must exhibit both multiple motor and one or more vocal tics in a period of a year, not necessarily at the same time. Tics usually start in the head area, as young as 3 or 4 years old, and progress down the torso as one matures. Tics are experienced as irresistible and (as the urge to sneeze) eventually must be expressed. Tics increase as a result of tension or stress, and decrease with relaxation or concentration on an absorbing task.

What Is Asperger Syndrome?

Asperger Syndrome (AS) is a neurological disorder. Characteristics of AS are: above-average intelligence, concrete thinking, inflexibility, communication deficits, problem-solving concerns, social deficits, behavioral issues, repetitive and stereotyped patterns of behavior and interests.

What Is Obsessive Compulsive Disorder?

Obsessions consist of repetitive unwanted or bothersome thoughts. Compulsions and ritualistic behaviors involving thinking that something must be done over and over and/or in a certain way.

What Is Attention Deficit Hyperactivity Disorder?

Attention deficit hyperactivity disorder with or without hyperactivity (ADHD) occurs in about 90% of persons with TS. Indications of ADHD may include: difficulty with concentration; failing to finish what is started; not listening; being easily distracted; often acting before thinking; shifting constantly from one activity to another; needing a great deal of supervision; general fidgeting; and difficulty with impulse control.

MEDICATIONS I TAKE AND HOW THEY MAKE ME FEEL

Medication _____ **I feel** _____

Medication _____ **I feel** _____

SYMPTOMS THAT INTERFERE WITH NEIGHBORHOOD ACTIVITIES AND SUGGESTIONS FOR DEALING WITH THEM

BEHAVIOR MANAGEMENT STRATEGIES

Additional Information

Helpful Information for the Paraprofessional

For paraprofessionals working with students with Tourette Syndrome, Asperger Syndrome, attention deficit hyperactivity disorder and obsessive compulsive disorder

Name:_____   **(I have the following)**
TS - AS - ADHD - OCD

Person at school I am comfortable talking to when needed:
_____

Basic Information About Tourette Syndrome, Asperger Syndrome, Obsessive Compulsive Disorder and Attention Deficit Disorder

What Is Tourette Syndrome?

Tourette Syndrome (TS) is a neurological disorder characterized by tics - involuntary, rapid, sudden movements or vocalizations that occur repeatedly in the same way. To receive a diagnosis of TS, a person must exhibit both multiple motor and one or more vocal tics in a period of a year, not necessarily at the same time. Tics usually start in the head area, as young as 3 or 4 years old, and progress down the torso as one matures. Tics are experienced as irresistible and (as the urge to sneeze) eventually must be expressed. Tics increase as a result of tension or stress, and decrease with relaxation or concentration on an absorbing task.

What Is Asperger Syndrome?

Asperger Syndrome (AS) is a neurological disorder. Characteristics of AS are: above-average intelligence, concrete thinking, inflexibility, communication deficits, problem-solving concerns, social deficits, behavioral issues, repetitive and stereotyped patterns of behavior and interests.

What Is Obsessive Compulsive Disorder?

Obsessions consist of repetitive unwanted or bothersome thoughts. Compulsions and ritualistic behaviors involve thinking that something must be done over and over and/or in a certain way.

What Is Attention Deficit Hyperactivity Disorder?

Attention deficit hyperactivity disorder with or without hyperactivity (ADHD) occurs in about 90% of persons with TS. Indications of ADHD may include: difficulty with concentration; failing to finish what is started; not listening; being easily distracted; often acting before thinking; shifting constantly from one activity to another; needing a great deal of supervision; general fidgeting; and difficulty with impulse control.

MEDICATIONS I TAKE AND HOW THEY MAKE ME FEEL

Medication _____ **I feel** _____

Medication _____ **I feel** _____

SYMPTOMS THAT I AM HAVING NOW
AND THINGS THAT YOU CAN DO TO HELP ME

My ADHD causes me to

If I am getting really anxious, fidgety or out of control, here are some strategies you can use to help me gain control:

🍎 Parent Journal

Date_____

Observations/Behaviors/Symptoms: _____

_____

_____

_____

_____

_____

Date_____

Observations/Behaviors/Symptoms: _____

_____

_____

_____

_____

_____

Date_____

Observations/Behaviors/Symptoms: _____

_____

_____

_____

_____

_____

Helpful Information
for My PE Teacher
For PE teachers having students with Tourette Syndrome, Asperger Syndrome, attention deficit hyperactivity disorder and obsessive compulsive disorder

Name:_____ **(I have the following)**
TS - AS - ADHD - OCD

Person at school I am comfortable talking to when needed:
_____

Basic Information About Tourette Syndrome, Asperger Syndrome, Obsessive Compulsive Disorder and Attention Deficit Disorder

What Is Tourette Syndrome?
Tourette Syndrome (TS) is a neurological disorder characterized by tics - involuntary, rapid, sudden movements or vocalizations that occur repeatedly in the same way. To receive a diagnosis of TS, a person must exhibit both multiple motor and one or more vocal tics in a period of a year, not necessarily at the same time. Tics usually start in the head area, as young as 3 or 4 years old, and progress down the torso as one matures. Tics are experienced as irresistible and (as the urge to sneeze) eventually must be expressed. Tics increase as a result of tension or stress, and decrease with relaxation or concentration on an absorbing task.

What Is Asperger Syndrome?
Asperger Syndrome (AS) is a neurological disorder. Characteristics of AS are: above-average intelligence, concrete thinking, inflexibility, communication deficits, problem-solving concerns, social deficits, behavioral issues, repetitive and stereotyped patterns of behavior and interests.

What Is Obsessive Compulsive Disorder?
Obsessions consist of repetitive unwanted or bothersome thoughts. Compulsions and ritualistic behaviors involve thinking that something must be done over and over and/or in a certain way.

What Is Attention Deficit Hyperactivity Disorder?
Attention deficit hyperactivity disorder with or without hyperactivity (ADHD) occurs in about 90% of persons with TS. Indications of ADHD may include: difficulty with concentration; failing to finish what is started; not listening; being easily distracted; often acting before thinking; shifting constantly from one activity to another; needing a great deal of supervision; general fidgeting; and difficulty with impulse control.

MEDICATIONS I TAKE AND HOW THEY MAKE ME FEEL

Medication _____ **I feel** _____

Medication _____ **I feel** _____

SYMPTOMS THAT INTERFERE WITH PE AND SUGGESTIONS FOR DEALING WITH THEM

BEHAVIOR MANAGEMENT STRATEGIES

Additional Information

Helpful Information for the Principal

For principals working with students with Tourette Syndrome, Asperger Syndrome, attention deficit hyperactivity disorder and obsessive compulsive disorder

Name:_____

(I have the following)
TS - AS - ADHD - OCD

Person at school I am comfortable talking to when needed:
_____

Basic Information About Tourette Syndrome, Asperger Syndrome, Obsessive Compulsive Disorder and Attention Deficit Disorder

What Is Tourette Syndrome?

Tourette Syndrome (TS) is a neurological disorder characterized by tics - involuntary, rapid, sudden movements or vocalizations that occur repeatedly in the same way. To receive a diagnosis of TS, a person must exhibit both multiple motor and one or more vocal tics in a period of a year, not necessarily at the same time. Tics usually start in the head area, as young as 3 or 4 years old, and progress down the torso as one matures. Tics are experienced as irresistible and (as the urge to sneeze) eventually must be expressed. Tics increase as a result of tension or stress, and decrease with relaxation or concentration on an absorbing task.

What Is Asperger Syndrome?

Asperger Syndrome (AS) is a neurological disorder. Characteristics of AS are: above-average intelligence, concrete thinking, inflexibility, communication deficits, problem-solving concerns, social deficits, behavioral issues, repetitive and stereotyped patterns of behavior and interests.

What Is Obsessive Compulsive Disorder?

Obsessions consist of repetitive unwanted or bothersome thoughts. Compulsions and ritualistic behaviors involve thinking that something must be done over and over and/or in a certain way.

What Is Attention Deficit Hyperactivity Disorder?

Attention deficit hyperactivity disorder with or without hyperactivity (ADHD) occurs in about 90% of persons with TS. Indications of ADHD may include: difficulty with concentration; failing to finish what is started; not listening; being easily distracted; often acting before thinking; shifting constantly from one activity to another; needing a great deal of supervision; general fidgeting; and difficulty with impulse control.

MEDICATIONS I TAKE AND HOW THEY MAKE ME FEEL

Medication _____ **I feel** _____

Medication _____ **I feel** _____

SYMPTOMS THAT I AM HAVING NOW
AND THINGS YOU CAN DO TO HELP ME

My ADHD causes me to

If I am getting really anxious, fidgety or out of control, here are some strategies you can use to help me gain control:

Helpful Information
for My Recess Monitor
For PE teachers having students with Tourette Syndrome, Asperger Syndrome, attention deficit hyperactivity disorder and obsessive compulsive disorder

Name:_____

(I have the following)
TS - AS - ADHD - OCD

Person at school I am comfortable talking to when needed:
_____

Basic Information About Tourette Syndrome, Asperger Syndrome, Obsessive Compulsive Disorder and Attention Deficit Disorder

What Is Tourette Syndrome?

Tourette Syndrome (TS) is a neurological disorder characterized by tics - involuntary, rapid, sudden movements or vocalizations that occur repeatedly in the same way. To receive a diagnosis of TS, a person must exhibit both multiple motor and one or more vocal tics in a period of a year, not necessarily at the same time. Tics usually start in the head area, as young as 3 or 4 years old, and progress down the torso as one matures. Tics are experienced as irresistible and (as the urge to sneeze) eventually must be expressed. Tics increase as a result of tension or stress, and decrease with relaxation or concentration on an absorbing task.

What Is Asperger Syndrome?

Asperger Syndrome (AS) is a neurological disorder. Characteristics of AS are: above-average intelligence, concrete thinking, inflexibility, communication deficits, problem-solving concerns, social deficits, behavioral issues, repetitive and stereotyped patterns of behavior and interests.

What Is Obsessive Compulsive Disorder?

Obsessions consist of repetitive unwanted or bothersome thoughts. Compulsions and ritualistic behaviors involve thinking that something must be done over and over and/or in a certain way.

What Is Attention Deficit Hyperactivity Disorder?

Attention deficit hyperactivity disorder with or without hyperactivity (ADHD) occurs in about 90% of persons with TS. Indications of ADHD may include: difficulty with concentration; failing to finish what is started; not listening; being easily distracted; often acting before thinking; shifting constantly from one activity to another; needing a great deal of supervision; general fidgeting; and difficulty with impulse control.

MEDICATIONS I TAKE AND HOW THEY MAKE ME FEEL

Medication _____ **I feel** _____

Medication _____ **I feel** _____

SYMPTOMS THAT INTERFERE WITH RECESS AND SUGGESTIONS FOR DEALING WITH THEM

BEHAVIOR MANAGEMENT STRATEGIES

Additional Information

Helpful Information
for My School Counselor

For school counselors working with students with Tourette Syndrome, Asperger Syndrome, attention deficit hyperactivity disorder and obsessive compulsive disorder

Name:_____   **(I have the following)**
TS - AS - ADHD - OCD

Person at school I am comfortable talking to when needed:
_____

Basic Information About Tourette Syndrome, Asperger Syndrome, Obsessive Compulsive Disorder and Attention Deficit Disorder

What Is Tourette Syndrome?

Tourette Syndrome (TS) is a neurological disorder characterized by tics - involuntary, rapid, sudden movements or vocalizations that occur repeatedly in the same way. To receive a diagnosis of TS, a person must exhibit both multiple motor and one or more vocal tics in a period of a year, not necessarily at the same time. Tics usually start in the head area, as young as 3 or 4 years old, eventually must be expressed. Tics increase as a result of tension or stress, and decrease with relaxation or concentration on an absorbing task.

What Is Asperger Syndrome?

Asperger Syndrome (AS) is a neurological disorder. Characteristics of AS are: above-average intelligence, concrete thinking, inflexibility, communication deficits, problem-solving concerns, social deficits, behavioral issues, repetitive and stereotyped patterns of behavior and interests.

What Is Obsessive Compulsive Disorder?

Obsessions consist of repetitive unwanted or bothersome thoughts. Compulsions and ritualistic behaviors involve thinking that something must be done over and over and/or in a certain way.

What Is Attention Deficit Hyperactivity Disorder?

Attention deficit hyperactivity disorder with or without hyperactivity (ADHD) occurs in about 90% of persons with TS. Indications of ADHD may include: difficulty with concentration; failing to finish what is started; not listening; being easily distracted; often acting before thinking; shifting constantly from one activity to another; needing a great deal of supervision; general fidgeting; and difficulty with impulse control.

MEDICATIONS I TAKE AND HOW THEY MAKE ME FEEL

Medication _____ **I feel** _____

Medication _____ **I feel** _____

SYMPTOMS THAT I HAVE
AND THINGS THAT YOU CAN DO TO HELP ME

Things that cause me a lot of stress

If I am getting really anxious, fidgety or out of control, here are some strategies you can use to help me gain control:

Information for the School Nurse

Student: _____

Helpful School Contact: _____

(circle applicable diagnosis)
TS - AS - ADHD - OCD

Parent/Guardian: _____ Work # _____

Parent/Guardian: _____ Work # _____

Basic Information About Tourette Syndrome, Asperger Syndrome, Obsessive Compulsive Disorder and Attention Deficit Disorder

What Is Tourette Syndrome?

Tourette Syndrome (TS) is a neurological disorder characterized by tics - involuntary, rapid, sudden movements or vocalizations that occur repeatedly in the same way. To receive a diagnosis of TS, a person must exhibit both multiple motor and one or more vocal tics in a period of a year, not necessarily at the same time. Tics usually start in the head area, as young as 3 or 4 years old, and progress down the torso as one matures. Tics are experienced as irresistible and (as the urge to sneeze) eventually must be expressed. Tics increase as a result of tension or stress, and decrease with relaxation or concentration on an absorbing task.

What Is Asperger Syndrome?

Asperger Syndrome (AS) is a neurological disorder. Characteristics of AS are: above-average intelligence, concrete thinking, inflexibility, communication deficits, problem-solving concerns, social deficits, behavioral issues, repetitive and stereotyped patterns of behavior and interests.

What Is Obsessive Compulsive Disorder?

Obsessions consist of repetitive unwanted or bothersome thoughts. Compulsions and ritualistic behaviors involve thinking that something must be done over and over and/or in a certain way.

What Is Attention Deficit Hyperactivity Disorder?

Attention deficit hyperactivity disorder with or without hyperactivity (ADHD) occurs in about 90% of persons with TS. Indications of ADHD may include: difficulty with concentration; failing to finish what is started; not listening; being easily distracted; often acting before thinking; shifting constantly from one activity to another; needing a great deal of supervision; general fidgeting; and difficulty with impulse control.

SYMPTOMS THAT MAY INTERFERE WITH LEARNING AND SUGGESTIONS FOR DEALING WITH THEM

1. Impulsivity, loud ticcing, inappropriate touching of others. Sometimes students with neurological disorders need to release tics, compulsions or other symptoms. Often the school nurse is the person who will provide support. Allowing student some quiet time or even a short nap can be beneficial.

2. Specific time limits for breaks should be discussed with the parents and student. Sometimes it is helpful to schedule these breaks at regular times, especially when the student seems to be going too often.

3. Students with these disorders ALWAYS react without thinking. This is neurological, so don't overreact to everything they say.

4. The more support the student receives from the school nurse, the better his/her day will be.

5. Documentation of questionable behavior will help others to address concerns.

6. It is important that all medications be administered as prescribed, especially if a specific time is prescribed.

7. Occasionally a student will need to take a short nap before returning to class.

Additional information specific to this student:

Helpful Information for School Staff

For individuals involved with students with Tourette Syndrome, Asperger Syndrome, attention deficit hyperactivity disorder and obsessive compulsive disorder

Name:_____

(I have the following)
TS - AS - ADHD - OCD

This information sheet was developed for the following individual:

___secretary   ___custodian   ___cafeteria staff   ___librarian

Person at school I am comfortable talking to when needed:

_____

Basic Information About Tourette Syndrome, Asperger Syndrome, Obsessive Compulsive Disorder and Attention Deficit Disorder

What Is Tourette Syndrome?

Tourette Syndrome (TS) is a neurological disorder characterized by tics - involuntary, rapid, sudden movements or vocalizations that occur repeatedly in the same way. To receive a diagnosis of TS, a person must exhibit both multiple motor and one or more vocal tics in a period of a year, not necessarily at the same time. Tics usually start in the head area, as young as 3 or 4 years old, and progress down the torso as one matures. Tics are experienced as irresistible and (as the urge to sneeze) eventually must be expressed. Tics increase as a result of tension or stress, and decrease with relaxation or concentration on an absorbing task.

What Is Asperger Syndrome?

Asperger Syndrome (AS) is a neurological disorder. Characteristics of AS are: above-average intelligence, concrete thinking, inflexibility, communication deficits, problem-solving concerns, social deficits, behavioral issues, repetitive and stereotyped patterns of behavior and interests.

What Is Obsessive Compulsive Disorder?

Obsessions consist of repetitive unwanted or bothersome thoughts. Compulsions and ritualistic behaviors involve thinking that something must be done over and over and/or in a certain way.

What Is Attention Deficit Hyperactivity Disorder?

Attention deficit hyperactivity disorder with or without hyperactivity (ADHD) occurs in about 90% of persons with TS. Indications of ADHD may include: difficulty with concentration; failing to finish what is started; not listening; being easily distracted; often acting before thinking; shifting constantly from one activity to another; needing a great deal of supervision; general fidgeting; and difficulty with impulse control.

SYMPTOMS THAT I AM HAVING NOW
AND THINGS THAT YOU CAN DO TO HELP ME

My ADHD causes me to

If I am getting really anxious, fidgety or out of control, here are some strategies you can use to help me gain control:

Helpful Information
for My Art Substitute Teacher

For substitute art teachers having students with Tourette Syndrome, Asperger syndrome, attention deficit hyperactivity disorder and obsessive compulsive disorder

Name:_____

(I have the following)
TS - AS - ADHD - OCD

Person at school I am comfortable talking to when needed:

Basic Information About Tourette Syndrome, Asperger Syndrome, Obsessive Compulsive Disorder and Attention Deficit Disorder

What Is Tourette Syndrome?

Tourette Syndrome (TS) is a neurological disorder characterized by tics - involuntary, rapid, sudden movements or vocalizations that occur repeatedly in the same way. To receive a diagnosis of TS, a person must exhibit both multiple motor and one or more vocal tics in a period of a year, not necessarily at the same time. Tics usually start in the head area, as young as 3 or 4 years old, and progress down the torso as one matures. Tics are experienced as irresistible and (as the urge to sneeze) eventually must be expressed. Tics increase as a result of tension or stress, and decrease with relaxation or concentration on an absorbing task.

What Is Asperger Syndrome?

Asperger Syndrome (AS) is a neurological disorder. Characteristics of AS are: above-average intelligence, concrete thinking, inflexibility, communication deficits, problem-solving concerns, social deficits, behavioral issues, repetitive and stereotyped patterns of behavior and interests.

What Is Obsessive Compulsive Disorder?

Obsessions consist of repetitive unwanted or bothersome thoughts. Compulsions and ritualistic behaviors involve thinking that something must be done over and over and/or in a certain way.

What Is Attention Deficit Hyperactivity Disorder?

Attention deficit hyperactivity disorder with or without hyperactivity (ADHD) occurs in about 90% of persons with TS. Indications of ADHD may include: difficulty with concentration; failing to finish what is started; not listening; being easily distracted; often acting before thinking; shifting constantly from one activity to another; needing a great deal of supervision; general fidgeting; and difficulty with impulse control.

MEDICATIONS I TAKE AND HOW THEY MAKE ME FEEL

Medication _____ **I feel** _____

Medication _____ **I feel** _____

SYMPTOMS THAT INTERFERE WITH ART AND SUGGESTIONS FOR DEALING WITH THEM

BEHAVIOR MANAGEMENT STRATEGIES

Additional Information

Substitute Information - Elementary School

For substitute teachers working with students with Tourette Syndrome, Asperger Syndrome, attention deficit hyperactivity disorder and obsessive compulsive disorder

*Helpful school contact person:*_____ Room #_____

Student:_____

(circle applicable diagnosis)
TS - AS - ADHD - OCD

Helpful Strategies

Opening:

Lunch:

Recess:

Dismissal:

Transition: (activities, hallway, lessons)

Special Classes or Para Assistance

Class_____Day(s)_____Room #_____Time:_____Teacher_____

Class_____Day(s)_____Room #_____Time:_____Teacher_____

Class_____Day(s)_____Room #_____Time:_____Teacher_____

MEDICATIONS DISPENSED by SCHOOL NURSE

Time_____Time_____Time_____Time_____

SYMPTOMS THAT INTERFERE WITH LEARNING AND SUGGESTIONS FOR DEALING WITH THEM

BEHAVIOR MANAGEMENT STRATEGIES

Instructions for Assigning Homework

Additional Information

Substitute Information
Junior and Senior High School

For substitute teachers working with students with Tourette Syndrome, Asperger Syndrome, attention deficit hyperactivity disorder and obsessive compulsive disorder.

*Counselor:*_____ *Room #*_____ *#*_____

Student:_____ (circle applicable diagnosis)
TS - AS - ADHD - OCD

Student's Daily Schedule

Time:	Classes:
1st	_____
2nd	_____
3rd	_____
4th	_____
5th	_____
6th	_____
7th	_____
8th	_____

MEDICATIONS DISPENSED by SCHOOL NURSE

Time_____   Time_____

SYMPTOMS THAT INTERFERE WITH LEARNING AND SUGGESTIONS FOR DEALING WITH THEM

BEHAVIOR MANAGEMENT STRATEGIES

Instructions for Assigning Homework

Additional Information

Helpful Information
for My Music Substitute Teacher

For substitute music teachers having students with Tourette Syndrome, Asperger Syndrome, attention deficit hyperactivity disorder and obsessive compulsive disorder

---

Name:_____

(I have the following)
TS - AS - ADHD - OCD

---

*Person at school I am comfortable talking to when needed:*_____

Basic Information About Tourette Syndrome, Asperger Syndrome, Obsessive Compulsive Disorder and Attention Deficit Disorder

---

What Is Tourette Syndrome?

Tourette Syndrome (TS) is a neurological disorder characterized by tics - involuntary, rapid, sudden movements or vocalizations that occur repeatedly in the same way. To receive a diagnosis of TS, a person must exhibit both multiple motor and one or more vocal tics in a period of a year, not necessarily at the same time. Tics usually start in the head area, as young as 3 or 4 years old, and progress down the torso as one matures. Tics are experienced as irresistible and (as the urge to sneeze) eventually must be expressed. Tics increase as a result of tension or stress, and decrease with relaxation or concentration on an absorbing task.

What Is Asperger Syndrome?

Asperger Syndrome (AS) is a neurological disorder. Characteristics of AS are: above-average intelligence, concrete thinking, inflexibility, communication deficits, problem-solving concerns, social deficits, behavioral issues, repetitive and stereotyped patterns of behavior and interests.

What Is Obsessive Compulsive Disorder?

Obsessions consist of repetitive unwanted or bothersome thoughts. Compulsions and ritualistic behaviors involve thinking that something must be done over and over and/or in a certain way.

What Is Attention Deficit Hyperactivity Disorder?

Attention deficit hyperactivity disorder with or without hyperactivity (ADHD) occurs in about 90% of persons with TS. Indications of ADHD may include: difficulty with concentration; failing to finish what is started; not listening; being easily distracted; often acting before thinking; shifting constantly from one activity to another; needing a great deal of supervision; general fidgeting; and difficulty with impulse control.

MEDICATIONS I TAKE AND HOW THEY MAKE ME FEEL

Medication _____ I feel _____

Medication _____ I feel _____

SYMPTOMS THAT INTERFERE WITH MUSIC AND SUGGESTIONS FOR DEALING WITH THEM

BEHAVIOR MANAGEMENT STRATEGIES

Additional Information

Helpful Information
for My PE Substitute Teacher

For substitute PE teachers having students with Tourette Syndrome, Asperger Syndrome, attention deficit hyperactivity disorder and obsessive compulsive disorder

---

Name:_____

(I have the following)
TS - AS - ADHD - OCD

---

*Person at school I am comfortable talking to when needed:*_____

Basic Information About Tourette Syndrome, Asperger Syndrome, Obsessive Compulsive Disorder and Attention Deficit Disorder

---

What Is Tourette Syndrome?

Tourette Syndrome (TS) is a neurological disorder characterized by tics - involuntary, rapid, sudden movements or vocalizations that occur repeatedly in the same way. To receive a diagnosis of TS, a person must exhibit both multiple motor and one or more vocal tics in a period of a year, not necessarily at the same time. Tics usually start in the head area, as young as 3 or 4 years old, and progress down the torso as one matures. Tics are experienced as irresistible and (as the urge to sneeze) eventually must be expressed. Tics increase as a result of tension or stress, and decrease with relaxation or concentration on an absorbing task.

What Is Asperger Syndrome?

Asperger Syndrome (AS) is a neurological disorder. Characteristics of AS are: above-average intelligence, concrete thinking, inflexibility, communication deficits, problem-solving concerns, social deficits, behavioral issues, repetitive and stereotyped patterns of behavior and interests.

What Is Obsessive Compulsive Disorder?

Obsessions consist of repetitive unwanted or bothersome thoughts. Compulsions and ritualistic behaviors involve thinking that something must be done over and over and/or in a certain way.

What Is Attention Deficit Hyperactivity Disorder?

Attention deficit hyperactivity disorder with or without hyperactivity (ADHD) occurs in about 90% of persons with TS. Indications of ADHD may include: difficulty with concentration; failing to finish what is started; not listening; being easily distracted; often acting before thinking; shifting constantly from one activity to another; needing a great deal of supervision; general fidgeting; and difficulty with impulse control.

<u>MEDICATIONS I TAKE AND HOW THEY MAKE ME FEEL</u>

Medication _____ **I feel** _____

SYMPTOMS THAT INTERFERE WITH PE AND SUGGESTIONS FOR DEALING WITH THEM

BEHAVIOR MANAGEMENT STRATEGIES

Additional Information

TOURETTE SYNDROME

Tourette Syndrome (TS) is a neurological disorder characterized by tics—involuntary, rapid, sudden movements that occur repeatedly in the same way. To receive a diagnosis of TS a person must have both multiple motor and one or more vocal tics, not necessarily simultaneously, throughout a span of more than one year. The tics may occur many times a day (usually in bouts), nearly every day or intermittently. Tics periodically change in number, frequency, type and location, and wax and wane in severity. Symptoms sometimes disappear for weeks or months at a time. While most persons with TS have some control over their symptoms, from seconds to hours at a time, suppressing them may merely postpone more severe outbursts. Tics are experienced as irresistible and (as the urge to sneeze) eventually must be expressed. Tics increase as a result of tension or stress and decrease with relaxation or concentration on an absorbing task.

MOTOR TICS

Eye blinking, rolling	Hair twisting
Squinting	Arm flailing
Head jerking	Arm flapping
Facial grimacing	Arm jerking
Facial contortions	Arm squeezing
Nose twitching	Smelling fingers
Body jerking	Smelling objects
Kissing hand	Shivering
Kissing others	Abdominal jerking
Hitting self or others	Throwing things
Clapping	Tearing books, paper
Pinching	Scratching
Shoulder shrugging	Squatting
Knee knocking	Skipping
Leg jerking	Stepping backwards
Stooping	Walking on toes
Jumping	Twirling in circles
Hopping, stomping	Deep knee bending
Kicking	Foot tapping
Ankle flexing	Foot shaking
Table banging	Foot dragging
Picking at lint	Chewing on clothes
Lip pouting	Pulling at clothes
Lip smacking	Somersaults
Lip licking	Body slamming
Tongue thrusting	Mouth opening
Hair tossing	Eyebrow raising

S Y M P T O M S

VOCAL TICS

Honking	Shouting noises
Grunting	Saying "hey, hey, wow," etc.
Sniffing	Guttural sounds
Belching	Noisy breathing
Spitting	Gasping
Snorting	Calling out
Squeaking	Squealing
Hiccupping	Clicking or clacking
Coughing	Making "tsk" & "pft" noises
Humming	Puffing expirations
Yelling	Hissing
Whistling	Laughing
Barking	Screaming
Yelping	Throat clearing
Gurgling	Blurting

COMPLEX TICS

Repeating of phrases, words
Animal sounds — cow, dog, etc.
Stuttering
Barely audible muttering — amplitude of speech
Talking to oneself
Pallilalia — repeating own words
Echolalia — repeating others' words or statements
Coprolalia — speaking obscenities, taboo phrases

ADHD

Often fidgets with hands or feet or squirms in seat
Has difficulty remaining seated when required to do so
Has difficulty waiting turn in games or group activities
Often shifts from one uncompleted activity to another
Has difficulty organizing work and playing quietly
Has difficulty following through on instructions
Often engages in physically dangerous activities without
  considering possible consequences
Often does not seem to listen to what is being said
Often loses things necessary for activities at school or home

ADHD occurs in many persons with TS. Many show signs of hyperactivity before TS symptoms appear.

Often blurts out answers to questions
Is easily distracted
Has difficulty sustaining attention in tasks/play
Often interrupts or intrudes on others
Often talks excessively

OBSESSIVE COMPULSIVE DISORDER

Obsessions consist of repetitive unwanted or bothersome thoughts. Compulsive and ritualistic behaviors refer to a person thinking that something must be done over and over and/or in a certain way. Research shows 80 to 90 percent of persons with TS also have obsessive compulsive disorder (OCD).

SYMPTOMS

OBSESSIONS

Being concerned with symmetry, exactness, cleanliness, order
Needing to know or remember things
Overfocusing on minute details
Having to have "JUST RIGHT" feeling
Overfocusing on one idea or action
Overfocusing on moral issues (right/wrong, fairness)
Focusing on specific numbers
Being concerned with colors of special significance
Needing to experience sensations (skin cut or burned)
Having a preoccupation with knives, scissors, blood
Worrying about harming self or others
Worrying that something terrible might happen (fire, death)
Being concerned about dirt or germs
Thinking about hoarding or collecting
Thinking about food and eating
Thinking about forbidden behaviors
Engaging in mental coprolalia (sexual thoughts, images, impulses)
Having aggressive thoughts, images, impulses

BEHAVIORAL

Quick temper
Overaction
Mood changes
Difficulties with impulse control
Oppositional behavior
Defiant behavior

COMPULSIONS

Overfocusing on one idea or action
Counting or grouping objects
Counting objects over and over again
Excessively ordering and arranging objects
Touching objects an exact number of times
Constantly fiddling with objects or clothes
Checking and rechecking (doors, locks, windows)
Repeating actions (in/out door, up/down from chair)
Needing to say or do what told not to say or do
Needing to finish verbalizations if interrupted
Needing to start over if interrupted
Repeatedly asking the same question
Having to respond to verbalization when not necessary
Persevering on a task
Unable to change to a new task or activity
Echopraxia (repeating the actions of others)
Copropraxia (making obscene gestures)
Repeating sounds, words, numbers, music to oneself
Playing computer video games over and over in mind
Pallilalia (repeating aloud own words)
Echolalia (repeating others' words)
Coprolalia (uttering obscene words)
Touching objects, others, self, wounds
Sexually touching self
Sexually touching others (breasts, buttocks, genitals)
Picking skin/sores
Cutting or burning skin
Sucking thumb
Cracking knuckles
Vomiting
Sniffing or smelling hands or objects
Licking or biting others
Excessive handwashing, bathing, cleaning
Erasing repeatedly
Writing and rewriting until paper looks perfect
Stealing
Biting nails
Adjusting/readjusting clothes to feel just right (socks, sleeves)
Evening things up (touching with one hand, then the other)

🍎 Teacher Journal

Date_____

Observations/Behaviors/Symptoms: _____

_____

_____

_____

_____

_____

Date_____

Observations/Behaviors/Symptoms: _____

_____

_____

_____

_____

_____

Date_____

Observations/Behaviors/Symptoms: _____

_____

_____

_____

_____

_____

Helpful Information
for the Vo-Tech Teacher

For vo-tech teachers working with students with Tourette Syndrome, Asperger Syndrome, attention deficit hyperactivity disorder and obsessive compulsive disorder

Name:_____

(I have the following)
TS - AS - ADHD - OCD

Person at school I am comfortable talking to when needed:
_____

Basic Information About Tourette Syndrome, Asperger Syndrome, Obsessive Compulsive Disorder and Attention Deficit Disorder

What Is Tourette Syndrome?

Tourette Syndrome (TS) is a neurological disorder characterized by tics - involuntary, rapid, sudden movements or vocalizations that occur repeatedly in the same way. To receive a diagnosis of TS, a person must exhibit both multiple motor and one or more vocal tics in a period of a year, not necessarily at the same time. Tics usually start in the head area, as young as 3 or 4 years old, and progress down the torso as one matures. Tics are experienced as irresistible and (as the urge to sneeze) eventually must be expressed. Tics increase as a result of tension or stress, and decrease with relaxation or concentration on an absorbing task.

What Is Asperger Syndrome?

Asperger Syndrome (AS) is a neurological disorder. Characteristics of AS are: above-average intelligence, concrete thinking, inflexibility, communication deficits, problem-solving concerns, social deficits, behavioral issues, repetitive and stereotyped patterns of behavior and interests.

What Is Obsessive Compulsive Disorder?

Obsessions consist of repetitive unwanted or bothersome thoughts. Compulsions and ritualistic behaviors involve thinking that something must be done over and over and/or in a certain way.

What Is Attention Deficit Hyperactivity Disorder?

Attention deficit hyperactivity disorder with or without hyperactivity (ADHD) occurs in about 90% of persons with TS. Indications of ADHD may include: difficulty with concentration; failing to finish what is started; not listening; being easily distracted; often acting before thinking; shifting constantly from one activity to another; needing a great deal of supervision; general fidgeting; and difficulty with impulse control.

MEDICATIONS I TAKE AND HOW THEY MAKE ME FEEL

Medication _____ I feel _____

Medication _____ I feel _____

SYMPTOMS THAT INTERFERE WITH MY VO-TECH CLASS AND SUGGESTIONS FOR DEALING WITH THEM

BEHAVIOR MANAGEMENT STRATEGIES

Additional Information

Weekly Report

The Weekly Report should be completed each Friday and sent home with the student so parents can address incomplete assignments and concerns over the weekend.

Name _____   Date _____

1st Hour/Subject _____

Missing Assignments: _____

Comments: _____

_____

_____

_____

Teacher's Signature _____

2nd Hour/Subject _____

Missing Assignments: _____

Comments: _____

_____

_____

_____

Teacher's Signature _____

3rd Hour/Subject _____

Missing Assignments: _____

Comments: _____

_____

_____

_____

Teacher's Signature _____

4th Hour/Subject _____

Missing Assignments: _____

Comments: _____

_____

_____

Teacher's Signature _____

5th Hour/Subject _____

Missing Assignments: _____

Comments: _____

_____

_____

Teacher's Signature _____

6th Hour/Subject _____

Missing Assignments: _____

Comments: _____

_____

_____

Teacher's Signature _____

7th Hour/Subject _____

Missing Assignments: _____

Comments: _____

_____

_____

Teacher's Signature _____